Angels in the Big Apple

SECRETS, SECRETS, SECRETS

BOOK EIGHT

A Novel

Gordon J. Goss & Teresa J. Richardson

ISBN: 9798867308469

Text Design by: Johnny Lowe
Cover Design by: Kimberly Calhoun

Published by N.S.D. Books
Website: www.secrets3.com
Email: books@secrets3.com

DEDICATION

This book is dedicated to Pastor Rick Brown, his family, and the entire congregation of Dry Creek Baptist Church.

Also, a special thanks to John Lowe, Suzanne Hatch, Brandon Meeks, Rick Brown, and the members of the Pearl and Richland Writing Clubs. Their suggestions and editing made this book a true team effort.

Contents

Part Two – *The Investment*

Part Three – *Matryoshka*

Part Four – *Divine Intervention*

Part 1
WORKING GIRL

Chapter 1

DREAM JOB

Eighteen-year-old MaryAna Lindley settled into her seat as the jet left the tarmac at the Jackson-Medger Wiley Evers International Airport in Jackson, Mississippi. Moments later the Boeing 737 made its familiar leisurely turn east toward Atlanta, the first leg on MaryAna's flight to visit her boyfriend, Tyler Richardson, in Pennsylvania. She stretched and smiled, luxuriating in the ample legroom afforded by her first-class window seat—*thanks, Mama!*—and peered out the window at the green passing in slow-motion below. MaryAna was glad to leave the heavy August humidity behind.

She glanced again at the passenger in the adjoining seat, a handsome middle-aged man with dark-brown hair and a touch of gray at the temples. She had noticed his smile and soulful eyes when he boarded the plane only a minute behind her. She also noticed how dapper he looked in his expensive three-piece suit.

After the flight attendant welcomed the passengers on the loudspeaker, she gave a rundown of the flight to Atlanta, ending with a practiced cheerful wish: "We thank you for choosing Delta and hope you will choose us again for your next journey!" As refreshments were served, MaryAna and her seatmate chatted, and the man—indicating the fashion magazine MaryAna was reading—asked her if she had noticed the ad in the issue for a company called Jacqueline Designs.

"I did, sir," she said. "It caught my attention, for sure."

The man then introduced himself: Mel Rubenstein, CEO of Jacqueline Designs. The fashion-conscious MaryAna was well aware of the company. Although not a fan of their fashions, she knew them to be an up-and-coming player in the competitive world of women's high-end apparel.

Mel turned the screen of his laptop toward her. "I don't wish to be presumptuous, Miss Lindley, but I wonder if you might browse our most recent proposed dress designs. I'd like your honest opinion of them."

"Sure, I'd be happy to," she said, smiling. She placed his notebook computer in her lap and began clicking through the images.

As they sailed eastward above the clouds, MaryAna shared her thoughts on the various designs—and was not shy about her impressions. Her insightful comments revealed an uncanny sense of fashion, and she poured out ideas about design as easily as Einstein would about physics.

For the balance of the flight, the two chatted, laughed, and—one might say—"hit it off." Before the plane touched down at Atlanta, Mel had offered MaryAna a job in the design department of his company.

"Thank you for the offer, Mr. Rubenstein," she said, somewhat taken aback. "It's very temptin', but I'm not really job-huntin' at the moment." Mel gave MaryAna his business card, however, in case she changed her mind. Once they deplaned, they shook hands and parted ways.

As MaryAna headed to her next gate, her mind was racing. The more she thought about actually living and working in NYC, the more excited she became.

How can I turn down a lifelong dream?

She stopped to consider her future, causing the retired couple following close behind to stumble into her backpack. Other travelers navigated around her as she lingered in the middle of the walkway. She took a breath, let it out slow, then pulled out her phone to text her new boss: Will take job. Changing ticket to Big Apple!

She stopped at the first Delta counter she saw, getting her Scranton, Pennsylvania, ticket changed to New York and a seat next to Mr. Rubenstein. Then she pulled out her phone once more, this time to text her boyfriend: Tyler, flying to New York for job. Will explain later.

On her way to her new gate, MaryAna spotted the CEO in an airport bar. She strode up to his table, announced "I'm back," and took a seat.

"I'm glad you accepted my offer, Miss Lindley," Mel said with a smile. He indicated his glass. "Would you like a drink before we take off?"

I probably should get something non-alcoholic.

MaryAna was sixteen the first time she wandered into a barroom. That decision led to an exciting adventure with Tony Russo, a man nearly twice her age. When she hit seventeen, her bar-hopping had morphed into a darker purpose—mostly excuses to meet older men, let them believe they were seducing *her*, and then a series of one-night stands.

That secret lifestyle drove the teenager into opioid addiction and mounting debt to pay for it. To earn extra money, she took a job as a cocktail waitress at a strip club, which ultimately led to a harrowing ordeal at the home of her drug dealer. Only by the grace of God did she survive mostly unscathed.

MaryAna finally quit opioids, but her drinking problem continued until she fell in love with Tyler Richardson earlier this year. That was the turning point—she went cold turkey and had not looked back.

But if I order a Coke, Mr. Rubenstein will think I'm a hick.

"What are you drinkin', sir?"

"Martini. Would you like one?"

Surprising herself, MaryAna nodded.

Mel motioned the waiter over, and when asked for her ID, MaryAna produced her fake driver's license that declared she was twenty-one.

When the drink arrived, Mel raised his glass. "To my newest employee."

She clicked her glass to his. "I've never had a martini before," she said, before taking a sip.

"What do you think?"

Her sudden toothy grin made Mel blink. "I love it." She finished the glass in one long gulp.

"Slow down, Miss Lindley," Mel said, waving his finger. "These can be quite potent."

"Don't worry, sir, I can hold my liquor. Is there time for one more?"

The CEO ordered her another, and once the waiter had left, Mel turned back to her. "Tell me—what changed your mind about the position?"

"I figured that when an opportunity this awesome knocks, I gotta rip the door off its hinges and go for it."

"I'm glad you did. I look forward to hearing more of your ideas."

When MaryAna finished the second martini, she covered her mouth to suppress a burp. "I suppose I shouldn't drink on an empty stomach."

"Do you want to grab a bite before we board? There's still some time."

"No, I'm too excited to eat."

Mel checked his Rolex and rose from the table, laptop in hand. "We should proceed to our gate."

MaryAna shouldered her backpack and handbag. "I was runnin' late this mornin' and just threw on this T-shirt and jeans. Do I have time to change?"

"We have several minutes. I'll wait for you."

Twenty minutes later, the CEO was pacing and checking his watch when the teenager re-emerged from the restroom.

A sophisticated French braid had replaced MaryAna's girlish ponytail. She had changed into a yellow off-the-shoulder peasant blouse, showcasing her generous cleavage. A white miniskirt and six-inch stilettos completed the eye-catching outfit.

"Miss Lindley?"

"Do I look OK?" she said, doing a quick pirouette.

He cleared his throat. "You . . . look older. Well, our flight is boarding, so we should go."

They flashed their boarding passes at the gate and were whisked aboard the waiting jet. MaryAna stuffed her backpack into the overhead bin and took her seat. Her new boss wiped his brow with a handkerchief and caught his breath before buckling in beside her.

"Sorry I took so long changing, sir," she said. "Thanks for the drinks, by the way."

"You said you just graduated. I assume that ID was fake?"

The teenager grinned. "Don't I look old enough to drink?"

"You do, yes. When I was your age, the drinking age was eighteen."

"They should've left it there."

"I agree. Young people are supposed to drink responsibly, but how can they if they're not allowed to drink at all? I prefer beer to mixed drinks myself."

"Me too," she said, smoothing a wayward curl behind her ear. "Hard liquor gives me a buzz, but sometimes it makes me sleepy."

"You should have plenty of time for a nap on this flight, if you wish."

A nap? What am I—four?

"When I changed my ticket, I asked to sit by you. I hope you don't mind."

"Of course not, Miss Lindley. I enjoy your company."

"If you want my opinion on any more designs, I'd be happy to look them over."

"Thank you, but I have some financial reports to review. Have you thought about where you might stay in New York?"

"Last year, my girlfriend and I stayed at the Plaza. I made a reservation but could cancel if you have another suggestion."

"The Plaza is a fine establishment and not far from our offices. Tell you what, my company will pick up your first month's expenses while you look for an apartment."

"Really? That's so sweet of you."

"We kill our employees with kindness but expect much from them," he said, waving another finger.

"I won't let you down, sir."

"A limo will meet us when we land, and we'll drop you at the hotel.

I'll pick you up at seven tomorrow morning on the way to the office."

"I can't wait."

Once airborne, MaryAna put in her earbuds and browsed the inflight magazine. The lead article, "What to Do in the Big Apple," soon caught her eye. The piece included photos of Central Park, Lincoln Center, Broadway, the Guggenheim Museum, the Statue of Liberty, and Yankee Stadium. She had visited a couple of them on her last visit, but wanted to see them again, as well as the other venues.

As a little girl, MaryAna dreamt about Prince Charming and fairytale castles. Now here she was, a modern-day Cinderella in a magic carriage flying her to the Big Apple.

By the time she was halfway through another article, "The Churches of New York," her attention began to wander. The martinis had kicked in, and she blinked, trying to concentrate on the story, which included photos of everything from grand cathedrals to tiny storefront churches bathed in neon. But she could not stop herself from yawning and soon leaned her seat back. The last image she saw before sleep took her was a place called Guardian Baptist Church that boasted a magnificent statue of the Archangel Gabriel at its entrance.

His face seemed familiar to her.

A dream job, limo rides, and a fancy hotel.

Big Apple, here I come.

Chapter 2

THE PLAZA

Brief turbulence interrupts MaryAna's sleep, and her eyes dart around the cabin before she remembers where she is. She checks her watch, noting that they should be landing soon.

Mel looks up from his laptop. "Nice nap?"

"Yes, thank you, except for that cloud we just went through or whatever it was." She unbuckles her belt, grabs her handbag, and shuffles toward the aisle.

Mel chuckles. "Another change of clothes?"

"Nope, just want to freshen my makeup."

"They should be announcing our arrival at JFK shortly."

"I won't be long this time. Promise."

She returns to her seat just as the flight attendant notifies the passengers to fasten seatbelts and prepare for final approach.

"So, what can I expect in New York, weather-wise?" MaryAna asks.

"Hotter than normal, but I'd say you're dressed appropriately," Mel noted, glancing at her blouse.

She fans her hands over her outfit. "These are a good example of the bold colors you should use in your designs. I also like pink, sapphire, turquoise, salmon and tangerine. For me, the brighter, the better."

"Well," Mel says, glancing at her attire once again, "that yellow blouse is certainly eye-catching."

"It's Tyler's favorite. He says it reminds him of the morning sun peeking over the mountains. Isn't that sweet?"

Mel grins. "He's a ballplayer, you said?"

"Yep. Tyler was traded from the Braves to the Yankees and assigned to their minor-league team in Scranton. Hopefully, he'll be playing in New York soon."

"Have you known him long?"

"We dated on and off in high school before I realized how much I love him. We'll probably get married sometime soon."

"Oh, so you're engaged then?"

"Not officially, but I'm guessing he invited me up so he could pop the question." She settles back in her seat and lets out a breath. "I suppose that's on hold for now."

Mel chuckles. "It's nice to be in love."

"It is."

I'll visit Tyler first chance I get. We can talk about the future then.

***

Once they are on the ground, the CEO picks up a *Wall Street Journal*. When they arrive at their baggage claim, MaryAna informs Mel she has three suitcases.

"Your luggage could well be on its way to Scranton, Miss Lindley."

"The Delta guy assured me they'd transfer my bags to my new flight."

"You have more confidence in the airlines than I. If your luggage does make it, I'll have a skycap assist us in getting it to the car."

Mr. Rubenstein couldn't be more of a gentleman.

Mel's one suitcase arrives first, and MaryAna soon wonders if he was right about her luggage being waylayed, as every other suitcase, duffle bag, and duct-taped container on the planet appears on the conveyor except hers. But finally, as if they had grown weary of torturing the anxious teenager, they appear.

"There they are!" she says. "The three pink ones."

"They're rather large, aren't they. It's a modern-day miracle they made it."

"You should have more trust in people, sir."

Mel snatches the first suitcase off the conveyor, surprised at its heft. "You don't believe in traveling light, I'm guessing." He grabs the other two as they roll up as well.

They find Mel's limo, a silver Rolls Royce Phantom waiting curbside, and are soon on their way.

MaryAna sits facing the CEO as they cruise through Brooklyn toward Manhattan and the Plaza. Her outfit stands in sharp contrast to the car's dark-red leather interior. She can't help but ramble on about the sights and sounds of the city, but Mel says little, his attention devoted to his paper.

MaryAna slips off her shoes, draws her knees under her, and peers through the limousine's sunroof once they are in Manhattan.

"I'm still blown away by all these skyscrapers."

Mel glances at her, then up through the tinted sunroof. "Yes, they're quite impressive."

She points to the sunroof. "Can we open it?"

"Maybe another time. For now, let's enjoy the air conditioning," he says, his attention returning to the financial news.

The Rolls Royce soon deposits them in front of the world-famous Plaza Hotel in Manhattan, across from Central Park.

"Our company receives a corporate discount, Miss Lindley. I'll need to register you."

MaryAna slips her shoes back on, then grabs her handbag and backpack. "Thanks. I hope this little detour didn't take you too far out of your way."

"Not at all."

The chauffeur, a tall black man in a gray uniform, comes around to the passenger side and opens the door. Mel and MaryAna step from the limousine into the bright August sun.

"Welcome to the Plaza." A burly black doorman with a broad grin tips his military-style hat as they approach the massive glass doors of the hotel. "Good afternoon. My name is Leon. I'll be happy to assist you."

Mel hands the doorman a folded bill. "See that the young lady's suitcases make it inside."

"Of course, sir."

"After you help him with the luggage, Roger, find someplace to park," Mel says to the driver. "I may be a while."

"Yes, sir."

Mel and MaryAna enter the hotel. Though she has been here before, the grandeur of the ornate marble lobby still takes her breath away. The plaster-coffered ceiling, mosaic floors, and gold-colored trim every which way remind her of a time when monarchs spared no expense to commemorate their reign.

As she follows Mel to the front desk, MaryAna realizes her stilettos make her about two inches taller than the CEO, which, though she does not know why, makes her grin. Simultaneously, she notices several men in the lobby have their eyes on her. Some are more obvious than others, but MaryAna has read every one of their minds—and she does a slow one-eighty as she walks, pretending to react in awe at the hotel's magnificent ceiling architecture.

Guys are always checking me out . . . and I love it.

Mel registers MaryAna into the hotel and hands her a plastic key card. "I upgraded you to a suite on the eighteenth floor overlooking the park. You're in room 1819."

"That's easy to remember. I'm eighteen, but I turn nineteen in a couple weeks."

"Well then, happy early birthday. You may charge food and whatever else you need to the suite. A bellhop will deliver your luggage shortly."

"Looks like you've thought of everything, sir. I'm thrilled to be startin' work tomorrow. This whole trip is like a dream."

"It'll be real enough at seven A.M. when I arrive to pick you up. Please be prompt."

MaryAna wants to give him a hug, but stops short.

Better not.

That wouldn't be professional.

She holds out her hand instead, but rather than shaking it, Mel offers his arm. "How about we go in the bar and celebrate you joining our company? You seemed to enjoy those martinis."

I thought we already celebrated, but I guess one more won't hurt.

12

"Lead the way," she says, taking his arm and glancing once more at the men still fantasizing from afar.

Once in the bar, they find an out-of-the-way table. Mel orders two martinis, and they once again toast MaryAna's new job.

They mostly make small talk, but MaryAna soon begins relating her family history.

"So," he says, "you were brought up by a single mom?"

"She told me my father died when I was a baby. I didn't learn the truth until I was sixteen. Turned out I also had a twin brother."

"That had to be a shock."

"It was," she says, finishing her current glass. "Thanks for the martini. It was even better than the ones in Atlanta."

"Would you like another? I'm not pushed for time."

"I think I've had my limit for the day. They'll be bringin' my suitcases upstairs soon."

"If you want to continue our conversation, Miss Lindley, room service could bring us a whole pitcher of martinis."

I probably shouldn't have had the first three, but they were so good.

"Maybe another time, sir. I need to get unpacked and make some calls. It's already been a long day, and I need to unwind."

Mel nods. "Of course. You have my number if you change your mind. My schedule is open this evening."

They say their goodbyes in the lobby, and MaryAna takes an elevator up to her floor to find her room. Minutes later, a bellhop arrives with her luggage. He takes them to the bedroom, and she gives him a generous tip.

"Thanks," the handsome young black man says. "The remote for the TV is in the top desk drawer. The maid restocks the minibar every day. Will there be anything else?"

"Nope, that's it. My name's MaryAna, by the way. What's yours?"

"Samson," he says, flexing his arms. "Like that guy in the Bible. But everybody calls me Sam."

"Nice to meet you, Sam." They shake hands. "You from New York?"

"Nope, Cleveland. Came here to be in musicals."

"Wow. Do you sing?"

"*And* dance."

"You're built like a dancer." She gives out a nervous laugh. "You know, tall and athletic."

Samson smiles, revealing his pearly-white teeth. He does a quick soft-shoe, and MaryAna squeals in delight. "That was awesome. Have you been in any musicals?"

"Not yet. The competition's pretty tough. But I'm keeping positive and hope to catch a break."

"I'm sure you will."

"Where you from?"

"Mississippi. I just landed a job in town designin' clothes."

"Well, congrats! Anything you need," he says, pointing to himself, "Sam's your man."

"Anything?" She gives him a mischievous grin.

"You bet. Just ask for me."

"I'll remember."

"Better get moving before my boss wonders where I am—he can be a pain in the you know what. Nice to meet you, Mississippi."

"Same here, Samson—I mean, Sam."

Once he has left, MaryAna does another pirouette, this time for herself.

Even the bellhops in this town are cool. I think I'm gonna love it here.

Chapter 3

PHONE CALLS

MaryAna opens her suitcases and hangs her clothes in the large walk-in closet. Most of her attire serve a singular purpose: highlight her long legs and hourglass figure. But, she realizes, they would probably not be considered appropriate office wear.

She envisions multiple shopping sprees. With a hefty checking account, the teenager has no money worries. She wants to invest some of it, *but clothes are important, dammit.*

With her suitcases unpacked, MaryAna's next order of business is to call Tyler. Her boyfriend's terse reply to her text hinted he had not shared her enthusiasm with the sudden change of plans.

"Hey," she says when he answers, "I'm at the Plaza Hotel in New York City. It's right across from Central Park."

"You should be with me, MaryAna. How the heck did you end up getting a job in New York?"

"I met the CEO of a company called Jacqueline Designs on the plane. They're an upscale design business. He liked my fashion ideas and offered me a job as a designer. I know it seems impulsive, but I couldn't pass it up."

"I know it's your dream, MaryAna, but you should've discussed such a big decision with me first. Your text seemed kinda cold."

"I didn't mean it that way. Everything just happened so quick. But, don't forget—when the Braves traded you to the Yankees, you let me know with a text."

"That was different. I had no choice in the matter."

"You'll be playin' at Yankee Stadium soon enough. By then, I'll have my own place, and we can live together. Won't that be awesome?"

"I don't know when that's gonna happen. The jump from double-A ball to triple-A hasn't been easy. I doubt I'll be playin' in New York any time soon."

"I believe in you, Tyler."

"That's great, but belief doesn't help me hit curveballs. Can you come visit this weekend?"

"I haven't even started my job yet. How about the followin' weekend?"

"That's better than nothing, I guess."

"Come on, don't be a stick in the mud. In the meantime, there's always phone sex. You wanna know what I'm wearin'—the yellow blouse you like so much. The one that shows off my—"

"MaryAna! You're so naughty."

"And you love it, don't lie. And before I left, I went to Victoria's Secret. I can't wait to model it all for you."

"I'm sure I'll like it. You always . . . make things interestin'."

"I try," she says with a giggle. "And if we get bored, there's always whipped cream."

"Do you stay up nights inventin' ways to get into trouble?"

"Sometimes. Tell you what, I'll make reservations for a week from Friday and try to get off early that day. Are you super-angry with me about not bein' there now?"

"Just disappointed. I thought . . ."

"When I get to Scranton, I'll make it up to you. I promise."

MaryAna hears a female voice in the background. "Who's that?"

"I'm at the ballpark for some extra battin' practice. How about I call you later?"

"OK. Love you so much. I'll be there before you know it."

"Good luck with your new job."

By the time I see him, he'll have forgotten all about being upset with me.

MaryAna draws the drapes closed and runs a hot bath, adding plenty of Epsom salts and lavender bath beads. For the past several months, a minor ache in her back has grown from an occasional twinge to a nagging ache. She has not been to a doctor, opting instead for hot baths, scalding showers, and over-the-counter pain medications.

After soaking for half an hour, the teenager slips into her fluffy pink bathrobe and dials the front desk to schedule a wake-up call for 6:00 the following morning.

In addition to a large wooden work desk, the living room boasts a leather sofa sandwiched between two elegant end tables and sumptuous wall-to-wall carpeting that makes MaryAna consider giving up footwear. And the picture window showcases a panoramic view of Central Park.

The living room also features a fifty-inch flat-screen and refrigerated minibar, which is stocked with a variety of beers, wine, and small bottles of liquor.

MaryAna selects a beer, Pilsner Urquell, and plops down on the sofa. She takes a long swallow and settles back.

I suppose I should call Mama.

Her mother, Sarah Lindley-Brown, is one of the wealthiest women in Mississippi. After inheriting a small fortune, her wise investments have made it substantially larger. She lives with her second husband, Scott Brown, the head football coach at the University of Southern Mississippi, in the city of Hattiesburg.

"Hey, Mama. Guess what—I'm in New York City."

"Did your plane get diverted, dear?"

"You won't believe what happened. I was offered a job at Jacqueline Designs. You know, that big fashion company. Isn't that crazy?"

"I have a couple of their dresses. You say someone offered you a job?"

"The CEO. I start tomorrow mornin' as an assistant designer. I can't believe it."

"Slow down, honey—I thought you were going to visit Tyler."

MaryAna tells her about meeting Mel Rubenstein, giving him her thoughts on their designs, and his offer of a job—and the radical change in plans.

"I'm gonna see Tyler in a week or so," MaryAna says, before taking another swig from her bottle. "I have a suite at the Plaza—you know, where Bonnie Lee and I stayed last summer."

"Back up a second, dear. So, this CEO offered you a job out of the blue?"

"What can I say? He was blown away with my fashion ideas."

"Are you sure he's the CEO?"

"I saw his business card, Mama. You know how I love to sketch ideas for clothes. Now I can make it my profession."

"MaryAna, you should be in college. If you want to study design, that's fine with me, but you need an education."

"Mama, this job is so much better than college. I'll gain firsthand experience and get paid to boot."

"But you are so young, dear."

"I'm almost nineteen. The sooner I get started, the better. This job is a fantastic opportunity."

"I understand, but I worry about your bipolar disorder. Taking your meds and AA seem to be helping. You shouldn't jeopardize all the progress you've made."

"I'm so much better now. Even Dr. Scanlon said so. I can't live in a bubble all my life."

"I'm glad your psychiatrist sees progress, sweetie, but it's not like a cold or the flu. Being bipolar is something you need to keep a check on. You don't want to get hooked on illegal drugs again, do you?"

She wants me hooked on prescription ones instead.

"I know, Mama. I brought my meds with me." MaryAna does not mention she did not take them today.

Sometimes they zombie me out worse than the oxy. Besides, I can't drink if I take those stupid meds.

"You know, everybody says I have a vivid imagination. You loved the dresses I designed for your weddin'. This will give me the chance to explore more of my ideas. And I get to live in a big city and meet new people."

"But New York City, dear? It's too big."

"It's a place to grow and learn. You know what Frank Sinatra said:

'If I can make it there—'"

"Since when did you become a Sinatra fan?"

"I'm not, but the point is still valid. I might become a famous designer. I've got to follow my heart."

"You may be settin' up your heart to be broken, honey."

"I've gotta take that chance."

Sarah sighs. "I know this has been a major goal of yours, but let's see how you like livin' in New York. It's far from your family and friends."

"It's not like I left the planet, Mama. I can fly home for visits. Besides, Tyler will be here playin' for the Yankees soon."

"Oh, sweetie, I hope you're right. Do you need extra money in the meantime? You know, until you get a paycheck?"

"Thanks, but I've got plenty. The company is payin' for my first month at the Plaza. Isn't that sweet of Mr. Rubenstein?"

"What do you know about him besides the fact he's the CEO?"

"He's a real gentleman. He made sure I got to the hotel safely and is picking me up in the mornin' on his way to the office—in a limo, no less."

"Is he married?"

"I didn't ask, but he wasn't wearin' a weddin' ring. He's interested in my talent and nothing else."

"You've got a lot to learn about the world, sweetheart. Girls have to be extra careful."

"I know, Mama. I'll find out more about him. I promise."

"Maybe I should fly up there and help you settle in."

"You need to let me grow up on my own."

"Do you want me to send you the rest of your clothes?"

"Hey, I'm in the best city in the freakin' world for shoppin'. I'll let you know if I need anything."

"What about your car?"

"Mr. Rubenstein says I don't need a car. Everyone here uses public transportation—taxis, subways, buses, Uber."

"Just be careful. New York isn't Mississippi."

"I'll be fine," MaryAna says, before finishing the bottle.

After she hangs up, she drops the empty into the nearby garbage can.

Mama is so old-fashioned. I'm not a little girl anymore.

She hops off the couch and heads back to the minibar.

Chapter 4

ELTON

Prior to sundown, sirens jolt MaryAna awake. She throws open the drapes of the bedroom window to see two fire trucks weaving their way up Fifth Avenue.

Once her heart rate has returned to normal, the teenager gazes out over Central Park and the streets surrounding it. She stands there, watching pedestrians scurrying about.

I shouldn't have taken a nap. I'll probably have trouble getting to sleep tonight.

Now wide awake, the teenager thinks about what to do next, determined not to waste a minute of her time in New York.

I need new clothes, but it's too late to go shopping tonight.

MaryAna recalls Mel's invitation—the thought of more martinis and stimulating conversation with the handsome CEO appeals to her.

I can tell he enjoys my company, but I shouldn't mix business with pleasure. Besides, he's my boss now.

She decides to watch TV, so she heads into the living room, pushing aside a room service table with what's left of a chicken Caesar salad and three empty bottles before plopping onto the couch.

She clicks on the TV, catching the end of a newscast concerning the "Manhattan Rapist," who is currently at large in the city. She flips through multiple channels before settling on a movie with Mel Gibson.

Then her eyes catch the empties on the cart during a commercial break.

It's OK. I can drink responsibly. One or two more martinis will help me get back to sleep. It's OK.

***

A half-hour later, MaryAna steps from the elevator into the lobby, now clad in an attractive mint-green cocktail dress. It has a short skirt but is one of her more sedate outfits.

In the bar, she seats herself at a table and orders a martini. A few minutes later, a young man with a mustache and goatee saunters in her direction.

"Hello," he says. "Would you like some company?"

She peers at him over the rim of her glass. "Sure, why not?"

He's one of the guys ogling me when I checked in.

MaryAna indicates the opposite chair. "Please."

"Thank you very much," he says taking the seat. "I'm Elton. Forgive me, but was that your father I saw with you before?"

"Not quite. He's my boss," she says, before finishing her glass. "I'm MaryAna. I'm guessing you're English, right?"

"London, to be exact. May I get you a refill?"

"If you wish."

He points to her glass. "Martini?"

She nods, then takes the olive from her glass and pops it into her mouth.

Elton motions for the waitress and orders a martini for MaryAna and a Scotch and soda for himself.

"So, what do you do in London, Elton?"

"I'm in banking. I'm here to contact potential customers. We're a private bank, catering to high-worth individuals like millionaires and billionaires. And what do you do?"

"I just got a job here at Jacqueline Designs. Have you heard of it?"

He shakes his head and hands her his card.

She looks it over. "I know a billionaire and a few millionaires."

"Really? Perhaps, you could let them know about us. That is, if you see them again."

He doesn't believe me.

She stuffs the card in her purse. "Maybe I should move my

22

accounts to your bank?"

He chuckles. "I don't think it's a good fit for a girl like you."

"A girl like me?"

"Don't get me wrong, babe. I'm just interested in you in other ways."

"What ways would that be?"

Before he can respond, the waitress arrives with their drinks.

"Keep the change, my dear," he says, handing her a twenty.

The waitress flashes a smile before leaving. "Thank you, sir!"

Elton turns back to MaryAna.

"You were explainin' why you're fascinated by my mind."

"You are a lovely young lady, MaryAna. After we chinwag a bit, I was thinking perhaps we could take the lift up to my room."

"And what, Elton?"

"Then,' he says, his gaze shifting to MaryAna's chest, "I will rip that little green frock of yours off your gorgeous body and show you why I'm interested in you."

"You basically wanna screw my brains out."

"Crudely expressed, but accurate nonetheless."

"You sure don't waste time."

"Well, life is short, isn't it. When I saw you before, you weren't shy about flaunting that exquisite body of yours. Every male in the lobby was laser-focused on you and you knew it. I fancied you a bit of a tart."

"A what?"

"The kind of girl who likes a certain type of fun. Promiscuous fun."

"And you think I'm that kind of girl?"

"No?"

"Not tonight, Elton. In fact, I won't waste any more of your time. I have a boyfriend and no intention of cheatin' on him."

"Is he here at the hotel?"

"No."

"Then if you don't tell him, he won't know, will he. It will be our little secret."

"I would know."

"If you have a good time, what's the harm?"

"I'm not even enjoying *chin-wagging* with you, Elton. You're arrogant, self-centered, smug, and oh—one more—condescending."

"What does that have to do with, as you call it: 'Screwing your brains out'?"

"You're a pompous ass too."

"Bloody hell, woman," he says, plopping his drink down. "You're certainly judgmental for someone in your position."

"My position? For your information, Elton, I've got more than a hundred thousand dollars in my checkin' account and millions more in my trust fund."

Elton blinks, exchanging his leer for a grin. "Well then—in that case, I would love to have your business."

"I bet you would. Tell me, Elton, have you ever been in love or in a committed relationship?"

He chuckles and takes a sip from his glass. "No, I can't say that I have."

"Then you can't understand how I feel."

Elton slides his chair back and gets up, tipping an imaginary hat. "This round goes to you, m'lady. Let's do lunch tomorrow and talk business. You have my card—give me a call."

MaryAna takes a sip from her glass and smiles. "Don't hold your breath."

Elton grabs his drink and heads off in the direction of another woman sitting alone.

Thank God Tyler's not like that.

***

An hour and several martinis later, MaryAna exits the bar. Though several other men attempted to pick her up, she turned them all down.

I love Tyler and won't jeopardize our relationship.

Still not sleepy, the teenager decides to go for a walk. She exits the hotel and strolls toward Fifth Avenue. Horse-drawn carriages line the street across from her, all waiting for customers to take scenic park tours.

I wish Tyler was here to take me on a romantic carriage ride.

"Geez, watch where you're going!"

"Sorry, I—hey!" The other pedestrian shoves MaryAna aside, and she stumbles off the curb.

HONNNNNK!

A pair of strong hands grabs her shoulders and yanks her back onto the sidewalk, and the taxi flies past, just missing her.

"Are you OK?"

Gathering her wits, MaryAna turns to her rescuer. "I think so. Tha—"

I've seen him before. He . . .

"You're welcome," he tells her in a calming voice.

An elderly black woman rushes over to MaryAna. "Are you okay, child? You should be more careful."

She turns to the woman. "I'm fine, ma'am. This nice gentleman snatched me back just in time."

"Excuse me?"

"The man who pulled me from the street." She turns back to her savior, but he has already disappeared.

"I saw the whole thing, dear. You stepped off the curb, then jumped back onto the sidewalk. You saved yourself."

"No, ma'am. He pulled me back."

"Honey, have you been drinking?"

"Well . . ."

"Sometimes we imagine things when we've had a little too much to drink."

"But . . ."

"You shouldn't be walking alone with that dreadful Manhattan Rapist on the loose. May I get you a cab?"

"Thanks, but I'm stayin' at the Plaza," MaryAna says, nodding toward the hotel in the distance. "I'm goin' back there right now."

"You do that, honey, and be safe."

"Thank you, ma'am. I'll try."

I didn't imagine it—he did save me.

Chapter 5

THE COMPANY

At 7:00 the following morning, Mel's silver limousine pulls up in front of the Plaza. The chauffeur opens the rear passenger side door for MaryAna, but the bleary-eyed teenager has not yet noticed the fancy vehicle.

He steps over to her and smiles. "Good morning, Miss Lindley."

She blinks and turns her attention to him. "Oh, sorry. I was a hundred miles away."

"Mr. Rubenstein is waiting for you."

"Oh, hey—it's Roger, right?"

"Yes, Miss."

"If you don't mind me askin', where are you from? Are you English?"

"I'm from Bermuda, ma'am. Have you ever been there?"

"No. I'd love to go someday."

"I think you'd like it," Roger says as MaryAna slips through the door.

She slides to the center of the seat facing back toward Mel. She is wearing a white blouse with a short navy-blue skirt. It rides up slightly, showing off her long tanned legs.

Mel wears a tailored business suit with a striped power tie. He sets today's *Wall Street Journal* in his briefcase and looks up.

"Did you have a nice conversation with Roger?"

"He told me he's from Bermuda."

"Really? I have to say, I didn't know that."

"How long has Roger worked for you?"

"Five years. You still excited about your first day of work?"

"You bet. I wanted to ask, by the way—I was wonderin' if it would be possible for me to leave early Friday next week. I want to visit my boyfriend. He's kinda upset I blew him off."

"It is all right with me, Miss Lindley, but you should discuss it with your direct supervisor. Just don't make this a habit."

"I won't." MaryAna glances out the window at the Manhattan skyline. "Are your offices in one of those skyscrapers?"

"It's nearby, but our building is only fifty-five stories."

"That's twice as tall as the highest buildin' back home."

"We occupy the top five floors. Your department is on fifty-one."

"How many people do you have workin' for you?"

"About five hundred worldwide, half of them here in New York. The design department is small, however—just five individuals."

"Wow, that *is* small, sir."

"There are two senior designers. Hannah and Sharree. Each has their own assistant. You will be Hannah's."

"And the fifth person?"

"Jacqueline Leblanc, manager of the design department. She's also the company's namesake and co-founder."

"I know the company has won a bunch of awards for its designs."

"Our advertising and marketing teams do a superb job polishing our image."

He sounds proud of their achievements, as he should be.

"We're a growing organization, Miss Lindley, with plenty of upside potential. I expect you to help us fulfill our destiny."

***

Once they have arrived at the company headquarters, the CEO escorts MaryAna to the Human Resources Department on the fifty-third floor and lets the manager know MaryAna will be filling the open position in design.

"Carl will take good care of you," Mel tells her. "I'll check back later."

The CEO smiles and whispers to the manager before heading to his own office.

What was that—something about me?

Carl is balding and in his early sixties. Though he seems pleasant, MaryAna's impression is that he is counting down the days till retirement. He shows her to a small conference room and hands her several documents. "Look these over, please, and sign them in the yellow highlighted areas."

"What are these?"

"Work history, medical info, yadda, yadda, yadda," he says without expression. "The usual stuff."

MaryAna goes to work filling out the forms, though some of the information is confusing to her. But, concerned that questions would make her appear unqualified, she goes ahead and signs each of the papers.

When Carl returns to retrieve the forms, he takes MaryAna to meet Hannah Goldberg, a woman in her late forties with light-brown hair pulled back into a bun. "Miss Lindley is your new assistant," Carl tells her.

"Yeah, Mel gave me a heads-up she was here. He knows Jacqueline doesn't like him meddling in her department. When she finds out about MaryAna, she'll probably throw another tantrum."

Carl snickers. "Tell me about it. But that's between her and Mel. She'll get over it." He turns his attention to MaryAna. "Okay, I'll leave you with Hannah, Miss Lindley. Nice to meet you, by the way."

"Thank you," MaryAna says, but Carl is already out the door.

She turns back to her new supervisor, who leans back in her chair, obviously sizing up the new employee.

"There a problem?" MaryAna says after a moment.

Hannah waves dismissively. "No, nothing for you to worry about. Have a seat."

"Thanks," MaryAna says, taking the chair across from Hannah's desk. "How long have you been with the company, Ms. Goldberg?"

"Call me Hannah. I was one of the first employees fifteen years ago. Mel says you're new to the city. Out of state—Michigan, was it?"

"Mississippi, actually."

"And eighteen."

"Correct, though I'll be nineteen soon."

Hannah shakes her head. "I can barely remember being nineteen. Anyway, let's introduce you to some of your co-workers."

Hannah takes MaryAna to a nearby cubicle where a young woman is busy on her laptop. She is pretty with hazel eyes and an athletic build. Her long brown hair features blond highlights.

"Kristen Kowalski, meet my new assistant designer, MaryAna Lindley."

The young woman turns and smiles. "She'll take over the new-girl duties, right?"

"Yes," Hannah says, "but you'll be training her."

"No problem." Kristen stands to shake hands with the new employee. "Nice to meet you, MaryAna."

"Likewise."

"Where's Sharree?" Hannah asks.

"In his office." Kristen then turns to MaryAna. "We'll talk later."

"I look forward to it."

Hannah taps MaryAna on the shoulder. "Let's go see Sharree."

She leads the way past file cabinets, stacks of various fabrics, and general clutter to an office door painted chartreuse, and knocks.

"Yes?"

"It's Hannah."

"Come in."

Sharree is a short man in his mid-forties, seated behind an ancient wooden desk covered in papers and books that threaten to spill over onto the floor. He has shoulder-length brown hair with green highlights and sports horn-rimmed glasses and a hot-pink western-style shirt.

"Sharree, this is MaryAna Lindley, my new assistant."

"Well, hello there." He rises and shakes MaryAna's hand. "I'm so glad to make your acquaintance. If there is anything, and I mean anything, I can do to make you feel more welcome, please, do let me know."

"It is nice to meet you, too."

He's got some Elton John vibes going on, for sure.

After they say their goodbyes to Sharree, Hannah takes MaryAna to a small cubicle near Kristen's.

"This will be your space, MaryAna. When you need to spread out, you may use the table in the conference room down the hall."

Soon they are back in Hannah's office. MaryAna asks her about wanting to leave work early the following Friday to fly to Scranton to visit her boyfriend. "I was on my way there when Mr. Rubenstein offered me this job. He said it was OK with him if it's OK with you."

"I have no problem with it. With Jacqueline still out of town, we're not up against any deadlines."

"Thanks."

"Mel told me you have some interesting ideas. He says you are pretty on the ball and could become an important part of our creative team. Right now, I'm designing a new blouse line. I'd like you to work up some sketches for me to review. You draw, don't you?"

"Yes, and I've got several cool ideas for blouses—they're kinda out there."

"Draw them up, and I'll take a look. If I approve them, they'll go to Sharree for comment. Jacqueline has the final say on all our designs."

"What's the boss lady like?"

Hannah shrugs. "Working for Jacqueline can be a challenge. She's brutally honest and a stickler for being on time."

"I'll make sure to remember that. Is she here today?"

"Not at the moment. Every summer, she goes to Paris to check on our competition and visit her family."

"So, she's French?"

Hannah smiles. "And she won't let you forget it. The French believe they are God's gift to fashion. Maybe they are."

***

That afternoon, MaryAna receives a call from Mel.

"So, how'd everything go on your first day? You settling in?"

"Hannah and the others have made me feel right at home. May I ask you something, sir?"

"Of course."

"Maybe it's none of my business, but this morning when you introduced me to Carl, just before you left you whispered something to him that, well . . . seemed to be about me."

"Oh, that." Mel clears his throat. "I just told him not to tell Jacqueline I'd hired you."

"Why not?"

"Jacqueline considers the design department her kingdom and doesn't like me to 'interfere.' She should've filled your position months ago but tends to procrastinate on such matters."

"When do you plan to tell her about me?"

"In our next phone conversation. She'll be upset, as usual, but she'll accept my decision."

"I don't want to cause trouble for you, sir, or have the boss lady mad at me."

"Everything will be fine. Would you like a ride back to the Plaza after work?"

"I won't turn down a limo ride."

"Most nights, I work late. I'll text you when I'm about to leave. Meet me around the corner at the Made Fresh Bakery."

"Got it."

"I cannot provide you transportation forever, Miss Lindley, but you're new to the city and need a helping hand. I'll pick you up same time tomorrow morning."

"I appreciate it, sir."

"And don't worry about Jacqueline. By the time she returns to the states, this whole thing will have blown over."

"When is she due back?"

"A couple weeks."

Looks like I'll cross that bridge in two weeks.

Chapter 6

DRINKING CONTEST

MaryAna learns her daily duties during her first week at the company. The routine includes filing, copying, entering data, answering the phone, and running errands. Not quite what the eighteen-year-old envisioned doing as an assistant designer. A plus, however, regarding errands includes frequent coffee runs to the Made Fresh Bakery, just a stone's throw from the office, and she is soon on a first-name basis with its employees.

MaryAna spends her first weekend and evenings at New York's finest department stores and boutiques stocking up on suitable office attire, and during the rides to and from work, she provides Mel an ongoing rundown on her purchases. He asks why she selected various items, and while his reactions to her new apparel are positive, MaryAna believes he is holding back some comments.

MaryAna takes full advantage of the Plaza's room service while her bipolar medication remains untouched. She enjoys appointments at the hotel's spa for facials, massages, and hair styling, all charged to her suite.

MaryAna gets to know the housemaids and other hotel staff. She especially enjoys talking with Leon. The doorman answers her many questions about the city and adds interesting historical facts, such as when she asked him about the Plaza. It was built in 1907 and stands twenty-one-stories tall. Although the chateau-style structure is dwarfed by newer buildings, it remains one of the city's iconic landmarks.

Whenever MaryAna sees Samson in the lobby, she smiles and

waves. The handsome bellhop always waves back with a big grin.

Late each evening, the teenager curls up on the sofa with a beer and calls Tyler. He is still not happy with her decision to work in New York. But she assures him it is part of God's plan to reunite them once he joins the Yankees.

"I can't wait to see you," she tells him near the end of their call Thursday night. "This time tomorrow, I'll be in your arms again. Won't that be awesome?"

"Are you for sure comin' this time? No detours to Philadelphia or Washington?"

"I'll be in your arms before you know it, Tyler. I love you so much."

It's nice to have someone I can count on.

***

On the second Friday, MaryAna leaves work early as planned on a flight to visit her boyfriend in Scranton. Upon landing, she takes a taxi to drop off her suitcase at his apartment. After changing into a V-neck blouse and skinny jeans, she heads off to the ballpark, where a game is underway.

"Tyler!" She jumps up and down waving when he heads in from the outfield for the bottom of the sixth inning, but he only acknowledges her with a tip of his cap.

What kind of a "Hey, babe—I missed you!" is that?

After the game, they ride his Harley Sportster to a local pizza parlor, where Tyler introduces her to six of his teammates who are gathered at a long wooden table with multiple pitchers of beer.

"Come join us," Todd, one of Tyler's fellow ballplayers, says.

"Thanks, but we want some private time," Tyler tells him and finds an out-of-the-way table.

"What would you like?" he asks MaryAna as they sit down.

"Beer, please."

"But what about—"

"I'm good. Nathan made me another ID."

Nathan Hale is one of MaryAna's former boyfriends and a crack computer expert. His checkered past includes a variety of illegal activities, one of which is the manufacture and sale of counterfeit IDs.

"How is Nathan?" Tyler asks.

"Still workin' at Hanberry Labs and on the straight and narrow—except for this little favor he did for me," she says, indicating her ID.

"I take it you quit AA."

She shrugs. "I never truly believed I had a drinkin' problem, Tyler."

"MaryAna . . ."

"What?"

"Nothing. I'll be right back." He heads to the front counter and orders a large pepperoni and a pitcher.

"Hey, Tyler!" Todd yells from across the room. "We're putting in twenty bucks apiece—whoever guzzles the most takes the pot. You want in?"

"I'll pass."

MaryAna turns and flails her arms at Todd. "Hey, what about me—can I play?"

Todd grins. "Sure, come on over."

"Some of those guys can really put away their beer, MaryAna," Tyler says, as he sits back down.

She grins and opens her purse. "C'mon, you know I can't resist a challenge." She sashays over to Todd and slaps him a crisp twenty. "Prepare to kiss your money goodbye, boys."

"You have to sit with us," Todd tells her, adding her bill to a pile of cash in the middle of the table, "so we can keep track of how much you drink."

MaryAna motions to Tyler. "Come on over, babe, and bring the pitcher."

A few minutes later, three young attractive women enter the restaurant and wave to all the ballplayers. They quickly invite the girls to join the group. Two of the girls sit at the far end of the table, but the third one walks up to MaryAna and Tyler.

The slender young woman wears a pinstripe Yankee's jersey, black shorts, long white socks and running shoes. She is cute with freckles and reddish-brown hair beneath a baseball cap.

"Hi, Ty." Her eyes scan MaryAna up and down. "So, who's this?"

Tyler stumbles to his feet, nearly overturning his mug. "Meghan, this is MaryAna."

"Ty has told us all about you, and that you just moved to New York. I used to live there when my father played for the Yankees."

MaryAna notes Tyler seems to not know whether to stand or sit, before he finally sits back down. "Meghan's daddy is our team's manager," he says.

MaryAna takes a swig and looks up at Meghan. "Yeah, I'm a Big Apple girl now. Tyler will be playin' there soon."

"Ty is certainly talented," Meghan says, giving him a smile, "but he needs to spend more time in Scranton to improve his skills."

"The guys are havin' a drinkin' contest," MaryAna says, before covering a burp. You want to participate?"

Meghan puts her hand around Tyler's shoulder. "I don't drink though, do I, Ty?"

One of Meghan's girlfriends waves to her. "Hey, come over and sit with us."

"Good luck in the contest," Meghan says to MaryAna with a smirk, then saunters over to her friends.

Between swigs from her mug, MaryAna soon regales the group with stories about growing up in Mississippi.

"So, you were a cheerleader," Todd says. "I bet you were pretty hot."

"Darn right I was. Right, Tyler?"

He nods and grabs another slice of pizza.

"I was also a cocktail waitress at a strip club," MaryAna continues. "I even went up on stage one time."

Tyler glares at her but says nothing.

Todd claps his hands and lets out a whoop. "Whoa, for real? You wanna do a lap dance for us right now—how about it?"

His teammates all chime in with jeers and whistles in agreement, but MaryAna waves them off.

"Sorry, but y'all are just gonna have to fantasize about that on your own." She chugs down another mug, her fifth. "Chalk up another one!"

Meghan and her friends share some chatter, then cackle like a brood of hens.

Tyler rises from his chair quick. "I think it's time we left."

"But what about the contest?" MaryAna says, refilling her mug. "I'm winnin'."

He grabs her arm before she can take another swig. "It's not like you need the money. Let's go."

"You go on," she says, pulling her arm free. "You'll give me a ride, won't you, Todd?"

Tyler glares at her once again but sits back down. "Okay, I guess we can stay a little longer."

They finally leave about an hour later, with MaryAna stumbling out the front door with a fistful of cash. Tyler catches her before she slips on the gravel.

"Put that money in your purse and count it later."

"Yes sir," she says, giving a salute. "You have any beer at your place?"

"Haven't you had enough?" he says, helping her onto the back of the Harley.

MaryAna wraps her arms tight around him once he mounts the bike. "Aren't you glad to see me?"

He kicks the engine to life before responding, but she does not hear his answer over the roar of the engine.

***

When they arrive at Tyler's apartment, MaryAna leads him to the bedroom and gives him a long X-rated kiss.

"Let me show you how much I've missed you." She drops to her knees, unbuckles his belt, and fumbles with his zipper.

But before she can pull his jeans down, Tyler lifts her back to her feet.

"MaryAna, we need to talk."

"Talk. Seriously?" She steps back and attempts to remove her blouse but gets tangled up in the process. "I want to make love, not conversation. Hey, where'd you go?" she says, before extricating herself from the stubborn blouse.

Tyler gapes at her and sighs. "Since I left Mississippi, I've been thinkin' a lot about our relationship, MaryAna."

"That's great." She plops onto the edge of the bed and peels off her skinny jeans, though it takes nearly a minute to do it. "I love you, and you love me. What else is there to say?"

"Plenty."

She removes her bra but nearly trips while slipping off her thong. Tyler watches but says nothing.

"Do I have to undress you?" she says.

He does not answer. With zero help from her boyfriend, she removes his T-shirt and jeans.

"MaryAna, I—"

But her lips smother his words. Undaunted by his reluctance, she directs him onto the bed. The lovemaking that follows meets her physical needs but leaves her wanting.

Afterward, they lie unmoving next to each other, the only sound their breathing. She is almost asleep when he turns to face her.

"You awake?"

"Barely."

"Can we talk?"

She rubs her eyes and sighs. "About what?"

"Our relationship?"

She sighs again. "What about it?"

"Sometimes, MaryAna, I don't think you care about me."

"Didn't I show you how much I care just a few minutes ago?"

"That's not what I'm talkin' about."

MaryAna scrunches up her face. "I didn't mean to talk about the strip club before—it just slipped out."

"That was just you bein' you. Which is kinda the problem."

MaryAna props herself up on her elbow. "Are you still mad because I went to New York?"

"You're missin' the point," he says. "We're like two ships passin' in the night, you and me."

"I have no idea what you are talkin' about, Tyler, and too tired right now to figure it out." She lies back on the pillow, her eyes weary. "I'll try to do better, OK?"

He does not respond.

She lets out a frustrated sigh. "It's been a long day. How about we discuss this tomorrow."

He rolls over, away from her. "Whatever."

Sometimes he's such a child.

Chapter 7

STRIKING OUT

Saturday is half gone by the time MaryAna crawls out of bed. She looks for Tyler before sending him a text asking where he is.

Tyler texts back: BALLPARK

An hour later, he returns with burgers and fries for lunch.

"How come you were at the ballpark so early?" MaryAna says, before scarfing down some fries. "The game isn't until tonight."

"I was doing some more battin' practice."

"I hope it's helpin'. After we eat, how about I model my new lingerie for you?"

"Maybe later. There's a Yankee game on TV."

She sighs. "In that case, I'm fixin' to take a bath and do my nails. I bought some new colors. Want to choose which one I should do?"

"You can do that."

"You're just a bundle of fun today, Tyler. Look, I'm really sorry about last night. I shouldn't have gotten involved in that drinkin' contest."

"Forget it," he says and walks to the kitchen. "I need more napkins."

That afternoon, Tyler receives multiple text messages. Each time, he goes outside and makes a phone call. After the fourth one, MaryAna asks him about it.

"It's just a friend who needs to talk privately," he answers. "No biggie."

They do not discuss their relationship, sticking to small talk. After the game, they make a beer run before returning to the apartment for a late supper. MaryAna finishes off a six-pack while they hunker down on the sofa to watch a movie, but as soon as the ending credits begin, Tyler decides to call it a night.

While he is in the bathroom, MaryAna changes into her newest lingerie. The fire-engine-red creation is a combination of one-inch straps and tiny patches of sheer lace. It barely covers the more vital areas while exposing nearly everything else.

Tyler climbs into bed without a word. MaryAna joins him but remains on top of the covers in an attempt to make him acknowledge her.

"So, what do you think about what I'm wearin'?"

"It's OK."

"OK? That's it? You're tellin' me it doesn't turn you on?"

"It's very sexy, but I'm kinda tired. I didn't sleep in today like someone else I know."

"I picked this out especially for you." Her voice is sing-song, child-like. "Don't you want to fool around—we can do whatever you want."

"Not tonight."

"I bet I can change your mind," she says, reaching under the covers.

Tyler grabs her hand. "MaryAna, I'm not in the mood, all right?"

"But I wanna make love," she says, cuddling up to him. "How about a massage? That'll relax you."

He turns onto his side away from her. "How about in the morning when I'm not so tired."

"What's the deal, Tyler?"

"Nothing. Go to sleep."

Instead, MaryAna rolls out of bed, turns on the TV, and starts another six-pack. Two hours later, she returns to the bedroom and snuggles up to her boyfriend once more. Although sex is still on her mind, she lets him sleep.

Why did I even come?

***

The next morning, MaryAna sleeps in once more. When she climbs out of bed close to noon, it is almost time to leave for an early afternoon game. Tyler's team wins, but he struggles, striking out three times.

After the game, he borrows a teammate's car to take MaryAna to the airport. On the way, she mentions her company's CEO is having his limousine pick her up at JFK.

"So, what, you're some sort of VIP now?"

"Mr. Rubenstein treats me like one. I get to ride in the limo to and from work every day. I feel like a celebrity."

"You seem to be spendin' a lot of time with this guy."

"Seriously, are you jealous?" She chuckles but sees no smile on his face. "You think I'm cheatin' on you, don't you—cheatin' with someone old enough to be my daddy?"

Tyler glances at her. "Are you?"

"Mr. Rubenstein has been a perfect gentleman. He's helpin' me get adjusted to the city. I took this job to become a designer, not to sleep with the boss."

"You haven't changed, MaryAna."

"Excuse me?"

"You're drinkin' again. Your clothes are too tight, and you flirt with every guy you see."

"You used to like what I wore. As for when I flirt, I'm just playin'. I told you I wouldn't talk about the strip club anymore. I've been faithful to you, Tyler. I'm practically a new woman."

"No, MaryAna, you aren't. You went to New York on a whim, with me just an afterthought. You still get wasted and make a fool of yourself. And now you're lettin' some old rich dude be your sugar daddy."

"What's wrong with that?"

"Don't you think he wants something in return? Maybe his own lap dance—or a lot more?"

"Low blow, man."

"Maybe, but you get wild and unpredictable when you drink. Who knows what you might do next?"

"You used to like wild and unpredictable."

"Used to is right. I hoped we could have a serious relationship built on mutual trust and respect."

43

"We have that. You'll be playin' with the Yankees, and then we can start talking about marriage."

"MaryAna, you don't get it. This isn't workin' out."

"What?"

"I thought seein' you this weekend might make everything better. You know, stir up old feelings. It hasn't. Even the sex was hollow."

"What are you sayin'?"

Tyler doesn't answer right away, his eyes on the road. "Like you've told me more than once: we should just be friends and go our separate ways."

MaryAna's insides do a one-eighty. "Are you . . . breakin' up with me?"

He does not reply.

"Did you meet someone? Have you been cheatin' on me?"

"We've only talked," he says, his face turning ruddy. "I was gonna tell you about her, but . . ."

MaryAna folds her arms and locks her eyes on the road ahead, her lip trembling.

"Are you OK?" he says.

"No, I'm not okay. You pursued me forever—till I finally fell in love with you and now you want somebody else. How do you expect me to feel?"

"You don't need me, MaryAna. You've got big plans—I'd just be in the way."

"Don't try and justify everything. I *have* changed, and we *do* have a serious relationship." She turns toward her window and wipes away a tear. "I need you. And you need me." She turns back to him. "Don't you?"

Tyler does not answer.

"Okay, if my drinkin' is such a big deal, I'll stop. I'll quit my job and move here to take care of you. Just tell me what you want me to do, and I'll do it."

"MaryAna, it's over. I want to be with someone else."

"You can't just push me aside like you don't care. I know you love me. This girl has got in your head. She's one of those baseball groupies, isn't she?"

"Does it matter?"

"Yeah, it does. Who is it?"

"Meghan. You met her at the restaurant."

"Oh, my God! She isn't even your type, *Ty*."

"She's a nice girl. She's helpin' me with my hittin'."

"You mean she's playin' with your bat."

"You'd like her if you got to know her."

"What, are we in sixth grade? Was she the one textin' you?"

"Yes."

"So, you want to be with that skinny baseball bitch instead of me? Fine! Go ahead, toss me out like a piece of trash. See what I care."

"You ever stop to think, MaryAna—it might be you who's the problem, not the guys you are with?"

"So, this is my fault now? I didn't screw around on you. You're the one seein' another girl. This is on you, mister."

Tyler keeps his gaze on the road ahead.

"Look," she says, "just drop me off in front of the . . . airport, OK? Then you . . . you can scurry back to your little Meghan in case she needs to talk *privately* again."

"Come on, don't be like that."

"How should I be? You dumped me. Just frickin' drive the damn car."

This trip has turned into a nightmare!

45

Chapter 8

THE VOW

MaryAna is surprised to find Mel in the car when Roger picks her up at JFK.

"I wasn't expecting you to pick me up yourself, sir, but it's nice to see you."

"I simply wanted to make sure you arrived safely, Miss Lindley. Will you be returning to Scranton anytime soon?"

MaryAna's eyes turn downward, then to the passing roadway outside. "I don't think so. My boyfriend and I broke up."

"Oh my. I am truly sorry to hear that."

She turns back to him. "At least I'll save a bunch on airfare. At least that's . . ." But the façade breaks, and tears break out on her cheeks. "I'm sorry . . ."

"No, no. I understand completely. Do what you have to do."

She sniffles and wipes her nose. "Thanks. I think."

"I know this is what they always say, but you're young, MaryAna. You're attractive. New York's a big place. You'll find someone else soon enough, I guarantee it."

Mel pulls out his handkerchief for her and she takes it. "Thanks."

They ride in silence for several minutes as she sobs quietly.

"It was . . . so unexpected. I thought he loved me, but—"

"But what?"

"He was seeing another girl," she says, her tone shifting now. "A baseball groupie, can you believe that?"

"You were right to break it off, it sounds like to me, Miss Lindley."

"Actually, he dumped *me*."

"It is true that long-distance relationships rarely work out, unfortunately."

"Tell me about it. At least now I can concentrate on my job. There's so much to see and do here. I don't need Tyler—screw him."

"That's the spirit," he says. "By the way, I don't mean to be impetuous, but I wonder if you'd like to join me for dinner this evening? There's a great little place not far from the Plaza. Nothing fancy, but the food is excellent."

"Thanks for the offer, sir, but I'm afraid I wouldn't be good company tonight."

"It might make you feel better, Miss Lindley, You need to eat, after all."

"Perhaps another time? I just don't feel hungry, really."

I want to hit the minibar and drown my sorrows, that's what I want.

"Certainly."

"So, how was your weekend, sir? I hope, better than mine."

***

The next morning, as per usual, Mel drops MaryAna off in front of the Made Fresh Bakery, where she picks up coffee and doughnuts for her department. She is in full-blown denial about Tyler, however, and does not want to talk about him.

"How was your trip to Pennsylvania?" Kristen asks when MaryAna offers her a coffee.

"Fine."

"Is your boyfriend doing well?"

"He's fine."

Kristen hands MaryAna several color sketches. "When you get a chance, Hannah wants seven copies of each of these."

"Sure. Anything else?"

"We've got a senior staff meeting at nine-thirty in the conference room on fifty-five," Kristen says, handing MaryAna another, smaller piece of paper. "This is a list of what you need to get from Made

Fresh for the meeting."

MaryAna scans the list. "I feel like I'm just a glorified waitress."

Kristen grins and leans back in her chair. "Before you got here, I was the coffee bitch."

"You want the job back?"

"Not a chance, new girl," she says with a wink.

***

MaryAna arrives at the conference room at 9:25, loaded with coffee and doughnuts. As she distributes them to the senior staff, Mel introduces her.

"Miss Lindley is Hannah's new assistant designer," he notes. "She comes to us from Mississippi and is new to the city."

I wish I could stay for the meeting—I bet I could learn a bunch.

"Thank you, Miss Lindley," the CEO tells her. "That'll be all."

"Yes sir. Nice meetin' y'all," she says to the group. "If you need anything else, let me know."

The day continues downhill from there. MaryAna's back begins to ache, and she develops a splitting headache. Adding to her discomfort, she starts her period.

When it rains . . .

***

That night, MaryAna contemplates various methods of revenge on her former boyfriend. Poisoning, crippling, or kidnapping the harlot named Meghan quickly come to mind.

On Tuesday, instruments of violence such as axes, swords, or chainsaws are googled. By midnight, however, she discards each as too messy to clean up.

By Wednesday, she concludes the breakup is due to one simple reason: falling in love with a guy who's too young and immature.

For the past three nights she has emptied the minibar of every beer inside. She has also sampled the wine and liquor, discovering a fondness for gin. Also for the past three nights, she curls up on the couch intoxicated, crying herself to sleep.

***

By Thursday, MaryAna resolves to take charge of her life and not depend on a male for happiness. To prove to herself she is serious, she deletes all photos of Tyler from her phone.

That'll show him.

Being with just one guy is a recipe for breaking your heart.

Never trust men, especially younger ones.

Thursday evening, in a change of pace, MaryAna decides a walk in Central Park is better than drinking herself into oblivion. She throws fashion to the wind, donning pink leggings, black shorts, and her USM sweatshirt.

The eighteen-year-old pulls her long blond curls into an impromptu ponytail and tops it off with a baseball cap. She elects to wear no makeup—a mortal sin for this Mississippi girl.

When she exits the elevator in the hotel lobby, despite her attire and no makeup, she still turns male heads. She usually revels in such attention, but tonight, she could not care less.

As she approaches the exit, the uniformed doorman opens the door for her.

"And how are you this fine evening, Miss Lindley?"

"Things could be better, Leon, but I'm making do. How's your wife doing—is her flu still got her under the weather?"

"Much improved," he says, flashing his trademark smile. "Thanks for asking. Would you like me to hail a cab for you?"

"Thanks, but I need to get some exercise. I thought I'd head over to the park. My lower back has been givin' me fits."

Leon's face turns serious. "It's a lovely evening, but this city does, I'm afraid to say, have its dangers. Especially at night. You be careful now."

"I will, thanks."

It's a park—how dangerous can it be?

Chapter 9

THE STRANGER

MaryAna crosses Fifty-Ninth Street and follows one of the footpaths into Central Park. It meanders for a bit, then intersects a serene pond where another path skirts the water's edge. She takes a slow breath and smiles.

How cool is that—wildflowers here in New York City.

She slips off her Air Jordans and skips through the evening grass, finally dropping to her knees to savor more of the floral scents. And even in the dim cool light, the colors of the flowers stir something in MaryAna's soul she can not quite understand.

Is this one canary yellow? No, more like lemon.

What about that one?

She flits from flower to flower like a bumblebee. After strange looks from several passersby, she slips her shoes back on and continues her walk.

Farther along the path, MaryAna crosses a concrete footbridge, which provides a panoramic view of the pond and a calming escape from the bustling Manhattan streets. Movement catches her eye—a lone bird flitting across the water to a tree seeking refuge for the night.

Her thoughts soften and sway with the branches of the trees in the evening air. More birds sail overhead in search of harbor until light. She closes her eyes and sees herself in the sky with them, wishing that she too could somehow be free of worry and obligation.

I spend more time delivering pastries and coffee than doing real work. I can do so much more.

MaryAna's eyes snap open at movement in the nearby bushes. She peers toward the source of the sound but sees nothing. She scurries across the bridge in the opposite direction, which leads her further into the park. Lights along the way illuminate the path but little else. Sensing someone is stalking her, she quickens her pace. The path continues into more trees, which now makes it impossible to see the pond or the surrounding buildings.

I might as well be lost out in the country back home.

Then she stops.

A fork in the path.

Which one leads out of the park?

Twenty feet ahead, a man in a dark hoodie steps from behind a tree and starts toward her.

He's got something in his hand!

MaryAna's heart cartwheels, but before she can even utter a cry, the man freezes.

"MaryAna."

MaryAna jumps at the sound of the voice, even as the hoodie man scrambles into the brush. She whirls around to see a middle-aged man in a plaid work shirt and jeans ten feet behind her on the path.

"Who—"

"Don't be afraid. We've met before."

A calming voice, MaryAna notes. The most calming voice she's ever heard.

She finally allows herself to breathe again. "Thanks for scaring off that guy. I think he was after me."

"He was up to no good, that's true."

MaryAna steps closer to the man, squinting in the nighttime light. "Hey, you're the guy who saved me from that taxi."

The man smiles. "Yes."

"I remember you at the nursing home a few years ago too. And then this spring, I saw you again at Carleigh's church. What are you doing here?"

"Keeping watch over you."

"What—did Mama hire you?"

"No, but she does worry about you."

"Tell me about it. Well, what's the deal then? What are you, a bodyguard or something?"

"I wouldn't say that. But I am here to warn you."

MaryAna chuckles. "About what—about drinkin' and not taking my meds? I'm a big girl—I can take care of myself."

"Just know that actions come with consequences. This can be a dangerous city, MaryAna. Not everyone here is as they seem."

"What—my boss? Somebody at the hotel?"

"Just choose your friends carefully. You will need allies to win this battle. Evil is all around you."

"'Evil is all around me.' What am I, in *The Hunger Games*? Who are you talking about?"

"Those who would align with Satan himself."

She stumbles back a step. "Say what? What are you, some sort of guardian angel?" Then she blinks. Hey—that statue in front of the church in the magazine. Gabriel—that's *your* face . . ."

"Do you believe in angels, MaryAna?"

"Well, yeah—the Bible talks about them. Are you . . . are you trying to tell me you're him—you're Gabriel?"

He smiles but does not answer.

"Well, if you're legit, which path should I take?" she says, nodding toward the park walkway."

"The path of righteousness."

"Well, of course that's what you would say. I mean, which footpath takes me out of the park?"

She turns back to him, but he is gone.

What the heck? Is this guy Batman, or am I tripping?"

MaryAna weighs the possibilities, then hustles down the leftward path. As she rounds a corner, she spots someone standing under a lamppost.

Oh, thank God, a policeman.

"Evenin,' officer," she says, her heartbeat easing down.

"Evening, ma'am. Are you walking alone?"

"Yes."

"It's not a good idea to walk in the park alone at night, especially for women."

"I'll remember. Can you tell me the nearest way out of the park? I'm kinda lost."

He points to a short set of steps nearby. "That'll take you back to the street."

"Thanks." She jogs over to the steps as the officer returns to his vigil.

Soon, MaryAna is back on Fifty-Ninth Street, walking among other evening pedestrians. She notes the line of horse-drawn carriages, waiting, as usual, to provide couples romantic excursions in the City That Never Sleeps.

A ride in one of them would be delightful, but not tonight.

***

Back in her suite, MaryAna orders a shrimp salad and strawberry cheesecake. Once it arrives, she washes it all down with a beer from the minibar.

Just as she finishes the bottle, her phone buzzes with a text from her longtime friend, Coree Butler: GREAT NEWS. CALL ME.

Coree is a freshman at the University of Southern Mississippi. After serving as a coach and placekicker for their high school, she was offered the position of receivers coach at the college level. For a female who loves the sport, it is a rare opportunity.

"What's up at Southern Miss, girl?" MaryAna says when Coree answers.

"Coach Brown just named your brother the startin' quarterback for the opener against Nebraska. I thought you'd like to know."

"Good for him. Since I've been in New York, JoeE and I have only texted a couple times. I'll call to congratulate him."

"I got your text about Tyler. Sorry I haven't called. I've been frantic with both football and school. How are you doin', other than Tyler, that is?"

"Awesome." MaryAna says. A lie. "You know me and Tyler—on

again, off again. But now it's done." Lie number two. "There's so much to do here. I haven't thought about him since we split." Lie number three.

"You found a place yet?"

"Workin' on it."

"How's your job so far?"

"The folks at work love my ideas." Lie number four. "I get my first paycheck tomorrow, but I'd be doin' this for free. I've been thinkin' about investin' some of the money JoeE gave me."

"Your mama should be able to help with that. She gave me some great advice on the stock I inherited."

"I know, Coree, but I want to do it myself."

"I'm proud of how you got a job and moved to the big city. Not to mention, you givin' up drugs and drinkin'."

MaryAna chuckles. "Yeah, it's nice *not* to be hungover, for sure." Lie number five.

"Sorry, but I've got to go. Coach called a meetin' tonight. With JoeE as our startin' quarterback, we have to adjust our offensive schemes."

MaryAna giggles. "Whatever that means. Hey, quick question—do you believe in angels?"

"Why would you ask that?"

"I think I just saw one."

"What makes you think it was an angel?"

"Long story, and you're in a hurry. I'll tell you about it another time. Love you."

"Love you more."

I shouldn't lie to my best friend, but I don't want her to see me screwing up.

Chapter 10

MARKET RESEARCH

At seven o'clock Friday morning, Mel's Rolls arrives at the Plaza to pick up MaryAna.

"Thanks, Roger," a bleary-eyed MaryAna says to the chauffeur as she slips through the open door.

"You are welcome, Miss Lindley."

As usual, she is seated facing her boss, Mel Rubenstein. "Good morning, sir."

But the CEO does not answer, his attention lost in today's financial news.

MaryAna clears her throat and repeats her greeting.

"Oh, pardon me, Miss Lindley," he says, folding his paper. "Good morning."

Today MaryAna is wearing an ivory dress with bright-red swirls running through the fabric. Like her other outfits, its short fringed skirt shows off her long legs.

"Is that a new dress?"

"Do you like it?" MaryAna shifts her weight, tugging at the hem in a gesture of modesty. "I got it at Neiman Marcus."

"Very nice. I believe it is from the Dolce and Gabbana spring collection?"

"You know your competition, sir. The Italian designers make excellent use of bright colors. That's why I like them."

"We don't require our female employees to wear our brand, but we do encourage them to do so, you might like to know. And we offer generous discounts."

"To tell you the truth, the store had several Jacqueline Design dresses, but I couldn't find one that really suited me. Like I said, I lean toward brighter colors. This got your attention, didn't it?" she says, indicating her outfit.

"You know, I did propose the idea of brighter colors at our weekly design meeting. Jacqueline was present, teleconferencing from Paris. But she wasn't as receptive as I'd hoped."

"Did you tell her it was my idea, sir?"

"Not as yet. Jacqueline can be rather sensitive when it comes to design concepts. I'll see that you receive full credit should we use your suggestions."

"I don't want her upset with me before we even meet."

"I'll take the heat for now, Miss Lindley. By the way, I was wondering—do you have plans for this evening?"

MaryAna blinks. "Nothing special. Do you have some work you need me to do?"

"I have an extra ticket to the Philharmonic. They're doing a tribute to Mozart. Do you . . . do you enjoy classical music, by any chance?"

"I don't know much about it, frankly."

"Well, I was thinking we could do some market research at the concert—you know, survey what women wear to such affairs this summer."

"That's a good idea. Who else is comin'?"

"Actually, it would be just us two."

Is he asking me out on a date?

"So, you want me to help you do market research?"

"Exactly."

"In that case, sure. I'd love to go."

"Splendid. It starts at eight o'clock. How about I pick you up around seven?"

"I've never been to that kind of concert. What should I wear?"

"How about one of our designs—if you wouldn't mind?"

"But I don't own one."

"We have a storage area with samples of all our products. You should be able to find at least one outfit to suit you. After lunch, see my secretary for a key."

"I can pick out whatever I want?"

"Of course."

"What do I tell Hannah?"

"Tell her I have a special task for you. She can get along without you for a couple of hours."

MaryAna grins. "This will be like goin' shoppin'."

"If you find something you like that doesn't quite fit, we have a department that can make alterations."

"I appreciate the opportunity to expand my knowledge about fashion, sir."

"My pleasure. We can compare notes after the concert."

It's nice that Mr. Rubenstein is attracted to me and my opinions, and not my looks. I mean—that's the deal, right?

***

After Mel drops MaryAna off at the bakery, she orders a black coffee for herself while waiting for the rest of her order. The eighteen-year-old hopes the caffeine will jump-start her brain after yet another restless night. Once back in the office, she distributes the coffee and doughnuts to the grateful recipients. Sharree makes his usual grand gesture of gratitude and raves about MaryAna's dress and how exquisite it looks on her. She hopes he will be as receptive to her blouse designs.

On her desk MaryAna finds an envelope with the company name and logo—her first paycheck has arrived. Hannah told her what her hourly wage as an assistant designer would be, which seemed generous, especially considering how much of her duties involves delivering coffee. But the amount left after taxes shocks MaryAna.

This is like half of what I was expecting—and what the heck is FICA? I took more home as a waitress at the strip club.

She marches into her supervisor's office with several burning questions, so Hannah explains FICA and deductions to her. But MaryAna is still miffed.

I gotta rethink my budget. That is, if I had a budget.

"By the way, Mr. Rubenstein has a special task for me this afternoon," MaryAna says before heading back to her desk. "I'll be goin' to the sample room after lunch. We're doin' market research tonight at the Lincoln Center, and he wants me to wear a Jacqueline dress."

Hannah sighs. "Why am I not surprised? Why don't you just . . . oh, forget it."

"Forget what?"

"Just because Mel's the boss doesn't mean you have to do anything he tells you."

"What are you sayin'?"

"I'm saying Mel is a rich, handsome guy, and you're a beautiful young woman. Do the math."

MaryAna cocks her eyebrow and folds her arms. "I've never been good at math."

"Just be careful, young lady. Don't do anything you'll regret."

"You're not my mama, Hannah. Besides, Mr. Rubenstein has been a perfect gentleman."

Hannah folds *her* arms. "Then you have nothing to worry about, do you, Miss Lindley."

"No, I don't."

I don't care if Hannah is my supervisor. Some folks should mind their own business.

Chapter *11*

THE DRESS

After lunch, MaryAna borrows the key from Mel's secretary and goes to the sample room, which is full of dresses, blouses, skirts, and accessories. The teenager grins and begins rummaging through the racks, shelves, and boxes in search of the perfect outfit for the evening.

MaryAna's deep dive into fashion wonderland soon culminates in a sleeveless formfitting crimson dress with spaghetti straps that cross in the back and shapes of flowers woven into the fabric. A white satin jacket and thin belt tops off the ensemble.

My white heels will go great with this, she thinks, checking herself out in a full-length mirror.

Almost perfect!

She locates a box to hold her new acquisitions and returns the key to the secretary. Mel spots her through the open door of his office and motions for her to come in.

The CEO's corner office is smaller than MaryAna had imagined, but nicely furnished: a large wooden desk, credenza, several chairs, and a black leather sofa complete with its own coffee table.

Mel nods toward MaryAna's box. "I take it you found something suitable for this evening."

"The color is darker than I prefer, but I love the style."

"You're a hard woman to please, Miss Lindley."

At least he called me a woman and not a girl or young lady,

"Not really, but I am particular about what I wear.

"I'm anxious to see what you selected."

"How about I keep it a secret until you pick me up."

He smiles. "A surprise it shall be then."

"It needs some minor alterations though. Where should I take it?"

"The north end of your floor. Alice Hempstead is the head of that department. Let her know I want the alterations done right away. If she has any questions, she can call me."

"Is it OK if I head out for the day after they're done? It takes me a while to get dressed."

He grins. "I'm aware of that, Miss Lindley. That will be fine. I'll inform Hannah."

MaryAna steps over to the ceiling-to-floor glass windows that form two walls of his office and gazes out at the Manhattan skyline.

"This view takes my breath away, sir."

"Truly breathtaking," Mel says, before clearing his throat. "It takes *my* breath away."

MaryAna turns to see his eyes on her and not the cityscape.

Was that a compliment?

"I'm kinda freaked out about doin' market research tonight. I hope I do a good job."

"I'm sure you will."

"I appreciate your having so much confidence in me, sir."

Mel leans forward in his chair, his hands clasped on his desk. "It's best if you didn't mention the concert to your co-workers. I don't want them to feel slighted. You understand, right?"

So, he wants to keep tonight a secret . . .

"I already told Hannah," she notes. "Is that a problem?"

He thinks for a moment. "It'll be fine, but no one else needs to know."

"I understand."

***

MaryAna stops by the lady's room while waiting for her alterations to be completed. Kristen is in front of one of the sinks refreshing her makeup. When MaryAna comes out of the stall, she begins washing her hands. "I love your skirt," she says. "It's very eye-catching."

"Sharree designed it for our spring collection, but Jacqueline ultimately rejected it."

"How come?"

"She claimed it was too provocative," Kristen says. "Sharree gave me this sample, and I sometimes wear it when Jacqueline's out of town."

"It reminds me of the Bible story about Joseph's coat of many colors—and the Dolly Parton song."

Kristen grins. "I doubt Sharee had the Bible or Dolly Parton in mind when he designed it."

"So, what's the deal with Sharree? He have a last name?"

Kristen returns the lipstick to her purse and looks around as if making sure they are alone. "Jenny in accounting told me his real name is Ezra Winklestein. He's very nice and a good boss. I've learned a lot from him."

"Hannah's nice, too," MaryAna says, drying her hands. "She hasn't taught me a whole lot yet, but I guess that'll come in time."

Kristen checks their surroundings once more. "I saw you getting out of Mr. Rubenstein's limo this morning."

"You did?"

"Yeah. I wasn't spying or anything, but I was across the street coming out of the drugstore."

"Mr. Rubenstein just gives me rides to and from work. It's not a secret, but he's concerned other employees might get jealous."

Kristen snickers. "Is that what he told you? Don't you think that's a bit strange?"

"I don't know what you think is goin' on. He's helpin' me because I'm new in town."

"Of course, what you do is none of my business. It's just . . ."

"Just . . . ?"

"You seem like a nice girl, MaryAna. I probably shouldn't say, but Rubenstein has a reputation around here."

"I don't listen to rumors."

"These are *facts*. You're not the first girl he's done *special* favors for. When I started here, he gave me rides too. That is, until I had to fight him off one night in his limo."

"He attacked you?"

"He grabbed me and tried to kiss me. Effing freaked me out."

"What did you do?'

"I threatened to report him to HR and he backed off. I should've filed a complaint, but I need this job."

"Maybe you misinterpreted his intentions . . . ?"

"His intention was to get me into bed. You just need to be careful."

"Thanks for the warnin'."

I'll give Mr. Rubenstein the benefit of the doubt—at least for now.

Chapter 12

THE CONCERT

At 7:05 that evening, Mel is waiting in the limo outside the Plaza. MaryAna texts him again to let him know she is nearly ready. Ten minutes later, she dashes through the doors of the hotel lobby and into the back seat of the car.

The crimson dress clings to all of MaryAna's curves, and with her hair in a sophisticated updo, she could easily grace the cover of any number of magazines from *Vogue* to *Playboy*.

"Sorry. It took me a little longer than I thought. Even with the alterations, it's kinda tight," she says, tugging on the front of the dress. "Does it look OK?"

Mel glances again at her bustline. "It . . . looks exquisite."

MaryAna giggles. "It's a Jacqueline Design. Ever heard of 'em?"

He grins as Roger pulls the silver limousine into traffic. "This dress is from our first year in business. I recall Jacqueline modeling it for us. I don't recall her filling it out quite like you, however."

"Was she a model?"

"She was, yes. She was doing magazine and runway work when we first met."

"Where did you meet?"

"A party at a friend's beach house. I was working on Wall Street at the time, and my dream was to run my own company."

"Hannah says Jacqueline has final say on all the designs."

"That's true," Mel says, "She's open to discussion, but the final decisions are hers."

"When I meet Jacqueline, I want to make a good impression. Any suggestions?"

He smiles. "Don't be late and don't disparage the French."

***

The house lights dim as Mel and MaryAna enter the Lincoln Center. The concert is about to get underway, so they hurry to their seats in the middle of the orchestra.

"These are great seats," she whispers, glancing around the famous hall.

"And the most expensive," Mel whispers back.

"I've got a pen and paper in my purse to take notes."

"Mental notes will be fine, Miss Lindley. There won't be a test."

The performance enthralls MaryAna, and she realizes she has heard some of the music before. At intermission, she checks out what other female attendees are wearing, though few appear to be as young as her.

After the concert, the teenager slips on her jacket and takes Mel's arm. She feels elegant and welcomes the admiring glances from many of the men they encounter.

"I made plenty of mental notes, sir."

"Excellent," he says as they leave the building. "The night is young. Why don't we discuss them over a late supper?"

They walk a few steps before MaryAna responds. "Sir, is someone waitin' for you at home?"

His face hints at a smile. "No, not even a dog or cat. Just an empty house, Miss Lindley."

Well then, that confirms it.

Kristen's words still echo in MaryAna's mind, however. "I'm kinda tired tonight," she says, faking a yawn. "I'm usually a night owl, but I haven't been sleepin' well. How about we discuss this market research Monday at work?"

"Better yet, Miss Lindley, how about dinner tomorrow evening while it is fresh in our minds?"

Roger pulls up in the limousine as MaryAna contemplates the offer.

That sounded like a date too.

Once they are inside the car, Mel says, "What do you say—we could also take in a musical."

Her face lights up. "More research?"

He nods and clicks the intercom to instruct Roger to return to the hotel.

"Have you ever been to a Broadway show, Miss Lindley?"

"Nope, never."

"The popular ones are often sold out Saturday nights. I have some connections, however, so I might be able to wrangle us some tickets. I can text you the choices tomorrow morning."

"Let me pay for the tickets, sir."

"Nonsense. I'm inviting you."

"At least let me pay for dinner."

Mel smiles. "If you insist. Would you like to make the reservation or choose a restaurant?"

"You choose."

He ponders for a moment. "How about T. J. Morgan's? It's an Irish pub and not expensive. Very old-world decor. The food is exceptional, and they're open late."

"Sounds great."

"Will you need another dress from the sample room?"

"I have a new Chanel I could wear. It's a perfect example of the bright-colored designs I like. You'll see what I'm talkin' about."

"Jacqueline's grandfather was a cousin of their founder, Coco Chanel."

"So, Jacqueline has fashion in her blood?"

"She does. Well, get some rest, Miss Lindley. We will have two nights of market research to digest along with dinner."

When the limousine rolls to a stop in front of the hotel, almost without thinking, MaryAna gives the CEO a quick hug, apparently blindsiding him.

By Kristen's standards, I just attacked him.

"Thanks so much, sir. I had a lovely evenin'."

MaryAna steps out of the car and turns to the chauffeur. "You do a great job, Roger."

He tips his hat to her with a big grin. "It's always a pleasure serving you, Miss Lindley." After he clicks the door closed, he adds, "I recall Miss Jacqueline wearing a similar dress."

"This one came from the company's sample room. I understand Jacqueline was a model."

"Like you, Miss Lindley, she is most attractive."

"Thank you, Roger," she says, beaming. "That's so nice of you."

She waves goodbye to him and turns to head in to the hotel lobby.

I wonder if Jacqueline and Mr. Rubenstein once had more than a business relationship.

Chapter 13

OLD FRIEND

MaryAna awakens just before nine Saturday morning and notes that Mel has sent her a list of possible musicals. She peruses the titles and texts him back: I'D LOVE TO SEE WICKED.

A few minutes later, she receives a reply: SHOW STARTS AT 7:30. PICK YOU UP AT 6:00.

He knows now to give me plenty of time to get ready—he's learning.

MaryAna orders breakfast, then calls her friend Tony Russo. They reconnected on her visit to New York City last summer after she thought he had died on a secret incursion into Iran. Her being back in town is a golden opportunity to reach out to him since their last conversation had not gone well.

"Mississippi girl! We haven't talked since . . ."

"Since you turned me down for a loan."

"Has it been that long?"

In desperation last fall, MaryAna had begged family and friends for cash to pay off the drug dealer who had her under his thumb at the time. But when they refused her, she subsequently accused them all of betraying her friendship.

"How's JoeE?" Tony says. "I understand he's playin' for USM."

"He's gonna be their startin' quarterback."

"Outstanding. And how are you doing these days, young lady?"

"Lots better. I'm off the pills and here in New York now. I work at a fashion company in Manhattan called Jacqueline Designs. By the way," she adds, her voice soft, "I really apologize for . . . well, for how I acted last time we spoke."

"Don't sweat it, MaryAna. Water under the bridge."

"Great. So, how's Dori?"

"We got a baby coming in a couple months."

"Hey, congratulations!"

"We're living in my grandparents' condo on Central Park West while I finish med school."

"We need to get together and catch up."

"Dori and I are at home today. Why don't you come over? She'll be happy to see you."

"Sounds good. Text me the address."

***

Two hours later, MaryAna steps outside the hotel, this time in a low-cut turquoise blouse and short tan skirt.

"Hey, Leon," she says, smiling at the doorman. "How's it goin'?"

"Just enjoying this fine weather, Miss Lindley. What're you up to today?"

"On my way to visit an old friend. And I'm not so young, Leon."

"Sorry. I have a teenage son, so anyone close to his age seems young to an old guy like me."

"You aren't old, Leon. How old is he?"

"Fourteen," he says. "Our Max is autistic."

"That must be difficult."

"Max is an artist. I think his work is damn good, but I'm biased."

"I'd love to see it sometime. Say, could you get me a taxi? I'm runnin' a little late."

"Sure thing." Leon hails a cab and opens the door for her when one pulls up to a stop."

"Thanks," she says, slipping him a twenty-dollar bill.

"That's not necessary, Miss Lindley."

"Buy Max some art supplies. Who knows—he might be the next Picasso."

***

When Tony answers the door at his apartment, MaryAna is shocked.

My God, he looks years older since the last time I saw him, like he hasn't slept in a week.

"Welcome to our home," Tony says, his voice upbeat.

She steps inside and hugs him. "This place is magnificent," she says, taking in the room.

The picture window in the condo's living room has a bird's eye view of Central Park. From the antique furniture to the oil paintings, the place screams "fancy."

Tony motions toward a pair of Georgian mahogany armchairs. "Make yourself comfortable."

"How's your hip?" she says, taking a seat.

"Tolerable." He limps over to the matching sofa. "Dori will be with us in a minute."

Iranian soldiers ambushed Tony's band of mercenaries during a secret incursion into the country. As the sole survivor of the failed mission, as well as being wounded, he eventually escaped the country with the aid of a local girl whom he promised to bring to the United States. To fulfill his promise, he ended up marrying the young woman. Her name was Dori.

She soon emerges from the hallway, looking every bit seven months pregnant. MaryAna rises to shake hands. "Nice to see you again." Dori joins her husband on the sofa.

"Until I find an apartment, I'd love to move into a place like this," MaryAna says. "It might be a good investment. Are there any units in this buildin' for sale?"

Tony chuckles. "The last one sold for several million, and it doesn't have a park view."

"Millions—really?"

"Yep. Anything nice in Manhattan is pricey. Would you care for something to drink?"

"Beer?"

"Your mother told me you'd stopped drinking."

"I started again. My addiction was with drugs, not alcohol."

"I see." Tony turns to his wife. "Anything for you, dear?"

"I want water, please."

"Be right back," he says before disappearing into the kitchen.

MaryAna turns her attention to Dori. "I understand your baby is due in a couple months. How're you feelin'?"

"All right." Dori arches her back as if it hurts. "I don't want Tony worry about me."

"Your husband should pamper you. He got you pregnant."

"Not his fault. I want baby."

"I didn't mean . . ." MaryAna realizes Dori's understanding of English is still probably limited.

When Tony returns, he hands the teenager a beer and his wife a glass of water, then takes his place beside her. He and MaryAna catch up, and he tells her about returning to medical school after so many years. Dori does not speak much, mostly listening quietly.

"My experience as a medic helps, but I still have a lot to learn," he says. "Tell me more about your new job. It's hard to think of you as a working girl."

"I'm an assistant designer. I'm hoping some of my ideas catch on. The CEO seems to like them. He's takin' me to a Broadway musical tonight. We're doin' market research to see what women are wearin' these days."

Tony raises his eyebrows. "Market research? What show are you going to see?"

"*Wicked.*"

"Dori and I saw it last year," he says to his wife. "It was awesome, wasn't it, honey?"

She nods.

Tony turns back to MaryAna. "So, you're going out with your new boss?"

"It's strictly business. We'll compare notes on the women's attire."

"It appears your CEO values your opinion."

"He and I talk on the way to and from work every day in his limo."

"A limousine, wow. And you're staying at the Plaza? You're certainly living the good life."

"The company is payin' for my first month. I wish I could live there full-time."

"Don't we all."

Is Tony jealous?

"So, how is your family, MaryAna? I haven't talked to your mother in a while."

"They're fine. Mama told me she'd asked you not to lend me any money," she says, the words spilling out before she catches herself, "but I was sure you'd come through for me."

"When you called, you weren't making much sense. I wanted to give you the money, but I was worried it might make things worse."

"I was probably high when I talked to you."

Tony's dark eyes lock on hers. "I should've come to see you. Maybe I could've helped. I wasn't much of a friend."

"I was stupid to get myself hooked. Only by the grace of God am I here today. But I doubt the fashion industry is as dangerous as the drug scene."

Tony chuckles and turns to his wife. "It's time you ate something. Why don't I pick up some Chinese takeout while the two of you talk, dear?"

Dori nods.

"You like shrimp fried rice, MaryAna?"

"Definitely."

"There's a great little place not far from here." Tony rises from the sofa. "When I return, you can tell us about Bonnie Lee and your grandparents."

After Tony leaves for the restaurant, Dori and MaryAna sit silently for a moment before Dori looks up at her. "You still love Tony?"

The question surprises MaryAna. "Ahh . . . yeah, but just as a friend."

"You no like him more than that?"

"Are you askin' if I still have romantic feelings for your husband?"

"When we in Iran, Tony tell about you. How he want marry you. When he with fever, he call your name, not mine. I think he in love with you very much."

"Dori, there's nothing between your husband and me. We're just old friends. You have nothing to worry about."

"Don't want Tony do drugs like you."

"I don't take drugs anymore."

"I see how Tony look at you," his wife continues. "Why you dress like that if you no want him?"

"I'm not tryin' to steal your husband."

"Best you go now."

MaryAna looks at Dori, her face now unsure of itself. Then she rises from the chair. "Tell Tony goodbye for me," she says, heading for the door.

"I tell him."

***

Once back at the hotel, MaryAna calls her friend, Carleigh Storm, back home. In Mississippi they had shared a four-bedroom house.

"I've gathered together everything you wanted," Carleigh says. "I'll FedEx them Monday."

"Just address it to the Plaza with my name and room number."

"You sure you don't want more of your clothes?"

"I've bought a bunch of new stuff here, but I might get you to send some other things later. By the way, something weird happened the other day. Remember when I went to your church and told you I talked to my guardian angel?"

"Yeah. You said he talked to you about forgiveness."

"I could swear I saw him again here, over in Central Park. He appears out of nowhere, talks all cryptic and everything, then disappears. This time he said something about choosing my friends carefully."

"That's good advice, angel or not."

"So, how are things with you, Carleigh?"

"Lookin' up. I told your mama I want to start payin' rent since you've moved away. It's not fair that my daughter and I are still gettin' a free ride."

"Mama has plenty of rental property and doesn't need the money.

Don't worry about it. She's not."

"A girl at the bank wants to move in here and share expenses. Sarah said it would be fine but to keep your room as is."

Mama doesn't believe I can make it here.

"Go ahead and get another roommate. I have no plans to come back any time soon. How's Kate?"

"Growin' like a weed. She already knows her ABCs. Hey, sorry to hear about Tyler."

"It was for the best. Young guys are so irresponsible."

"Tell me about it. So, what have you been doin' in New York besides work?"

"I went to a concert last night. Tonight I'm goin' to dinner and a Broadway musical."

"With someone?"

"My company's CEO. We're doin' market research—checkin' out what women are wearing."

Carleigh giggles. "Is that what they call it up there? Sounds like a date if you ask me. Tell me about this guy."

"He's handsome, sophisticated, and has a limo."

"How old is he?"

"In his forties, maybe early fifties. Does it matter?"

"I know you like older guys, MaryAna, but you're really pushing the envelope here."

"He's in great shape for his age, and he loves my design ideas."

"Well . . . as long as he's good to you and makes you happy."

"He is good to me, Carleigh. Hey, I've got to go—kiss Kate for me."

"I will."

Why doesn't anyone believe me about my market research?

Chapter 14

WICKED

That evening following the show, Mel takes MaryAna's hand to guide her through the crowded lobby. The simple gesture hints of intimacy, intended or not.

I love how Mr. Rubenstein takes care of me.

"That was amazin'," she says, once they're outside the theatre. "That was fantastic. Thanks for invitin' me."

"You're most welcome. Did you take note of what the women were wearing?"

"A little, but I have to admit I was so engrossed with the show that I forgot. I don't think I really did what I was supposed to tonight.

"I made plenty of notes to bounce off you," he tells her. "By the way, once again, I just want to say your Chanel is definitely eye-catching."

"Well, thank you, sir," she says, bobbing a curtsy. Her mid-thigh length white dress is short-sleeved with a high collar and a spiral band of tiny pink flowers woven into the fabric. "This is a perfect example of what I like—elegant, yet bright and sassy."

"It fits your personality, Miss Lindley."

The limousine soon arrives, and Mel opens the door for her. MaryAna slips into the rear-facing seat while the CEO slides in across from her. As the vehicle pulls into traffic, she hums the song "Popular" from the musical.

"I take it you like that one."

"It's catchy."

"Do you identify with the Glinda character? She's blond and

outgoing like you."

"I identify with both her and Elphaba. Most of the time, I'm upbeat like Glinda, but sometimes, I can be moody and sullen like Elphaba."

"I'm guessing you were popular in high school, Miss Lindley."

"I was voted onto the homecomin' court all four years and was prom queen as a senior. If you don't me askin', what were your high school days like, sir?"

"I was privileged to be at the top of my class at an exclusive prep school."

"Did you play any sports?"

"Lacrosse."

"I saw my first match last year when I visited my grandparents. It was exciting. I even went out with one of the players."

"Have you dated many guys?"

"Quite a few."

"Were they all around your age?"

"Some, but most were several years older than me."

I should be honest with him.

"Guys around my age . . . well . . . they aren't very dependable. Take Tyler. He said he loved me, then took up with another girl because I didn't discuss movin' to New York with him. How do you like that."

"It seems unfair."

"Darn right it's unfair. I want someone who will be there when I need him."

"Someone older and wiser who appreciates your finer qualities?"

"Exactly," she notes, grinning. "Do you know anyone like that?"

Mel grins as well. "I might."

Maybe Mr. Rubenstein is attracted to more than just my mind.

***

It hits her the moment MaryAna and Mel enter T.J. Morgan's: mahogany. The tables, chairs, bar, walls—impossible to ignore, but not overwhelming, the scent permeates the busy pub. A tall balding man shows them to a booth in the back of the restaurant. "Will this be all right, Mr. Rubenstein?"

"Yes, perfect," he says, handing the man a folded bill.

Whoa—was that a fifty?

"Your waiter will be right with you."

"Thank you, Sidney. I appreciate your discretion."

As the man walks away, MaryAna opens her purse. "Do I need my ID?"

Mel waves her off. "You won't need it here, Miss Lindley."

A waiter in an emerald-green shirt arrives with two mugs, a frosted pitcher, and menus. "I'll give you a few minutes," he says before leaving.

Mel fills their mugs, and MayAna takes a quick sample. "Interesting. What kind of beer is this?

"Golden Ale, from a brewery on Long Island. It's a bit stronger than beer."

She takes another swallow and takes in the room. "They seem to know you here."

"I come here often. We go to higher-end establishments for business, but here I can kick back."

"This place rocks," she says, picking up a menu. "What do you suggest?"

"I prefer the garlic chicken or the grilled salmon, but everything is good. Tonight, I'm going with the salmon."

"Sounds awesome. Remember, this meal is on me." She takes another gulp, then turns back to him. "May I ask a personal question?"

"Of course," he says before taking a sip from his mug.

"I heard some disturbin' rumors at work."

Mel shifts in his chair. "Rumors?"

"Did you sexually harass a female employee in your limo?"

"You're very straightforward, Miss Lindley." The CEO takes another a drink. "Are you referring to Kristen Kowalski?"

MaryAna maintains eye contact. "I'd like to hear your side of it."

Mel takes another swallow. "I invited Miss Kowalski to dinner. We had a pleasant evening, but she was giving mixed signals. On the way back from the restaurant, I attempted to embrace her, but she reacted quite negatively. I immediately apologized."

"You don't seem like the type of guy who would force himself on anyone. Maybe she did overreact."

"My thoughts exactly. Still, I should've waited for her to make the first move."

MaryAna drains her mug and suppresses a burp. "Maybe you just picked the wrong girl to hug."

"What are you saying, Miss Lindley?"

"Just that all females don't think alike. I hugged you last night. You could have taken that as a first move."

"I took it as a friendly gesture."

"It was meant that way," she says, pouring herself more ale. "So, changing the subject, you want to talk about what the women wore at the concert last night?"

"Uh . . . yes, of course."

For the rest of the meal, and two more pitchers later, they stick to the topic of women's fashion.

***

The CEO summons his car just before midnight. When Roger opens the rear door, MaryAna sees Mel whisper something to him. Once inside the vehicle, the chauffeur raises the tinted privacy glass between the passengers and the front seat.

"It's hot in here," MaryAna says, pointing to the sunroof. "Can we open it now?"

Mel pushes a button and the roof door slides open. MaryAna slips off her high heels, stands up on the seat and pops her head out of the opening. "Teenagers in movies always hang out of the sunroof—c'mon," she says, waving him up.

"I'm not a teenager," Mel notes, craning his neck. "It's dangerous and probably illegal."

MaryAna spreads her arms wide as her hair flails in the rush of the cool night air, and she squeals with joy. "I'm defyin' gravity just like Elphaba—join me!"

Mel shakily gets to his feet, struggling to maintain his balance as he pokes his head through the opening.

As the limousine cruises up Fifth Avenue, MaryAna spreads her newfound wings once more. "I'm the queen of the world!" she yells, lost in her own Titanic fever dream.

"Please be careful," Mel says, his eyebrows losing their composure.

When the car changes lanes MaryAna loses her balance and latches onto Mel for support.

"We should sit back down, Miss Lindley. Please."

But she lets go of him when they stop at a traffic light. Mel takes his seat and refastens his belt, asking her again to come down. She does not hear him and waves to the occupants of nearby vehicles. Some even wave back.

"Come back up," she says. "The city's callin' to us."

"I like the view from here just fine," he says, glancing at MaryAna's long legs.

"Oh, you do?" She giggles and waves to a young man in a delivery truck who is gawking at her.

The limousine lurches forward when the light changes. MaryAna loses her balance again, this time plopping into Mel's lap. He cradles her, and their eyes lock. The next thing she knows, her lips are on his.

At first, Mel does not return the kiss, but MaryAna is persistent. She presses her body against his, and soon they are lost in a passionate embrace.

The moment is short-lived as the limousine arrives at the Plaza. The teenager scoots off the CEO's lap and returns to the seat across from him. While she straightens her dress, he clicks the button to close the sunroof.

"Would you like to go somewhere else, sir? Maybe a club. I'm in the mood to dance."

"It's late," he says, smoothing down his windblown head. "Perhaps another evening."

She slips on her heels. "Isn't this supposed to be the city that never sleeps?"

"It doesn't, Miss Lindley, but I do."

"We could play some disco tunes and dance in my suite."

"It's a tempting offer, young lady, but I should refuse."

"Why?"

"Because you're my employee."

"We're not at work." MaryAna leans over and whispers in his ear. "There's more to me than my legs."

Mel swallows hard. "I wouldn't want to be accused of sexual harassment."

"I'm not Kristen and don't care if you're my boss's boss's boss. Wouldn't you like to dance with me?"

"I'd like to do more than that, Miss Lindley."

She grins. "What's stoppin' you?"

Mel pushes the intercom button. "Roger, I'll be here at the Plaza for a while. I will let you know when to pick me up."

"Yes, sir," Roger says over the speaker.

After they exit the limousine and head toward the lobby arm in arm, the CEO turns to her. "I cannot believe I'm with a beautiful young lady in a Chanel dress. It's like betraying my own company."

MaryAna feels no pain as they swoop into the Plaza. Her new world sparkles like the lobby's gold trim. The teenager overflows with excitement she could only imagine back home.

Her new companion checks most of the boxes on her list of desirable male attributes and believes a romantic relationship deserves serious consideration. Their age difference has faded like melting snow. Still, the teenager harbors a few gnawing doubts.

I don't know Mr. Rubenstein that well.

There's plenty of time to remedy that.

Chapter 15

LET'S DANCE

Once at the door to her suite, MaryAna digs through her purse, looking for her room card.

"I know it's here someplace."

"May I?" Mel says, taking her purse.

He searches through it, then opens her wallet. He finds the keycard wedged between her ID and several packets of condoms.

"Did you learn anything about me from rummaging around in there?" she says with a grin as they step inside.

"That you're sexually active, yet take precautions."

"Do you have one with you?"

Mel shakes his head.

MaryAna hands him one of the packets. "You never know when you might need it."

The CEO slips it in his pocket while she goes to the minibar and grabs a beer.

"Whatcha want, sir?"

He settles himself on the sofa. "Maybe something later."

"Suit yourself." She plops down beside him. She slips off her shoes and digs her toes into the soft carpeting. "Southern girls love to go barefoot."

"The color of your toenails matches your eyes."

"It's called electric blue." MaryAna giggles before taking a swig of beer. "Tyler never noticed things like that. Older guys are much more observant."

Mel takes her hands in his. "What else do you like about older gentlemen?"

"You're more dependable and don't go runnin' off with every girl who bats her eyes at you."

"I would hope so," he says, before stifling a yawn.

"Hey, if you're tired, we could do this another night."

He smiles. "I'm fine." He takes her in his arms, and they kiss. When they finally break apart, he nods toward her dress. "May I help you out of that?"

"How about you tell me all about yourself first? What was your childhood like? Where'd you go to college? What was your first job?"

"I had a normal childhood before attending Yale, then working on Wall Street."

"Is Wall Street like in the movies? Do people really make fortunes every day?"

Mel loosens his necktie and chuckles. "It's not really that exciting. Let's save the history lesson for another time," he says, pulling her close once more.

Usually in these types of situations, MaryAna feels tingles of romance that spur her on, but tonight seems different somehow, and second thoughts suddenly run through her head.

She snatches her phone from her purse. "How about I play some music so we can dance?"

Without answering, Mel draws her into another tight embrace. Despite her misgivings, she does not resist. But when his hand moves to her zipper, she decides they have gone far enough.

How can I get him to stop without hurting his feelings?

She gets up and takes his hand. "Follow me," she says, leading Mel to the bedroom. She places her phone on the bedside table and sets it to play the ABBA song, "Dancing Queen."

Mel removes his watch and sets it on the dresser. When he turns back around, MaryAna is standing in the middle of the bed, dancing to Abba. "Miss Lindley, what are you doing? Be careful!"

"I told you I wanna dance—so, let's dance."

He offers his hand to help her down, but she keeps going. "Come down, you're scaring me."

"No, you come up," she says, but he waves her off.

It's working. He thinks I'm crazy and will leave on his own.

"I thought you wanted to party!" She purses her lips in a mock pout.

"It's not safe."

"Do you always do what's safe?"

Mel puts his hands on his hips and just watches as MaryAna sways to the music. She nearly falls but keeps her balance, despite the pitchers of ale swirling around in her brain.

To MaryAna's surprise, Mel removes his jacket and vest. After neatly hanging them on the back of the chair, he slips off his shoes and slides onto the bed.

OMG!

The CEO manages to get to his feet and performs some halfhearted dance moves, his tie swinging to its own rhythm. After a truly heroic effort, he takes hold of MaryAna's waist to steady himself.

"I cannot believe I'm doing this, Miss Lindley."

"Me neither."

"How about I take you to a disco this week?" he says, as the song ends.

MaryAna throws her arms around his neck. "Promise?"

"You can drink and dance all you want. That is, if we can get down now?"

"OK."

Mel steps off the bed with a sigh of relief. She grabs his shoulders and jumps to the floor.

If that didn't scare him off, nothing will.

MaryAna collapses onto the bed and looks up at him with a newfound respect for his sense of adventure.

"Did you have fun?"

"I would prefer something less vertical, Miss Lindley."

MaryAna blinks.

OMG!

Her tingle is back and it's ready to rumble.

MaryAna rolls over with her back to the CEO. "You can help me out of this dress now."

He eagerly pulls down the zipper, and she slips off the dress, tossing it to the floor. Now clad only in her fire-engine red lingerie, she slides over to make room for him.

I hope my guardian angel isn't working late tonight.

"You like what I'm wearin'?"

"You're stunning, Miss Lindley." His eyes glide over her, but he stays put.

MaryAna props up on one elbow. "Come join me."

Mel looks at her, swallows hard, then grabs a pillow instead. "I'm going to check out that comfortable sofa. See you in the morning."

"What's going on? I thought you wanted to."

"You've had too much to drink, it wouldn't be right. Not to mention, I am indeed exhausted."

"Don't you want to fool around?" she says, now stone cold sober.

"Let's save it for another time." Mel leaves the room, closing the door behind him.

MaryAna stares at the door in disbelief.

And people call me crazy?

Chapter 16

MORNING COFFEE

Ugh! What time is it?

MaryAna stretches, fumbling for the ibuprofen on the bedside table. On the way to the bathroom, she notices that Mel's jacket and vest are gone from the chair, but her dress is neatly folded there instead.

She brushes out her hair and puts on makeup while considering what to wear. The eighteen-year-old decides on a hot-pink cut-off T-shirt and matching short-shorts.

The CEO's Rolex is still on the dresser. She picks it up and sees an inscription on its back: NOW & FOREVER.

Somebody loves him, or at least did once.

When MaryAna opens the door to the front room, she finds Mel on the sofa with a cup of coffee and *The New York Times*.

The CEO looks up and smiles. "Good morning, dancing queen."

Without returning his smile, she hands him the watch. "You left this on the dresser."

He slips it back onto his wrist. "Thank you."

"That's a nice inscription. Who gave it to you?"

"Someone I used to care for very much."

"Old girlfriend? Ex-wife?"

"Business partner."

Was it Jacqueline?

"Did you sleep well?"

MaryAna shrugs. "I haven't been sleepin' well at all lately. My back has been givin' me fits. Guess I'm gettin' old."

Mel chuckles. "You're far too young for that excuse."

He still sees me as a child. Is that why he didn't sleep with me?

She takes the coffee pot from the room-service table and pours herself a cup. "Anything of interest in the paper?"

"Last night, a blonde was spotted hanging out of the sunroof of a Rolls Royce. NYPD is combing the city for her."

"Oh my God, really?" she says, biting her lip. "I don't want trouble with the law."

He breaks into a grin.

"You're kiddin', right?"

"Will you pull something like that every time we go out?"

"Maybe." The eighteen-year-old gives him a coy smile.

"I don't know what to do with you, Miss Lindley."

She sits down beside him. "That was obvious last night when you left my bedroom."

Mell looks away and blushes.

I've embarrassed him. That's so cute.

"Who knows, next time I might just hang out of your sunroof like Lady Godiva."

"No doubt the authorities would indeed be after you. I can see the headline now: SOUTHERN GIRL ARRESTED FOR INDECENT EXPOSURE."

"You think I'm indecent?"

"Perhaps a bit of an exhibitionist."

I'm a walking cliché: Small-town girl goes wild in the big city.

"I take it, sir, you're not a fan of crazy stuff."

"Sometimes I enjoy it. Last night was, let's call it, different. I'll never be able to think of ABBA in the same way, that is certain."

MaryAna giggles. "You're kinda weird, but in a nice way." She sips from her cup. "I should be honest with you. I wasn't happy when you left my bedroom last night."

"I had the feeling you wanted to take things a little slower. Was I wrong?"

"Well, yeah. No. I had mixed feelings. I like you, but I don't know you that well. And there's the age difference."

"Does it bother you I'm much older, Miss Lindley?"

"Not when we're together like this. But what will people think?"

"Does it matter what they think?"

"Yeah, kinda." She giggles. "And there's the problem of elderly gentlemen needin' so much rest."

"Elderly?" Mel chuckles. "I have been around the block a time or two. I consider my age and the experience that comes with it one of my best qualities. It helps me understand women and their needs."

"So, you think you understand us?"

"Maybe more than you realize."

She gives a little twist of her head. "So, what's my best quality?"

Mel thinks for a moment. "Your enthusiasm."

"Really?"

"That impromptu dance made my heart pound in more ways than one. I find you both unique and charming. That's a potent combination."

He's so observant. And mature.

MaryAna scoots closer. "Do you want to do something together today?"

"Unfortunately, I have a previous engagement this afternoon that I cannot cancel."

"What's so important?"

"My brother Isaac and I go to Sunday dinner at our parent's home on Long Island."

"That's so sweet. I used to go to luncheons with my mama after Sunday services. I was goin' to check out Guardian Baptist Church this mornin', but it's too late now. Which one do you attend?"

"I go to synagogue on Saturdays."

"You're Jewish?"

Mel draws back. "Is that a problem?"

MaryAna shakes her head. "I've just never known any Jews."

"Quite a few people at our company are of the Jewish persuasion, Miss Lindley, including your boss, Hannah."

"Really? Y'all seem the same as Christians to me." She lays her head on his shoulder. "Too bad you gotta leave."

Mel puts his arm around her. "If you want, we could get together this evening. Would you like that?"

"Definitely. We could see some of the sights. Afterward, we can come back here for a candlelight dinner. Then we'll dance to ABBA songs. That is, if you aren't too sleepy."

"I think I can handle it," he says, checking his watch. "You choose."

"I'd like to see the Statue of Liberty. I missed it on my last trip."

"How about I pick you up, say around five? The Statue tours will be over for the day, but we can take the Ferry across the harbor. It's a nice ride and passes near Miss Liberty. After that, we can come back here."

"Awesome."

"Have you found an apartment yet?"

MaryAna shakes her head. "I should be lookin' today, but I want to go to an art museum."

"Which one?"

"The Guggenheim. I'll be back in time for our date. It's a *date*, right? Not market research?"

Mel smiles. "It's definitely a date." Mel kisses her on the forehead as he rises from the sofa. "I sent a text to Roger. He should be here by now."

MaryAna sets down her cup and stands up. "You know, I didn't plan last night. It just sorta happened."

"You're very spontaneous, Miss Lindley. Still, I'd prefer not to dance on the bed again."

"I can do horizontal."

Their lips meet in a short kiss.

Mel points to her skimpy attire. "You'll need some warmer clothes this evening. And bring a jacket. It can get chilly on the ferry."

He's always looking out for me. Is that why I like him?

After Mel has left, she plops back on the sofa. All the events of the past couple of days race through her mind and back again.

All I can do is follow my heart.

Chapter 17

THE GUGGENHEIM

MaryAna strolls through the lobby on her way out two hours after Mel has left. Today she sports a blue skirt and a long-sleeved red blouse with little white hearts. Leon is at his post as usual, and he tips his hat to her, along with his as-usual broad smile.

"Good afternoon, Miss Lindley."

"Hey, Leon. Do I look patriotic?"

"You could pass for an American flag," he says and salutes her.

She giggles. "Later today, I'm gonna see the Statue of Liberty."

"Did you know the Statue itself is only a thin sheet of copper about the thickness of two pennies? Its light green color is due to natural weathering."

"You're a walking Mr. Google, you know that?"

"Thanks. Also, thanks again—I bought Max some art supplies with that money. He was thrilled and asked if you were an angel."

"I wish it were true." The teenager sighs. "By the way, I understand the Guggenheim is nearby?"

"About a mile and a half up Fifth Avenue," he says, pointing in that direction.

"I'll have to walk since my angel wings are at the cleaners."

Leon gives out a belly laugh. "Just stay along the park. You'll see the Guggenheim across the street."

***

When MaryAna reaches the museum, she is impressed. The building, designed by Frank Lloyd Wright, is circular and a piece of artwork itself.

91

The eighteen-year-old pays the entrance fee and begins her trek up the spiral walkway. She takes her time to study each of the paintings on display. After nearly three hours, she has made it only halfway through all the exhibits. She decides to check out one last painting and then call it a day.

I can come back another time and pick up where I left off.

When the teenager approaches her final painting of the day, she finds a well-dressed young man already there studying the artwork. He glances at her, then turns back to the painting.

He looks like he just stepped out of GQ.

"Is that a camel-hair jacket?" MaryAna says without thinking.

The young nan turns to her, seemingly surprised by the question. His hair is short, and he stands ramrod straight like a soldier.

"Why yes, it is a Ralph Lauren. You know your fabrics."

That accent sounds eastern-European.

MaryAna smiles at his compliment. "I work at a fashion company called Jacqueline Designs. I'm an assistant designer there."

"How nice for you." He turns back once again to the artwork.

The painting before them portrays a gaunt laundress leaning on her iron. Shades of blue and gray underscore her bleak existence.

MaryAna reads the plaque next to the impressive work of art. "Oh, this is a Picasso," she notes, louder than intended.

The young man glares at her like she just laughed out loud at a wake.

"Sorry. It's just that I have a friend whose grandparents have a Picasso. It's similar in style to this one."

"A Picasso?"

MaryAna tells him about her visit to Tony's grandparents' home in the Hamptons. As she describes the painting, the young man nods.

"I've seen that work in an exhibition here in the city. So, you're acquainted with the owners?"

"The Russos are friends of mine."

"Might they be interested in selling their Picasso? I could get them an excellent price."

"I doubt it. It was a gift to the family from the artist himself. Are you an art dealer?"

He hands her his business card. His name is Vladimir Volkow, and he is indeed an art dealer.

"I specialize in private collectors, like your friends. I work with buyers and sellers for a commission. Art can be a good investment. Do you paint, Miss, ah. . ."

"Lindley, MaryAna Lindley."

Vladimir extends his hand. "It's nice to meet you."

"I like to paint, but I'm just a novice. I take it you know a lot about art."

"I majored in art history at the School of Visual Arts here in the city. You don't sound as if you are from this area."

"I recently moved here from Mississippi."

Vladimir puts his finger to his temple. "I believe that is somewhere in the southern United States."

She nods. "I'm stayin' at the Plaza until I find an apartment."

"That's a nice place to live. I hail from Moscow and came to America for college. After graduation, I started my business. It has proven quite lucrative."

She smiles and nods toward the painting before them. "I'll bet you can tell me all about this one."

Vladimir returns her smile. "During Picasso's early life, he lived in poverty in Paris. The painter empathized with the workers around him like the woman in the painting."

"So, he painted what he saw."

"That's correct," he says, and then points out the form and composition of the piece. "Do you understand?"

MaryAna nods even though most of it goes over her head.

"These elements foreshadow Picasso's later abstract works," he continues.

"You sure know a bunch about this paintin'. Thank you so much."

"My pleasure. Are there other paintings you would like some information about? Or possibly we could discuss art over a cup of coffee."

I think he likes me, but I need to leave, darn it.

MaryAna checks the time. "Unfortunately, I have to go. It was nice meetin' you, Vladimir."

"Please, let me know if your friends will part with their Picasso. Maybe they'd be interested in investing in other art."

"When I talk to them, I'll find out."

"It was delightful making your acquaintance, Miss Lindley."

As MaryAna descends the spiral walkway, she glances up to see Vladimir watching her.

Everyone in the Big Apple is so friendly.

Chapter 18

STORM WARNING

Mel's limo arrives to pick up MaryAna at ten minutes after seven the following morning, the first time he has ever been late.

After Roger has let her in and closed the door, she gives Mel a peck on the cheek. He follows up by giving MaryAna a deep, passionate kiss before she buckles in. She notes that the privacy glass is still up.

"That was a nice hello," she tells him. "You're runnin' a little behind schedule, sir. Did I keep you up past your bedtime?"

He smiles. "My world wobbled on its axis this weekend, but I enjoyed the ride."

"My world wobbles every day," she says, taking his hand. "I hope you can keep up with me."

"If necessary, I'll start going back to the gym to get into better shape."

"I think you're in awesome shape, sir."

"Thank you. You seem quite chipper for a Monday morning."

"I finally got a good night's sleep. What time did you leave last night?"

"A little before eleven," Mel answers as the limousine motors down Fifth Avenue. "When I returned from the bathroom, you were zonked out on the sofa. That piece of furniture has become a popular destination."

She giggles. "You should've woke me up. I wanted to fool around."

"I started to, but you looked so peaceful. Almost angelic. I just covered you up and left."

"That's so sweet. It must've been all that fresh air I got yesterday. I loved the ferry and seein' the Statue of Liberty. It gave me goosebumps."

"I was afraid you fell asleep on the sofa to pay me back for leaving your bedroom the night before."

"Oh, no, sir. I wouldn't do that to you."

"Why do you call me sir? Is it because I'm so much older than you?"

"It's a Southern thing. Why do you still call me Miss Lindley?"

"So I don't slip up and use your first name at work. People might get the wrong impression."

"I take it you want to keep our relationship a secret. I'm cool with that, but Kristen already knows about the rides. Maybe others do too. Won't they figure out the rest?"

"Let's hope not."

"Are we going to get together tonight?"

"Some buyers are in from out of town, and I'll be going out with them after work. These things can run pretty late. So, how about we get together tomorrow evening instead?"

"Works for me."

"Will you wear that sexy red number you wore Saturday? I'd love to peel it off of you."

"Oh, you would?" she says, grinning. "I'm lookin' forward to that too. And then we could make love for the first time. Have you been with many women?"

He chuckles.

"What?"

"It is just I've never met a female as straightforward as you, Miss Lindley."

"Does it bother you?"

"It's refreshing but will take some getting used to. To answer your question, I've dated my share of women over the years. How about you?"

"I want to be honest with you, sir. I've been with about a dozen or so guys in the last year and a half. In the past several months though, I've only slept with Tyler."

"I appreciate the honesty." Mel kisses her again. "You'll need to find another way back to the hotel after work today. I need the limo for the buyers."

"No problem. I'll just get a cab."

"Would you like to take a helicopter ride over the city on Wednesday?"

MaryAna's eyes light up. "Can we do that?"

"I'll make a reservation."

"What about work? Hannah is finally givin' me time to draw up my ideas for the blouse line."

"Explain to her I have another special assignment for you. With Jacqueline still out of town, there's no rush on those designs."

"I've never ridden in a helicopter."

"I also owe you a trip to a disco. How about this Friday we check out Paul's Casablanca in Soho? It's one of the city's hot spots. It should be fun."

"My social calendar is quite full, but I'll squeeze you in." She gives him a long, tantalizing kiss. "You're so good to me."

"And you're so appreciative."

The limousine soon arrives at their usual spot in front of the bakery.

"It feels like we're sneakin' around," she tells Mel. "I've had secrets come back to haunt me."

"All this is for the best," he says as they embrace one more time.

She gives the CEO a parting peck on his cheek just before the chauffeur opens the door.

After Roger lets her out and closes the door, he leans close to her. "Storms are in the forecast."

MaryAna scans the sky. "You sure? It looks like it's gonna be a great day today."

"Storms come in many shapes and sizes," he says, before whispering, "I like you, Miss Lindley, but you should be careful."

The teenager whispers back. "About what?"

"It's not really my place to say, Miss, but . . ."

"But what?"

Before the chauffeur can answer, Mel rolls down the window. "Is everything all right?"

"Oh yeah," MaryAna says. "We were just talkin' about the weather."

"Oh." The CEO looks relieved. "Roger, we're running late."

His chauffeur hustles around to the driver's side.

"I'll call you later, Miss Lindley," Mel says as he rolls up the window.

What was Roger gonna tell me?

Chapter 19

I THOUGHT YOU KNEW

After distributing this morning's coffee and doughnuts, MaryAna settles back at her desk. She pulls out her sketch pad and plays with some blouse designs, letting her imagination run wild.

Some of these are pretty out there . . .

By noon, the teenager has completed half a dozen unique designs and decides to break for lunch at the diner across the street. It is packed, however, and not seeing an open table, MaryAna is about to leave when she sees Kristen waving from a booth in the back.

"MaryAna, come sit with us."

The teenager slides in across from her co-worker and another young woman. Like Kristen, her friend is in her twenties with an athletic build. The other girl has black hair in a butch cut and piercing dark eyes.

"We just got here, so we haven't ordered yet," Kristen says. "This is Heidi Friedman. She works in accounting."

"Thanks for lettin' me sit with you. I hate to eat alone. Nice to meet you, Heidi."

"Same."

When the waitress arrives to take their orders, the other girls opt for a hot pastrami on rye while MaryAna orders a Reuben, which Mel introduced to her the night before.

"What do you do in accounting?" MaryAna asks.

"I'm in charge of the payroll." Heidi's accent is similar to Tony's Brooklyn one. "I make sure you get your paycheck."

"I wish you didn't take out so much for taxes."

Heidi gives her a half-hearted smile. "We don't have a choice."

"Y'all are havin' some fine weather here. When do you reckon it'll get cold?"

"All too soon." Kristen turns to her friend. "MaryAna's from Mississippi. Don't you love her accent?"

"It's different." Heidi takes a sip of water. "What's it like in Mississippi?"

"In the summer, you can fry an egg on the sidewalk. We rarely have snow, at least where I lived. I'm goin' to need some warmer clothes for sure."

"You'll get plenty of use of them here," Kristen adds. "So, you do anything fun this weekend?"

"Went to a concert at the Lincoln Center, saw a Broadway musical, visited the Guggenheim, and rode the ferry past the Statue of Liberty."

Kristen chuckles. "You sound like a tourist. I'll bet our CEO took you to those places."

I guess Kristen let the cat out of the bag. I told Mel word would get out.

"Mr. Rubenstein took me to most of them. You have to admit, ridin' in that limo is a trip. He even opened the sunroof so I could hang out. Did he take you places?"

Kristen nods. "Yeah, before he made his move. Just wait till he wants to collect for those rides."

Heidi snickers. "Isn't that the truth?"

"Did Mr. Rubenstein give you rides, too?" MaryAna asks.

"I'm from this area," Heidi explains. "And I'm not as hot as you guys, so he never hit on me. But Kristen's told me all about his shenanigans."

MaryAna shifts in her seat. "Do you believe he's dangerous?"

"Some guys are unpredictable," Kristen says. "One minute they're all perfect gentlemen, the next they want to rip your clothes off."

She is interrupted by the waitress bringing their sandwiches. For a moment, the three young women eat in silence.

Kristen takes a bite from her dill pickle, then turns to Heidi. "Tell MaryAna about the girl in accounting."

"Her name was Tierra Jenkins, and she was from Indiana. On her first day, Rubenstein told me he had a special assignment for her. After that, she'd go straight to his office every morning. I hardly ever saw her."

"Did he actually have assignments for her?"

Heidi shakes her head. "I'm a supervisor in accounting and never heard of any results from one. When I asked Tierra, she said she was helping Mel check out some figures. I suspect the only *figure* he was checking out was hers."

MaryAna swallows a bite from her sandwich. "When was all this?"

"Last spring," Heidi answers. "While Tierra was a probationary employee."

"A what?"

"For your first three months, you're on probation, so to speak. You can get canned without warning or cause."

"That doesn't seem fair," MaryAna says before one again biting into her Reuben.

"It's in the paperwork you signed. You also signed a non-disclosure that keeps you from working for a competing company. It's all legal crap."

"I should've read through all those forms. I just went ahead and signed them."

"Nobody reads them," Kristen says. "If you leave Jacqueline Designs, you can't work in design for any competitor for the next five years. It's supposed to protect company secrets."

"Is Tierra still workin' here?"

"Rubenstein told me to fire her," Heidi says. "He didn't give a reason. Through the grapevine, I heard his wife found out what was going on and made him do it."

MaryAna goes pale. "You mean Mr. Rubenstein is married?"

"You didn't know?" Heidi asks.

MaryAna shakes her head.

My guardian angel warned me some people in this city aren't what they seem.

Kristen lets out a sigh. "Sorry, I thought you knew."

101

MaryAna pushes her sandwich away, her complexion in flux. "No wonder he wants to keep me a secret. I don't feel . . . so good."

The teenager clamps her hand over her mouth and rushes to the restroom, returning fifteen minutes later.

"Are you OK?" Kristen asks.

"No." MaryAna's eyes are red and puffy. "I hate men and will never trust them again."

Heidi gives her a knowing smile. "Right on, sister."

"I thought Mr. Rubenstein cared for me." MaryAna uses a napkin to wipe her cheeks. "Can you believe I almost slept with him. How could I be so stupid?"

Kristen pats her on the arm. "You shouldn't be alone tonight. After work, Heidi and I are going to Boots 'n Heels. It's our favorite club and not far from here. Come with us."

MaryAna sighs. "I don't know . . . I don't think I'd be good company."

"Come on," Heidi says, a newfound warmth in her voice. "We can drink and bitch about guys."

"That's my favorite sport," Kristen adds. "MaryAna can call Rubenstein all the bad names in the book, and we'll drink a toast to every one of them."

MaryAna attempts a smile. "I know some pretty nasty ones."

"We'll make up some new ones," Heidi says, slamming her fist into the table.

"I'll think about it and let you know." MaryAna's phone buzzes. Someone is texting her. She checks the sender and looks up at her co-workers. "It's him."

Kristen plops her sandwich onto her plate. "What does *he* want?"

"He says he misses me," MaryAna notes, while typing a reply.

"I'll bet he does," Heidi adds. "What did you tell him?"

"That I can't wait to see him." MaryAna holds up her phone so they can read the response. "It's true, but not in the way he thinks."

OK, yet another failed relationship.

When it comes to men, I'm always screwed.

Chapter 20

BOOTS 'N HEELS

Following the bombshells dropped at lunch, MaryAna is unable to concentrate on work that afternoon. She aches to storm into Mel's office and give him a substantial piece of her mind, but she also knows such unprofessional behavior would only appear childish and probably get her butt fired.

I'll confront him tomorrow morning after I've had time to cool off.

MaryAna clings to the hope that Kristen and Heidi are unaware of Mel's current marital status.

Maybe he's separated and getting a divorce.

Her brief romantic relationship is not as easy to dismiss as she thought it would be. A week ago, the eighteen-year-old considered being with the much older CEO unfathomable. Now, the idea of losing him creates an unexpected heartache.

How did I develop such feelings so quickly?

MaryAna has no answer. She considers herself an independent woman, yet still enjoys someone taking care of her.

My psychiatrist says I have daddy issues.

Maybe I do.

Just before five o'clock, MaryAna closes her sketch pad and leans back in her chair. She still has not decided if she will go clubbing with her co-workers.

Maybe I'll meet some cute guy who'll help me forget about Mr. Rubenstein.

Her phone alerts her to a text from Mel: COME TO MY OFFICE.

MaryAna responds: Why?

His reply: Free until six. Secretary left. My sofa is quite comfortable.

In that second, MaryAna pushes aside her anger and forgets how he deceived her. The prospect of making love with the powerful CEO with one of the greatest cities in the world as backdrop kicks her romance novel fantasies in gear. She flips the coin but already knows the outcome.

I should give him a chance to explain.

MaryAna bursts into Mel's office and asks flat out if he is married. His response: He and his wife are separated and have filed for divorce.

"I love you, Miss Lindley . . . MaryAna. Only you—now and forever."

"Oh, sir. I love you, too," she hears herself say, although somewhere in her mind she is unsure if that is in fact true.

The teenager's clothes disappear as if by magic, and she melts into his arms. They make mad, passionate love on the black leather sofa and nothing else matters. They are the only two people on Earth and all that exists in space and time is this moment, this joining, this *now.*

I'm queen of the world!

But the daydream fades as fast as it had begun. Without the influence of alcohol, her moral compass asserts itself, telling her to avoid the slippery slope to which such reckless adventures inevitably lead.

Before I get with him, I want to know the truth about his marriage.

She picks up her phone and texts Mel her response: Meeting friends at a club. See you tomorrow.

My guardian angel will be so proud of me—at least for tonight.

***

Thirty minutes later, a taxi drops MaryAna at the address Kristen gave her. One letter at a time, and then all together, the neon "Boots 'n Heels" sign calls to all who dare to enter the rather plain wooden door. She hustles inside to the dimly lit room that suddenly bursts with pools of multicolored neon.

A long wooden bar takes up most of the far wall. To its right is a hallway leading to restrooms. Against the right wall sits an old-time jukebox and a small dance floor. Across the room from the bar are several booths that provide a modicum of privacy. The remainder of the club has small tables and chairs scattered about, filling out the room.

MaryAna spots her friends sitting at one end of the bar, and they wave to her. She hurries over and grabs the empty stool next to them.

Kristen gives MaryAna a hug. "I'm glad you came. We saved that for you. So, what would you like?"

"Martini."

Kristen signals to the attractive red-haired female bartender, who is wearing a short-sleeved western shirt and jeans. "A martini for my friend. Put it on our tab."

MaryAna notices two more girls entering the club. One is short with long black hair and bronze skin. She looks around the room before settling onto the barstool beside MaryAna. The other girl, with pale skin and purple hair, finds a spot at an empty table.

The bartender brings MaryAna's martini, and MaryAna pops out her ID.

"We don't see that many Mississippi girls."

"I just moved here a few weeks ago," MaryAna says, noting the tattoos blanketing the bartender's arms.

"My name's Chipper."

"MaryAna. Say, can I get a burger?"

"Sorry, honey, this isn't a restaurant. I can bring you a bowl of mixed nuts."

"But your sign says 'Bar and Grill.'"

Chipper grins. "Actually, it's Bar and Girl."

MaryAna quickly scans the club again and realizes all the customers are female. "Oh, got it." She turns to Kristen. "This isn't what I expected."

"You said you were down on men."

"I was . . . I am."

Chipper returns with a large dish of nuts. "If you need anything else, honey, just let me know. Love that accent, by the way."

"Oh, um . . . thanks."

The bartender smiles. "I get off at midnight. If you're still around, maybe we can get to know each other better."

"We'll probably be leavin' much earlier, I think."

"Whatever." Chipper grabs a handful of nuts and heads to the other end of the bar.

"What is it with female bartenders?" MaryAna asks Kristen. "The one I worked with back in Jackson was always hittin' on me too."

"You're very hittable." Heidi chuckles as soft music begins to play. "I mean that in a good way."

As several girl-girl couples make their way to the dance floor, a young woman in a tailored suit and cropped-back hair approaches MaryAna. *She could almost pass for a man*, MaryAna thinks. Only the bulges of her chest betray her gender.

"Wanna dance?" she asks, her voice soft and feminine.

"Ah, no. I mean, no, thank you. I'm not actually . . . you know."

"Oh.' The young woman turns and heads toward another woman sitting at the bar.

"It's all right," Kristen says. "Straight girls come into this club all the time. It's no big deal."

"I think I hurt her feelings. I take it you and Heidi are a couple."

Kristen nods. "For five months now."

"We're thinking about getting married," Heidi says. "So, did you talk to Rubenstein?"

"I'm goin' to confront him on the way to work tomorrow. If I catch him off guard, he won't have time to make something up."

Heidi leans in. "It's a good plan, but you better be prepared to be fired on the spot."

"I'll cross that bridge when I come to it." MaryAna takes a sip of her martini. "I came to New York to be a designer, not a mistress."

"Good for you," Heidi says. "Kristen and I are going to dance now. When we come back, let's work on some nasty names for Rubenstein."

MaryAna grins. "I've got some good ones already."

As the teenager nurses her martini, another young woman

approaches, a tall brunette wearing a short dress with a plunging neckline.

"Hi, I'm McKenzie. Want to dance?"

MaryAna shakes her head. "Thanks, but I'm not gay."

"That's OK," McKenzie leans up against her and whispers: "I could blow your world apart."

"Thanks, but my world is already in pieces, I have to say."

"Too bad." McKenzie says with a smirk. "Maybe later you'll change your mind."

She saunters farther down the bar. Another girl apparently accepts her invitation, and they head to the dance floor. On the way, she brushes against MaryAna, even though there is plenty of room to pass by.

"Oops, sorry."

I've done that same move to get a guy's attention.

The short girl on the barstool next to MaryAna taps her on the shoulder. "If you're talking to someone, you won't get hit on so much."

"Can I talk to you?"

"Sure. I'm Isadora."

"MaryAna. You probably heard I'm straight."

"Yeah." Isadora tosses her long hair back over her shoulder. "Is this your first time at a lesbian bar?"

"Yeah. I work with Kristen and Heidi, but I didn't know they were a couple until tonight."

"Where do you work?"

"Jacqueline Designs. Are you familiar with them?"

"I love their dresses, but they're way out of my price range. Doesn't stop me from looking though—I love to shop."

"This city is fertile ground for us shoppers to plow. What do you do?"

"I'm an interpreter at the UN. I moved here from West Virginia a few months back."

"I'm from Mississippi. I bet you speak a bunch of languages."

"Spanish, Russian, mostly, plus a few others."

"You come here a lot?"

Isadora shakes her head. "I've been to a couple other places but didn't hook up with anyone. The fact that I look like I'm in junior high doesn't help."

"I think you're cute," MaryAna says, intrigued by her new friend. "What about the girl you came in with?"

"We just happened to walk in at the same time."

"If you want, Isadora, we could be shoppin' buddies. That is, if you don't mind that I'm straight."

Isadora takes a sip of her rose-colored drink. "Sure, if you don't mind I'm not. My friends call me Izzy."

"Are you Hispanic?"

"My father is Russian, and my mother is from Cuba. They met while he was working there, and soon got married. I was born in Miami when they escaped to the U.S. Later, we moved to West Virginia when my dad got transferred.

"What's that you're drinkin', Izzy?"

"Maiden's Blush. It's gin, Triple Sec, grenadine, and lemon juice. Want to try it?"

MaryAna takes a sip. "Oh, that's delicious. I'm gonna get one for myself when I finish my martini. You want to exchange phone numbers?"

They do, then continue chatting and working on their drinks. After several minutes, the girl with the purple hair steps to the bar, and in an Eastern European accent, asks MaryAna to dance.

"No thanks. My new friend Izzy might like to."

The purple-haired young lady hesitates before turning to Isadora. "You like to dance?"

"Yes, I would."

As they head to the dance floor, Isadora glances over her shoulder at MaryAna and mouths "Thank you."

The teenager finishes off her martini and orders her first Maiden's Blush.

OK, time to drown my sorrows.

Chapter 21

CONFRONTATION

MaryAna rides into work Tuesday morning with a throbbing hangover and a substantial chip on her shoulder. She has not said a word since getting into the car.

"Hey, how about you sit with me over here," Mel says, patting the seat beside him, but MaryAna says nothing in response, preferring her glare do the talking.

He leans forward and places a hand on her knee. "Is there something wrong?"

She removes his hand but keeps her eyes on his. "What makes you think something is wrong?"

He sits back and sighs. "I haven't a clue."

"Of course you don't—you're a guy." But before he can respond, MaryAna continues. "Tell me about Tierra Jenkins."

"You've been listening to rumors, haven't you? Whatever you heard, it's not true."

MaryAna folds her arms and crosses her legs. "Why don't you tell me what's true then."

"There's not much to tell."

"Humor me."

"If I do," he says, "you must keep it to yourself. Some parts of Tierra's job were secret, and I'd like them to stay that way."

"I'm waiting."

Mel takes a deep breath and lets it out in a huff. "I noticed suspicious activity in our financial accounts, so I hired Tierra to make an independent audit."

"And?"

"We spent a couple weeks going over the books. It turned out my suspicions were unfounded."

"Did you give her rides to and from work too? Or take her to concerts, dinners, and musicals?"

"No."

"Why did you fire her?"

"She was a probationary employee. There was no open job for her to fill. She understood that when I hired her."

"Did you have an affair with her?"

"Certainly not. Is that what you heard?"

"The story is your wife found out about Tierra, and she made you fire her."

"That's ridiculous. My wife knew all about my suspicions and why I hired her."

"So, you admit you're married?"

"Of course I am," he says, the first time MaryAna has heard him raise his voice. "I thought you knew."

"Why does everyone think that? I didn't know until yesterday. You don't wear a ring."

"I find them uncomfortable."

"Oh, please. Well, bein' with a married man makes me uncomfortable. Did you think about that?"

"I wasn't trying to deceive you, Miss Lindley. You never asked, so I assumed you knew I had a wife. Or you didn't care."

"Oh, I care. Married men are supposed to wear their weddin' rings—it's a job requirement. The other night, you told me you had no one to go home to, not even a pet."

"My wife is out of town, and our dog is with her. That's why I had the extra ticket for the concert."

"What about you and your brother visitin' your parents on Sundays? You made it sound like it was just the two of you.

"Issac isn't married, and my wife never comes. She and my mother don't get along. I'm sorry you got the wrong impression."

MaryAna's foot begins tapping.

"My marriage has been in name only for years, Miss Lindley. I enjoy your company and would've settled for simply taking you places. *You're* the one who pushed things along."

"What, now it's *my* fault?" MaryAna brushes away a tear. "What were you gonna do when your wife got back? Dump me like Tyler did?"

Mel reaches out his hand, but she does not take it. "I was hoping we might continue seeing each other. Discreetly, of course."

"I'm not that kind of girl. If your marriage was so bad, why don't you get a divorce?"

"Believe me, I would love one, but my wife is Catholic and doesn't believe in them. There are also major financial entanglements to consider. It's complicated."

MaryAna's face is burning. "Why the heck is everything always complicated?"

"That's just how it is, Miss Lindley. Can we just still see each other?"

"No way! We're done."

"What if I were to leave my wife and share an apartment with you? Would you consider a romantic relationship?"

"Shack up with a married man? I won't commit adultery just for your convenience." She wipes away more tears. "Well, if you're gonna fire me, go ahead."

"I have no intention of firing you."

"That's a relief, but this is my last ride to work with you. It's time I learned to use the subway."

"Miss Lindley, you don't have to—"

She holds up her palm. "Stop calling me that. From now on, I'm just another employee."

"If that's the way you want it."

"It's *not* what I want," MaryAna wipes her cheeks again. "As long as you're married, it's what must be."

What the hell—two breakups in just over a week? Even if one of them was by choice!

111

How come my relationships always end in death?

***

After work, MaryAna takes a taxi to her hotel. Once in her suite, she grabs a beer from the minibar, curls up on the sofa, and pulls out her phone.

"Hey, Mama. Sorry I didn't call you back last night. I've been really busy."

"That's all right, dear. You sound a bit down."

"Just tired. We're workin' up a new line of blouses. Every time I sketch one, my supervisor suggests all kinds of changes and I have to start over. Of course, that's what they pay me to do."

"I . . . I heard about your breakup with Tyler. Do you want to talk about it?"

"That's old news, and I'm over it."

"You're too young for a serious relationship."

"I'm almost nineteen, Mama. Can we talk about something else? How's Coach Brown and my brothers?"

"To tell you the truth, I hardly ever see the boys. They were here Sunday for dinner and upbeat about the opening game. Scott only comes by for a few hours each day, and that's mostly to sleep and change clothes. I'm a football widow, and the season hasn't even started. By the way, Dr. Scanlon called."

"What does my psychiatrist want?"

"She told me you haven't responded to her text."

"She's probably just checking to make sure I'm takin' my medication. So, how're your investments goin'?"

"Ah . . . fine, dear. You've never asked about them before. I didn't think you were interested."

"I'm tryin' to broaden my horizons. I went to the Guggenheim last weekend. Have you ever considered investin' in fine art?"

"No, but Sheldon has had some good luck in investing in art."

"Just more money to add to his billions." MaryAna says. "As if he needs it."

Sheldon Hanberry, who owns Hanberry Labs, is Sarah's longtime friend, business associate, and political ally. She has also provided him with financial advice over the years, which has often proven invaluable.

"Have you talked to Sheldon lately, MaryAna?"

"Not since last fall. He probably doesn't want anything to do with me anymore since I'd just asked him for money to pay for drugs."

"Sheldon's happy to learn you're off the opioids. I'm sure he'd be thrilled to hear from you."

"I'm still embarrassed about askin' so many people for money."

"It's all history, dear. You need to let it go."

"I might call him—you know, to talk about his art investments."

"Has someone approached you about buyin' a paintin'?"

"Oh, no. It just occurred to me when I was at the Guggenheim."

"If you buy anything, use a reputable art dealer, and always keep your emotions out of it. Fear and greed lead to bad investment decisions."

"Thanks, Mama. I'll keep that in mind."

Once off the phone, MaryAna accesses her online checking account. Since coming to New York, her debit card has rarely had a day off.

I didn't spend that much though, right?

The teenager checks her recent transactions and discovers otherwise.

MaryAna digs around in her purse for Vladimir's business card and dials his number.

"Vladimir Volkow. May I help you?"

"Hi again. It's MaryAna Lindley. I met you at the Guggenheim Sunday."

"Oh, yes—the blonde with the funny accent."

He's one to talk about accents.

"That's me. I'd like to invest in some art."

"Fine art can be expensive, Miss Lindley."

"I don't have access to my trust fund for a couple of years, but I've got another account."

"I'll keep you in mind should an opportunity arise. To make a substantial profit, I match desperate sellers to anxious buyers. My clients have done well on such transactions."

"Well, I'm kinda in a hurry."

"These situations don't come up that often. When they do, I must move quickly."

"Will you let me in on your next one, Vladimir?"

"I will consider it, Miss Lindley, but your funds must be readily available."

"It's all in my checkin' account."

"How much money are we talking here?"

MaryAna tells him her balance, which is still above a hundred thousand dollars.

"That's a lot to be sitting around, Miss Lindley." The line goes quiet for a moment, but before she can say anything, Vladidmir continues. "I don't do business with strangers. We should get better acquainted."

A fresh tingle surges through MaryAna. "Would you like to come to the Plaza tonight? We could have dinner and hang out."

"Thank you, but I don't mix business with pleasure. I'll call you tomorrow to arrange a meeting. What time is good for you?"

"Around seven. I'll be off from work then."

"Seven o'clock then. Goodnight, Miss Lindley."

"It was nice talkin' with you," she says, but the Russian has already hung up.

Vladimir's not the friendliest guy in the world, but he is very professional.

Part 2

THE INVESTMENT

Chapter 22

DINNER PLANS

On Wednesday evening, MaryAna receives a call from Vladimir.

"Have you found me some art to invest in?"

"I am working on it. Last night, you suggested we get together. What about dinner this Friday? Somewhere of your choosing."

"How about the Todd English Food Hall here at the Plaza. I can charge it to my suite. That way my company will pay for it."

"If you wish, Miss Lindley. You also mentioned you're seeking an apartment for rent. As it so happens, my sister and I are in the market for one also."

"Where do you live now?"

"In Brooklyn, but not in a good neighborhood. We've found a suitable three-bedroom in Greenwich Village, but it's pricy. Would you consider becoming our roommate?"

"That's an awesome idea."

"Of course, you'd need to see the place and meet my sister, Natasha. If it's all right, I'll invite her to join us Friday evening."

"I'd love to meet her. What time?"

"Let's say around eight o'clock? Do you have a boyfriend who might want to join us?"

"No, but I have a friend, Isadora, who might like to meet y'all."

"That would be fine. I'll text you Friday when we're close to your hotel and meet you in the lobby. Maybe Saturday we can show you the apartment."

"That works for me. Does your sister like to shop?"

"Don't all women?"

"Some more than others. I look forward to meetin' Natasha. I'm sure we'll become the best of friends."

***

After her conversation with Vladimir, MaryAna slips on her silk pajamas and arranges a wake-up call for the next morning. She grabs some white wine from the minibar, curls up on the sofa, and calls Isadora.

"Hey, shoppin' buddy."

"MaryAna? It's good to hear from you. How did it go with that CEO guy?"

"As far as our personal relationship, he's history. But he hasn't fired me—at least not yet. So, what happened after I left the club?"

"You mean before we stuffed you into that taxi and told the driver to make sure he got you to the Plaza?"

"I shouldn't have had that Maiden's Blush."

Isadora laughs. "It was the second, third, and fourth ones that were the problem. You sure like to dance."

"The girl with the purple hair."

"Kira."

"She had an interesting accent."

"She's Russian. Do you remember the other six girls you danced with?"

"It's all still kinda fuzzy. I think one was named McKenzie."

"She wanted to take you home with her."

"Thanks for lookin' out for me, Izzy. I do remember Kristen and Heidi leavin'. I probably embarrassed them to death."

"You broke me up when you told Kira you weren't a lesbian, but that there were definitely some good selling points about being one."

"I said that?"

"The bartender kept refilling your glass just to keep you talking. We didn't know what you were gonna say next."

"So, I made a fool of myself."

"You're naturally funny and so innocent."

"Believe me Izzy, I'm far from innocent. Did I mess up your night?"

"I had an awesome time, and Kira came home with me."

"I'm glad things worked out. Hey, how would you like to go shoppin' tomorrow evenin'? I need a new dress for a dinner on Friday with an art dealer and his sister. They're potential apartment mates. And I'd love for you to come with me to dinner too if you're free."

"Sure, why not."

"You can bring Kira too if you want."

"She's on her way to Russia to visit her family, so it'll be just me."

"How about we meet at Bloomingdale's tomorrow after work? Say about six?"

"It's a date."

***

MaryAna pours another glass of wine and then phones Coree. They have exchanged some texts in the past few days, where MaryAna told her longtime friend about attending the concert and the musical, but left out her relationship with Mel.

"Sounds like you've been busy. What about your new girlfriends?"

"They're all really nice. I'm goin' shoppin' with Izzy tomorrow."

"She's a lesbian too?"

"Izzy's cool. It's not the big deal people make it out to be."

"Have you found an apartment?"

"I might be sharin' one with a brother and sister. He's an art dealer, and they're originally from Moscow."

"You've certainly met a variety of people. How's the job goin'?"

"The CEO likes my ideas, but says the head designer isn't so keen on them. I hope I can change her mind when I meet her."

"You've always been unconventional, MaryAna. Most people resist new concepts. Not everybody here likes my ideas about football, but I just plug away, workin' to convince them to open their minds."

"Coree, you know I don't have your patience. Of course, I've only been on the job three weeks. And last weekend, I made the situation more complicated."

"How's that?"

"By seein' Mr. Rubenstein outside of work."

"The CEO? Isn't he, like older than our parents?"

"Yeah, he's older, but handsome, really rich, and treats me well."

"How far did this relationship go?"

"I didn't sleep with him, but I wanted to, and kinda still do, frankly. I'm so messed up. When I learned he was married, I broke it off."

"You're supposed to find out if a guy is married before you go out with him. It's a house rule."

"I know. It was dumb. Combined with Tyler dumpin' me, I'm really down. Mama calls every day to check on me, but I can't talk to her about my love life. If she knew the truth, she'd put me on the next flight back home."

"You want to talk about it?"

"You have a few minutes?"

"All the time in the world."

It's time to tell Coree the whole truth.

Chapter 23

SAMSON

Later that evening, MaryAna is about to go to bed when she hears a knock on the door. She throws on her pink bathrobe over her pajamas and peers through the peephole.

A young black man in a blue T-shirt and jeans stands in the hallway, but MaryAna does not recognize him.

"Who is it?"

"It's me, Samson."

Since they first met, MaryAna has seen the bellman several times. She always waved to him, but they have not spoken since the day she arrived.

When the teenager opens the door, the bellman flashes a toothy smile. "Hey, Mississippi. What's up?"

"Sorry, Samson. I didn't recognize you without your uniform. Come on in."

"I just finished my shift. How have you been?"

"Could be better." She shrugs. "How about you—any progress on your musical career?"

"I got a callback yesterday. Nothing certain, but it's promising."

"Hey, that's awesome."

"That's why I stopped by. I'm going to my favorite jazz bar to celebrate and wondered if you might join me. It's a great place to chill."

"Thanks, but I've got to get up early tomorrow." She sees the light go out in his eyes and takes his arm. "So, how about instead we get something from the minibar and celebrate here?"

Samson stops. "They don't like us fraternizing with the guests. If my boss finds out, he's liable to fire me."

She grins. "It'll be our secret."

The two get beers from the minibar and make themselves comfortable on the sofa. After some chitchat, Samson pulls out a joint and a lighter and lights up.

"Would you care to partake?"

It's been a while since I've had any weed, but what the heck?

He takes a hit and hands it to her.

MaryAna does the same. "So, tell me about the callback."

"The musical is called *Hamilton* and set around the time of the American Revolution. It casts non-white characters as the Founding Fathers."

"Really? I thought they were all white guys."

Samson shrugs. "It may not be historically accurate, but the music is great. It's a combination of hip-hop, R & B, pop, soul, and traditional-style show tunes."

"I hope you get the part. When will you know if you got it?"

"Soon. It just opened on Broadway, and they're looking to replace a couple of the cast members."

"I'm sure someday you'll be a Broadway star. Just don't forget all us little people."

He grins and takes another hit. "I'll leave tickets for you at the box office."

MaryAna takes the joint back and fills her lungs.

"Tell me all about growin' up in Ohio, Sam."

For the next half hour, the bellman relates stories about surviving inner-city Cleveland. One of them is from when he was a senior in high school.

"I got the lead role in a musical put on by a local theater group. My co-star was a white girl from the suburbs. We started dating and became rather involved."

"Did she come with you to New York?"

"She wanted to, but her parents found out about us. They convinced her to break up with me."

"Why?"

"They said my ambition to be on Broadway was unrealistic. But I'm sure there was more to it than that."

"I had a black boyfriend my junior year," MaryAna says as she grabs another beer. "You remind me a lot of him. I really liked Matthew, but we had to break up."

"How come?"

"He was a super athlete with all kinds of scholarship possibilities. But after we started datin', his grades began to tank. I was a bad influence. You know—stayin' out late, drinkin', and all. For his sake, we called it quits."

"That's a switch," Samson says with a half smile. "Usually, it's the guy who corrupts the girl. What about your parents? What did they think about you dating a black dude?"

"Mama was cool with it. At that time, my daddy wasn't around. Tell me more about Cleveland."

Samson pours out his experiences in the hood while MaryAna continues visiting the minibar. When she finishes her fourth beer, Samson leans close and kisses her on the lips. It is soft and hesitant.

No harm in making out. It might cheer me up.

MaryAna does nothing to encourage him, nor does she do anything to discourage his advances. Each succeeding kiss is more probing and less hesitant. After several, they take a break to catch their breath.

"Do you have a girlfriend?"

"Not since I left Cleveland. You have a boyfriend?"

MaryAna shakes her head. "Not anymore."

Feeling a nice buzz from the joint, she pulls him closer. He loosens the belt of her robe and slips it off her shoulders. She leans back on the sofa, soaking up the attention like a sponge.

Samson slips his hands beneath her pajama top. Only then does MaryAna recall her vow to not be involved with "younger" men.

"How old are you, Sam?"

He blinks. "Twenty. Why?"

"Just curious, is all."

Darn it. He's Tyler's age—why couldn't he be older?

Samson blinks again and resumes where he left off. He raises her pajama top for a closer look. But when his hand drifts downward between her legs, MaryAna freezes. Seeking only a diversion and not another serious relationship, the conflicted young woman realizes this is the point of no return.

Is that my guardian angel tapping me on the shoulder?

MaryAna pushes his hand away. "Please, don't."

"I thought that's what you wanted."

I shouldn't do this. I can't do this.

Samson looks up at her. "Just relax, Mississippi. I know how to make a girl feel good."

"I'm sure you do, but please don't."

He hesitates. "You sure?"

"I'm sure."

Samson sits up. "Is it because I'm a bellman?"

"Heavens no," she says, pulling her top back down.

"So, what's the problem?"

"Nothing with you. I'm sorry, but I just can't."

Samson sits unmoving, his eyes darting around the room. "Another time, maybe?"

"Yeah, sure. Maybe once I've gotten settled and don't have so much going on."

He sighs, then gives her a little grin. "OK, Mississippi."

Darn it. I hurt his feelings.

"I really enjoyed hearin' about your life, Samson. You're sweet."

"Like Matthew?"

MaryAna nods. "Both of you are tall, good-lookin', considerate, and very talented."

He kisses her on the cheek and gets to his feet. "If you need anything, Mississippi, remember, Sam's your man."

"I will."

I can't risk getting my heart broken again.

124

Chapter 24
GETTING TO KNOW YOU

Just after six Thursday evening, MaryAna meets her new friend Isadora in front of Bloomingdales. After three hours of non-stop shopping, they take a cab to the Plaza where they will order room service for dinner.

"You sure bought some expensive clothes, MaryAna. I wish I could afford to spend that kind of money."

"The man who raised my twin brother died three years ago. He had tons of life insurance. My brother shared a bunch of it with me."

"Sweet."

"I'm lookin' for a good investment. If you hear of something, let me know."

"What kind of investments do you have in mind, MaryAna?"

"The art dealer we're havin' supper with tomorrow is lookin' for the right opportunity. I don't know if art is the way I should go. My mama has made tons of money in stocks, real estate, and things like that."

"The news is always talking about paintings selling for millions of dollars," Isadora says. "You said you're an amateur artist, and you love art, so you should invest in what you know."

"That seems logical." The teenager thinks a moment. "Vladimir seems very professional, but I only just met him at the Guggenheim last Sunday."

"That's not exactly a hangout for bad guys."

"Yeah, but I don't know much about him."

"Do we ever really know anyone?"

"I thought I knew my ex-boyfriend, but you know how that turned out."

"After I meet Vladimir, I'll let you know what I think of him. I'm a pretty good judge of character."

Once they reach the hotel, Leon helps them unload their purchases from the taxi.

"Another double shift?"

"You guessed it, Miss Lindley."

"Could you have Samson bring everything up to the room?"

"Of course."

"Leon, this is my friend, Isadora. We're shoppin' buddies." MaryAna hands Leon a folded bill.

"Miss Lindley, you're too generous," he says, tipping his cap to both girls.

***

Samson soon arrives at the suite with the afternoon's spoils piled on a cart. MaryAna instructs him to move all but two specific boxes into the bedroom.

"Those are Izzy's. Just set them on the sofa, please."

He does so, and the teenager hands him a nice tip.

"Thanks, Mississippi."

"Samson is a singer and dancer," MaryAna tells Isadora. "You should get his autograph before he hits it big on Broadway."

Her friend, however, does not respond.

The young man turns to MaryAna. "I enjoyed the other night."

"Me too. Maybe we can get together again soon."

"I'm off tomorrow afternoon—I could show you around town."

"That sounds awesome, but I've already got plans. How about Sunday afternoon?"

"Working a double shift Sunday. Filling in for Eddie."

"Oh, OK. Maybe next Saturday then?"

"I'll check my schedule." The bellman nods to Isadora, but she just stares at him.

He turns back to MaryAna. "Take care, Mississippi. If you need anything, let me know."

"I see you haven't given up on guys completely," Isadora says after Samson leaves, "but the bellman? Really?"

"What about him?"

"He was practically drooling when he looked at you, MaryAna."

"He was not! Sam's a fun guy, but he's only twenty—too young for a serious relationship."

"I don't think you realize the effect you have on guys—or girls, for that matter. You turn heads wherever you go."

"Even yours?"

"Hey, if I was into straight girls, I'd jump your bones right now," she says, giggling.

"Wanna help me put away my new clothes?"

"Sure."

In the bedroom, Isadora looks around, wide-eyed. "This room is bigger than my efficiency apartment."

"What's that?"

"Basically, a room with a sofa that makes into a bed. There's also a small kitchenette and a tiny bathroom. It's all I can afford."

"That's why I'm hopin' the apartment in Greenwich Village works out." MaryAna hands her friend a room-service menu.

"Order what you want. My company is payin' for it. At least for another week. The CEO promised me that long before I told him to take a hike."

"That's the guy who's married?"

"Yeah—another failed relationship. My expectations for men may be too high."

They order dinner and make themselves comfortable on the sofa.

"Mr. Rubenstein caught me on the rebound. It seems like I bounce from one guy to the next. They say if you kiss enough frogs, you'll find your prince. Looks like I'm workin' my way through the swamp."

Isadora giggles. "I wonder if that works with princesses?"

"Have you always liked girls?"

"It's more like I never liked boys. At least, not like my friends who went boy crazy in junior high. Were you boy crazy?"

"I had a major crush on my best friend's older brother in junior high, but he treated me like a little sister. In high school, I dated a bunch of guys. How about you, Izzy?"

"My life went haywire in college. My parents hired a math tutor for me, and she and I used to talk about things—you know, the stuff you can't discuss with your parents. Turned out my tutor wasn't into guys either. As they say: one thing led to another. After that, I met several other girls, but the relationships never lasted."

"Have you ever been with a guy?"

"Once, at a sorority party when I was intoxicated."

"I've been wasted more times than I care to remember," MaryAna says, letting out a long breath. "I wish I could kick my habit of fallin' for unreliable guys. You're lucky you don't have to deal with them."

"Women can be jerks too. I'm hoping Kira's the real deal."

MaryAna looks at her friend and grins. "So, you aren't interested in me at all?"

Isadora chuckles. "I make it a rule *not* to sleep with straight girls, and you're as straight as an arrow. I think we'll be great friends, but only friends."

"We already are."

I think I've found a new best friend.

Chapter 25

NATASHA

MaryAna gets a call from Tony Russo Friday morning at work. She has not talked to her old friend since being at his apartment the week before when his wife Dori abruptly suggested that MaryAna leave.

"So what happened you had to leave so suddenly? All Dori told me was that something came up."

"Yeah, I . . . um, forgot I needed to pick up a couple of things before my date."

"Did you like *Wicked*?"

"It was awesome. I want to check out more musicals."

"I have this afternoon off and wondered if you could join me for lunch. You need to bring me up to date on your family."

"What about Dori? Will she be coming too?"

"She has a strict diet, so she won't be joining us. Why?"

I might as well tell him what happened.

"Your wife believes you still have feelings for me and thinks I might lead you astray."

"She told you that?"

"In so many words, yeah."

Tony takes a moment before he continues. "She's not entirely wrong. I still think about you often and what might have been."

"You're married and about to have a child. When I received your bracelet, whatever there was between us died."

"Not for me. I literally owe Dori my life, but I can't help my feelings for you. I've tried to keep them secret from her, but apparently

I'm not that good at it."

"I'm not that carefree girl you met in Syracuse. A lot has happened since then."

"You mean the drugs?"

"That and so much more. You only know the tip of the iceberg."

"I don't care about all that. Can we get together and talk about us?"

"You're married, Tony. There is no *us*."

"I don't love Dori. I was considering divorce when she told me she was pregnant—I'm not even sure the kid is mine."

"You need to work all that out with her. As long as you're married, we shouldn't be seein' each other."

"We're still friends, aren't we?"

"Of course, but gettin' together, even for lunch, could be misconstrued."

"Even if we only talk?"

"Others might see it differently."

"You mean like my wife?"

"And anyone else who might see us, Tony. We shouldn't even be talkin' now. At least, not about feelings."

"If that's how you want it. Goodbye, MaryAna."

***

On Friday evening, Isadora is with MaryAna in her suite at the Plaza. For over an hour they have been getting ready for their dinner date with Vladimir and his sister.

MaryAna receives a text from Vladimir: WILL BE AT PLAZA IN 15.

From the bedroom, MaryAna yells to Isadora in the bathroom. "We need to head downstairs in a few minutes. How're you doin'?"

"Finishing my makeup. How about you?"

"Just gotta put my dress on."

Isadora soon emerges from the bathroom in a long-sleeve animal print dress, her dark eyes shimmering like the unique creation. "How do I look?"

"Fantastic," MaryAna says, giving her a thumbs up. "I told you at Bloomingdales that dress would look perfect on you."

MaryAna sports a pink satin dress that is slit up one side. Her breasts push at the low neckline, and in her six-inch heels, she towers over her friend. She rushes over to Isadora and turns around, holding up her hair.

"Zip me up, Izzy?"

"Hey, this isn't the dress you bought for tonight."

"I changed my mind. Vladimir might like this one better."

"Are you trying to do a business deal or seduce him?"

"I want him to let me in on his next big art deal. If he thinks I'm hot, maybe it'll increase my chances. He is a guy after all."

"I thought you were down on men."

"I am, but I can make exceptions."

"As a reputable art dealer," Isadora says, "Vladimir may not appreciate you coming on to him. That dress screams 'Take me to bed.' If you want him to take you seriously, you should wear something more professional."

She's got a point. Maybe I should save this one for another night.

"You're right, Izzy. I'll change."

***

Vladimir and his sister are waiting in the lobby when the other two young women join them. For MaryAna, it is a personal best: changing in under ten minutes. She is now attired in a more conservative rose-colored dress with a high neckline.

MaryAna introduces Isadora. Vladimir follows suit by introducing his sister who is wearing a black evening dress, matching her long black hair. Like her brother, she has a creamy complexion.

Vladimir sure looks sharp in that houndstooth tweed jacket.

They make their way to the Plaza's Food Hall. When they have been seated, MaryAna turns to Vladimir. "So, do you have an investment for me yet?"

"In fact, there is a promising one on the horizon."

MaryAna's eyes light up. "Tell me about it."

"A collector I've done business with previously died suddenly. His widow needs some quick cash, so she's willing to part with her late husband's paintings. She has one in particular that could make us some serious money if I find the right buyer."

"Oh, that's exactly what I'm lookin' for," MaryAna reaches out to squeeze his arm, but he pulls it back. "You'll give me first crack at it, won't you?"

"We can discuss it next week when I know more. Let's not talk any more business tonight. The food here is considered some of the best in the city."

"The buffets looked amazing on the way in," Isadora says. "I'm starving."

***

After the meal, they all check out the decadent display of desserts. Once they have returned to their table, Natasha suggests they go to a club to dance. MaryAna votes in favor of the idea while Vladimir and Isadora are less enthusiastic.

The art dealer receives a call and glances at his phone to see who the caller is. "Excuse me, ladies, I must take this."

He scoots back from the table, turns toward the wall, and speaks to the caller in Russian. After a minute in conversation, he hangs up. "I must apologize," he tells his companions, "but my sister and I must leave."

"I hope it's nothing serious," MaryAna says.

"My uncle needs us, Miss Lindley. Thank you for dinner. It was most enjoyable."

"What about the apartment? Are we still on for tomorrow?"

"Natasha won't be available, but I can pick you up here in the afternoon." He and his sister rise from the table. "Say two o'clock?"

"That'll work."

"So, what do you think of my new friends, Izzy?" MaryAna says, after Vladimir and Natasha have left.

"I like them. Vladimir seems very professional and trustworthy. I believe they'll make lovely roommates."

"I'm surprised you didn't mention you speak Russian." MaryAna takes another bite of her cream cake.

"It would've been rude of us to speak another language and leave you out of the conversation."

"Thanks. Any idea what that phone call was about?"

"Hard to tell much from only one end of the conversation."

"I caught the word *Kalashnikov*." MaryAna takes another bite of her dessert. "Isn't that some kind of gun?"

"Yeah, what the Russians call an AK-47. Didn't you tell me they live in a bad section of Brooklyn?"

"Yeah, that's why Vladimir wants to move. I've got to admit, I'm kinda attracted to him."

"Has he made any advances toward you?"

MaryAna shakes her head. "Unfortunately, no."

Isadora taps her fingers on the table. "Maybe I should ride along tomorrow. You know, just to be on the safe side."

"That's not necessary. I'll be fine."

"OK, but you should keep everything business-like. Don't flirt with him or you might be looking for another art dealer."

"This deal is important to me," MaryAna assures her friend. "I'll be on my best behavior."

But if Vladimir does flirt with me, all bets are off.

Chapter 26

THE APARTMENT

MaryAna wakes up just before 9:00 Saturday morning and crawls out of bed with a splitting headache. Isadora had come back to her suite after dinner the night before, and they'd ordered a couple Pay-For-View movies and again sampled the minibar. MaryAna pops some ibuprofen and throws on her fluffy bathrobe.

She finds Isadora on the couch watching *Thelma & Louise* on TV, but the morning sun from the window is too much to bear, and she quickly pulls the shades closed.

"How can you stand all that light?"

Isadora smiles. "I'm not the one with a hangover."

"How can you be so cheery, Izzy? Doesn't your head hurt?"

"I stuck to wine while you cleaned out the beer before tackling the hard stuff. Maybe you have some Russian in you."

"Maybe. While I shower, would you call room service and order a pitcher of orange juice, coffee, and whatever you want?"

Isadora picks up the room's phone. "You don't want anything to eat?"

"No thanks."

MaryAna soon rejoins Isadora in the living room. As her friend chows down on a club sandwich, the teenager drains two glasses of orange juice.

"Maybe I'm dehydrated or something," MaryAna says, pouring herself a third glass. "Vladimir will be here at two. I was thinkin' more about him last night. And that gun thing still bothers me."

"He and his sister seem nice," Isadora reassures her. "If you want, I could still go with you this afternoon—to make sure everything is all right."

"That's not necessary. I'm just bein' way too suspicious. They'll make awesome roommates."

"Remember, MaryAna, it should be all business with Vladimir. No hanky-panky."

"I could use a little hanky-panky, Izzy. I'm feelin' kinda antsy, if you know what I mean."

"Well, don't look at me. And you shouldn't be expecting Vladimir to solve your problem either."

"I know—it's strictly business. But still . . ."

"MaryAna!"

"OK, Izzy," the teenager grins. "You're worse than Mama."

Geez.

Can't a girl have any fun?

***

That afternoon MaryAna waits outside the Plaza, this time in a white silk blouse and skinny jeans. Vladimir soon pulls up in a black BMW X5 wearing a gray golf shirt and black slacks.

She slides into the passenger seat. "Right on time," she says. "You look comfortable."

"I'm done with work for the week. Please, fasten your seatbelt."

"Nice car."

"It belongs to my uncle. He lets me borrow it from time to time."

"Does he live in Brooklyn too?"

"He does." The art dealer pulls into traffic. "He owns some buildings that occasionally get broken into. I help him guard them on occasion. That's why we had to leave so early last night."

Does that explain the rifle?

"What about the police—shouldn't they be doin' that?"

"They show up after the break-ins but never catch the perpetrators. The buildings are located in high crime areas."

"Has your uncle been in this country long?"

"He came here right after the fall of the Soviet Union and has done well for himself."

"How about your parents?"

"They live in Moscow," he answers as they stop at a traffic light. "My father is what you call a bureaucrat at the Kremlin. Do you have any brothers or sisters, Miss Lindley?"

"I have a twin brother, a stepbrother and four half-brothers."

"They're renovating the apartments in the building we are going to check out. It'll be at least a month before we'll be able to move in. Is that a problem?"

"Not really. I'll just stay at the Plaza."

"Have you had lunch yet, Miss Lindley? I was thinking perhaps we could get something after we look at the apartment."

Izzy would tell me to refuse, but she's not interested in guys.

"Could we go to a Russian restaurant? I've never been to one."

"Certainly."

They soon arrive in the area of Manhattan known as Greenwich Village and find a place to park. The afternoon is quite warm with a gentle breeze from the west. With only a touch of her hangover remaining, MaryAna enjoys the fresh air.

Before they leave the car, Vladimir pulls out a pack of Marlboros. "Do you mind if I smoke?"

"Go ahead. I notice a lot of Europeans smoke—in the movies anyway."

"It's still common in Russia." He takes out a cigarette and a matchbook. "My lighter stopped working this morning," he explains, striking a match.

"I need matches for the scented candles I bought," MaryAna tells him as they exit the car.

"Take these." He flips her the book of matches. "I've got more."

"Thanks," MaryAna notices the writing on the matchbook is Russian. "What's *Matryoshka?*"

"It's the Russian word for nested wooden dolls. Have you ever seen any, Miss Lindley?"

"Mama brought me some from New Orleans when I was young." She slips the matchbook into her purse. "I'll have to remember that word."

Vladimir motions toward a nearby building. "The apartment is in there."

When they enter, they see several carpenters at work. Vladimir talks to one, who apparently is the supervisor, but MaryAna cannot hear what they are saying due to the saws, hammers, and other tools in use.

The Russian leads her up to the third floor, where they find the door to one of the apartments open. It is empty except for a table saw and other carpentry equipment.

"This is the one my sister and I selected," Vladimir says, and tells her what the rent will be. "You'll be responsible for one-third."

"That seems fair."

"We'll also split the utilities three ways." He points to a closed door. "Your room is through there."

MaryAna goes inside and peers out the bedroom's only window. *Not much of a view. I'm sure gonna miss the Plaza.*

"Do you want me to write you a check now as a deposit?" she says.

"We'll take care of that, Miss Lindley. We trust you."

***

Once they have toured the apartment, they go to a nearby Russian restaurant for lunch. MaryAna peruses the menu as Vladimir explains the cuisine.

She decides on the chicken schnitzel with truffles, dill butter, and potatoes. Vladimir opts for the beef stroganoff with kasha, a porridge made from roasted buckwheat.

Vladimir drinks a Vodka Collins while they wait for their meal, and MaryAna has a martini.

"Any updates on the investment front?" she asks, anxious to earn some extra money.

"There is some news. As I suspected, the widow I mentioned has agreed to sell a painting I am interested in. Now to locate a buyer."

"Who's the artist?"

"Jacob von Ruisdael, a seventeenth-century Dutch master. Not as well-known as Rembrandt and Van Gogh, but his work is quite remarkable and sells consistently."

"I love classic Dutch paintings."

"This transaction should have an extremely quick turnaround—a matter of days. Are you still willing to invest?"

"I am." She finishes her martini and orders another.

"When I've nailed down the details, I'll contact you. At that point, we must move fast."

Vladimir drives MaryAna back to the Plaza after lunch. When they pull up in front, she notices the horse-drawn carriages along Fifty-Ninth Street.

"I've been wanting to take a carriage ride through Central Park ever since I got here," she says wistfully.

"I believe those carriages are more for tourists."

"I know, but it would be so romantic. Do they have anything like that in Moscow?"

"Possibly at Gorky Park."

"If we took a carriage ride, you could be my Prince Charming," she says with a grin.

"Prince who?"

"You know, from *Cinderella*."

"But that's just a fairy tale."

"My favorite one." MaryAna unbuckles her seatbelt and opens her door. "I'm a pushover for romantic stories. How about you?"

Vladimir's phone buzzes. He checks the message, then thumbs a quick reply. "Natasha, wondering when I'll be home. As always, she has tasks for me. My sister will be thrilled to learn you're going to be our apartment mate."

"I had a wonderful time, Vladimir. Thanks for lunch. We'll have to do it again soon. Next time it's my treat."

"I look forward to many more enjoyable dinners with you, Miss Lindley," he notes with a smile.

MaryAna lingers before getting out of the car, hoping Vladimir will kiss her goodbye. He does not.

I can't believe he's not attracted to me.

Nah, that can't be it—he has *to have a girlfriend.*

***

After returning to her suite, the eighteen-year-old receives a text from Kristen asking MaryAna to give her a call.

"Hey, girl. What's up?"

"Heidi and I are going to the beach tomorrow—you wanna come too?"

"Can I bring my friend Izzy? She's the girl I met at Boots 'n Heels."

"Are you two . . .?"

"No, not what you're thinking—we're just friends. We've been hangin' out shoppin' and stuff."

"That's cool. You'll need to come to Heidi's place in Brooklyn. I'll text you the address."

"What time do we need to be there?"

"We want to get a fairly early start—shoot for ten o'clock. We have plenty of beach towels, so all you'll need to bring is sunscreen. And wear your swimsuit under your clothes so we won't have to find a place to change."

After they hang up, MaryAna calls Isadora, who readily accepts the invitation.

"I'll get a taxi and pick you up at your place around nine. What's your address?"

Isadora gives it to her. "Send me a text when you leave the Plaza, MaryAna. I'll be waiting in front of my building. So, how did things go with Vladimir?"

"I'm definitely sharing the apartment with him and his sister."

"Did he try any hanky-panky?"

MaryAna giggles. "Unfortunately no, he was a perfect gentleman. See you in the mornin'."

I've certainly made some awesome friends here.

Chapter 27

BRIAN

On Sunday morning, a taxi drops Isadora and MaryAna off at Heidi's four-plex apartment building in Brooklyn. They see Kristen loading beach bags, towels, and a large cooler into the trunk of a dark-blue Buick Lacrosse.

"Is this your car?" MaryAna asks.

"It belongs to Heidi's older brother. She shares an apartment with him, and we use it when he's out of town. We've got beer, soft drinks, and sandwiches. I hope you like chicken salad."

"Yum-yum." MaryAna piles into the back seat with Isadora. "So, where are we goin'?"

"A barrier island on the south shore, not far from where I grew up," Heidi answers. "Do you have many beaches in Mississippi?"

"Some, but I prefer ones along the Alabama and Florida Coast like Gulf Shores, Destin, and Panama City. We call it the Redneck Riviera."

The other girls laugh.

"Were you girls into sports in high school?" Kristen asks.

MaryAna is the first to respond. "I did gymnastics, karate, and cheerleading."

"I was a cheerleader, too." Isadora holds up her left arm. "I got tossed up in the air and hoped the girls caught me. The pin in this wrist is from one time they didn't."

***

Once on the warm sand of the beach, the four girls spread out towels and shed their outer garments. Kristen is wearing a pink two-piece

141

while her girlfriend has on an identical one in blue. Isadora's petite figure in her black and white polka dot suit makes it hard to believe she is in her twenties.

MaryAna sports a lime-green, Brazilian-style string-bikini, which stands in sharp contrast to her bronze tan. Below her navel, a kitten tattoo peeks out to keep an eye on their surroundings.

Heidi takes a long look at her. "I'm surprised you don't have something hanging from your belly button to go with that tattoo."

"I love jewelry, but I'm not into those kinds of adornments," MaryAna tells her. "How about you?"

"I've got several piercings." Heidi sticks out her tongue, revealing a silver stud. "Kristen has some too. What about you, Izzy?"

"I don't even have pierced ears," she says. "There isn't enough of me to punch any extra holes."

The girls giggle and Heidi pulls suntan lotion from a beach bag. "Turn around, Kristen, and I'll do your back."

MaryAna takes out her sunscreen and turns to Isadora. "You look like you've been in the sun all summer."

"It's all natural thanks to my mother. You've got a great tan, MaryAna."

The teenager laughs. "All thanks to tannin' beds."

Once the girls are satisfied they are safe from damaging UV rays, they settle on their towels and enjoy the fresh sea air. The area they have staked out is not crowded, but sunbathers continue to pour onto the inviting sand.

About fifteen minutes later, two young men approach the girls. The taller is north of six feet with long brown hair, and MaryAna thinks that with his build, he could be a lifeguard. His shorter, dark-haired friend is nowhere near as muscular, but both saunter along as if they own the beach.

"Is it time to reapply some lotion, ladies?" the tall guy says in an accent similar to Heidi's. "We'll be glad to help you out."

"Thanks," MaryAna says, sitting upright, "but I think we're good."

"I'm Brian. This is my buddy Kevin," he says, indicating his shorter friend. "I haven't seen you around before, Blondie. I would've remembered that kitty cat."

"It's my first time here."

"Awesome. Mind if we join you?"

MaryAna glances at the other girls who are shaking their heads. "We'd rather you didn't."

Brian's smirk does not waver. "What's your name?"

"You're blocking my sun, dude," Heidi says, her eyes on his.

"Sorry, babe." He moves a couple of steps. "My friends and I have an awning set up just down the way. You and your friends are welcome to join us."

"Thanks, but we're fine," MaryAna reiterates.

Brian steps closer and crouches only a few feet from her. "Hey, we've got beer and some dynamite weed." He places two fingers on his lips as if smoking. "Might loosen you up."

"Maybe later."

Brian smiles like a cat who has cornered its prey. "You do that, Blondie, and we'll have some fun."

Kevin taps Brian on the shoulder and nods toward Heidi, who is clasping Kristen's hand.

"Yuck!" Brian says, lurching upright. "I didn't know you were a bunch of dykes."

MaryAna leaps to her feet. Only a few inches shorter than Brian, she locks eyes with him. "And what if we are?"

"It'd be a waste of female flesh, that's what," he says, his smirk back in full force. "Especially you, Blondie. We could've had a nice time together."

"I'd rather be with my friends than with a jerk like you."

Heidi jumps up, and steps toward him. "Get lost, Bozo."

Brian shoves her hard. She staggers backwards but manages to keep her feet.

"Stay away from me, dyke. You don't want a piece of me."

Kristen cowers behind her girlfriend, and Isadora scrambles away backwards on the sand.

Heidi takes another step toward Brian. "Take your best shot, butthole."

"Ladies first, you bitch," he says, sticking out his chest.

MaryAna dives between them, keeping them apart. "Hey, there's no need for this. These guys are going to leave us alone, *aren't* you?" she says, jerking her eyes up at Brian.

"You dykes make me sick. I could take out every one of you if I wanted to."

"Just try it!" Heidi yells, jabbing her finger in his chest.

Brian tries to yank MaryAna aside to get to Heidi, but she stands her ground.

"I'm warnin' you, Brian. Don't touch me again."

"Or what?" He reaches out to grab MaryAna, but she moves low and with a lightning kick sweeps his right leg out, sending him to his knees. She then takes his right arm and twists it behind his back. He yelps and grunts as she holds him down, but he cannot extricate himself.

She leans in close, increasing the pressure on his arm, and in a guttural tone she didn't know she had, gives Brian helpful advice: "Never threaten me or my friends again."

Kevin takes a step toward her, but she snaps her glare toward him.

"Back off or y'all will both need a hospital."

He holds his hands up and backs away.

"Now," MaryAna says, her attention back to Brian, "apologize for being a dumb ass dick."

He does not respond, so she applies even more pressure to his arm.

"OK! I'm sorry, I'm sorry."

The commotion has attracted a group of onlookers who witness the beatdown.

"Now apologize to Heidi for pushin' her and callin' her that bad name . . . do it!"

White heat ripples through Brian's arm. "*Uhh* . . . I'm sorry I pushed you and . . . for cursing at you. I'm sorry!"

MaryAna lets him go and backs away. "Good boy. Now get lost."

As Brian drags himself to his feet, the crowd gives a smattering of applause.

"It's all over, folks," MaryAna tells them. "I was just teachin' this guy some manners." The onlookers disperse, with several giving MaryAna a thumbs up as they go.

"Come on, Kevin," Brian says as he jiggles his arm, trying to get the blood back. "Let's get out of here. These dykes are crazy."

MaryAna watches them disappear down the beach before collapsing on her towel, her heart still pounding.

Heidi takes Kristen's hand. "Remind me to never mess with MaryAna. Those were some insane moves, girl."

"All those years learning karate came in handy. Is Kristen all right?"

"She'll be fine." Heidi puts her arm around her girlfriend. "She's had some scary experiences with guys."

"You got a taste of what we often face," Kristen adds, "if you don't fit in or go along. Thanks for standing up for us."

"No problem." MaryAna lies back down and lets out a long breath.

Those punks were lucky I was in a good mood.

Chapter 28

CARSON

When the four young women return to Heidi's apartment, they order pizza and swap tales about their families, friends, and upbringings. Around eight o'clock, MaryAna and Isadora catch a cab back to Manhattan.

"I'd love to see your apartment, Izzy."

"Ahh . . . yeah, sure. Not much to see though."

When the taxi lets them out, they walk the four flights up to Isadora's apartment.

"You want something to drink?" she says once they're inside.

"Whatcha got?"

"Let me see." Her friend walks to the kitchenette, opens the refrigerator, then the cupboard above it. "We've got rum, canned pineapple, and cream of coconut. Want me to make piña coladas?"

"Awesome." MaryAna plops on the sofa and slips off her sandals. "After all that fresh air, salt water, and encounter with Brian, I'm gonna sleep well tonight."

"You and me both." Isadora gets ice from the fridge for the blender.

"Can you believe that guy?" MaryAna sighs. "Some men can be damn ugly."

"Kristen was scared to death, but you were so cool," Isadora says, dumping the rest of the ingredients into the blender. She hits the switch, and blender's motor reverberates through the apartment.

"I just reacted to the situation like I was taught, "MaryAna replies once the blender stops. "Were you scared of those guys?"

"I just wanted to hide."

MaryAna leans back on the sofa and yawns. "In karate we learned runnin' away is often the best strategy. Today, though, it wasn't."

Isadora brings the blender and glasses to the sofa. She fills them, hands one to MaryAna, and then joins her on the couch.

"Oh, that's good," MaryAna says, before emptying the glass. "How about we go shoppin' again Thursday after work? It's my birthday."

Her friend pours the teenager another glassful. "Sounds like fun."

"Mama always took me shoppin' for my birthday. I had parties, but the trips to the mall are my fondest memories."

Isadora nods. "I loved to shop with my mom even though we didn't see eye-to-eye on clothes. She always wanted to buy me little girl stuff even when I got older."

MaryAna finishes off the second pina colada, then pours herself a third. They chat about high school, being cheerleaders, and a myriad of other topics that become more and more personal.

As they talk, a warm, fuzzy feeling engulfs MaryAna. She is unsure whether it is from the alcohol or the coziness of being with Isadora.

"I had so much fun with you girls today, Izzy. It got me thinkin'. Men have caused me nothing but heartache. Maybe I should expand my horizons—you wanna be more than just shoppin' buddies?"

Isadora draws back. "I told you I don't sleep with straight girls."

"When my best friend, Coree, and I were ten or eleven, we sometimes practiced kissing with each other. There wasn't anything sexual about it. In fact, I would close my eyes and pretend she was her brother. I don't know, maybe I'm bisexual."

"A lot of young girls experiment like that. It's just curiosity."

"Izzy, what if I kissed you right now?"

"Well . . . ahh . . . please don't."

"Aren't you attracted to me?"

"I don't wanna mess with our friendship."

"Why so pessimistic?"

"Because I know you like men. Being with me would simply be an experiment. You could go back to guys at any time. I don't want

148

my heart broken again."

MaryAna takes her friend's hand, but Isadora pulls it back. "You don't really want that kind of relationship, MaryAna."

"How can you be so sure?"

"If you really wanted me, you would've kissed me when we first stepped into this apartment. That's what Kira did."

***

When MaryAna returns to the hotel later Sunday night, she is in the mood for a martini. Still wearing her lime-green bikini beneath her T-shirt and shorts, the eighteen-year-old meanders into one of the hotel bars and finds an empty barstool.

Soft music plays from speakers somewhere in the room; MaryAna does not recognize the song. A few tables are occupied, but only one other patron is sitting at the bar. He gives her a glance before turning his attention back to his glass.

The bartender takes MaryAna's order, checks her ID, and brings her a martini.

"We close in less than thirty minutes, by the way."

"In that case, bring me two more."

The bartender shuffles off to make the drinks. When he returns with the other two martinis, she has already finished the first one.

The man sitting at the bar, who in his mid-thirties, slides over to the stool next to hers. He looks comfortable in a gray golf shirt and tan slacks. His medium-length brown hair is combed forward as if to hide a receding hairline.

"My name's Carson," he says. "Mind if I join you?"

"Be my guest. I'm MaryAna."

He's kinda cute, and I like his smile.

Carson clears his throat. "I hate to drink alone," he says.

"Me too. You stayin' here at the Plaza?"

"Sure am." He points to her drinks. "Are you in a hurry to get wasted?"

She giggles. "I just like the taste. So, are you in town for work or pleasure?"

"I work for a financial firm. I flew in from Chicago for a seminar this weekend."

"That sounds interestin'. Tell me about it."

"It was on risk management and boring as hell. My company invests in commercial real estate—malls, office buildings, that kind of stuff."

The bartender reappears, telling them it is last call. Carson tells him to bring them another round on him.

"Thanks," MaryAna says, finishing off her second martini. "You were sayin'?"

Carson tells her about the commercial real estate market and his job in Chicago. Before long they are talking about cars, movies, and the latest music.

About the time MaryAna finishes her fourth martini, the bartender announces the bar is closing. The teenager grabs her purse and slides off the barstool, but one of the martinis has already found its way to her head and she grabs Carson's arm for support.

"Thanks," she says, looking up at him. "You aren't wearin' a weddin' ring, sir. Are you married?"

"Divorced," he says with a chuckle. "I'm sorry they're kicking us out. I could listen to your cute southern drawl all night."

The romantic tingle missing when MaryAna was with Isadora earlier in the evening now reverberates through her body in high gear.

Izzy's right—I do love men.

She takes Carson's hand. "I've got a minibar. Why don't you come up? You can tell me more about investin' in commercial real estate."

"I'd love to, but I should get some sleep. I'm flying out early in the morning."

"If you change your mind, I'm in suite 1819."

"How can you afford a suite here?"

"My boss pays for everything."

"So, you really are a working girl."

"I am five days a week, but not tonight," she says with a grin. "You should see the view of the park from the eighteenth floor. It would take your breath away."

150

"Is the park the only great view I'll see up there?" he says with a hint of a smirk.

MaryAna giggles. "I'll guarantee you'll see a whole lot worth stayin' awake for."

"How can I refuse such a charming offer? On the way, I need to grab something from my room. Then we can check out those fantastic views."

My guardian angel ain't gonna be happy with me tonight.

As they stroll to the elevators arm-in-arm, MaryAna spots Samson and waves to him. The bellman glances at her but does not wave back.

Whoa, is Samson jealous?

Chapter 29

LATE FOR WORK

Monday morning, MaryAna awakens on the carpet in her living room. Beside the sofa are her shoes, T-shirt, shorts, and lime-green bikini. Empty beer bottles adorn the end tables.

On one of them is an ashtray with several smushed-out joints. The marijuana smoke has dissipated, but the pungent odor clings to the room like an unwanted guest. The teenager looks around for Carson who is nowhere to be seen.

MaryAna recalls the businessman removing her clothing as they made out on the sofa. He had peeled off each piece like someone unwrapping an expensive present. The anticipation stoked the fire burning within her.

When she was naked, Carson had her step to the large plate-glass window as if he were directing a movie. In the moonlight, the eighteen-year-old stared out over Upper Manhattan like a queen surveying her domain. He sat back, lit up another joint, and enjoyed the view of her body silhouetted against the New York skyline.

As MaryAna stood in front of the window, she felt like a work of art on public display. The teenager continued to gaze out over the twinkling lights until Carson removed his clothes and joined her.

"You were right," he said, taking her in his arms from behind. "The view is worth every penny."

The teenager's breath fogged up the cool glass. "I told you it was worth stayin' awake for."

As Carson pressed her face and upper body against the window, he made love to her. It felt as if she was doing it with the entire city. Her mind wandered, and she fantasized about being with other lovers.

This is what it would've been like in Mr. Rubenstein's office, but about thirty stories higher.

MaryAna shelves her memories of the night before and pulls the drapes closed. With a yawn, she stretches, gathers up her clothes, and sighs.

I haven't smoked that much weed in a while. Now I remember why.

On the desk, she spots a business card, two hundred-dollar bills, and a handwritten note.

It reads: Hope this is enough to cover the beer, the great views, and everything else. If you're ever in Chicago, call me.

What's the money for? I told him my boss pays for everything.

MaryAna stuffs his card and the bills into her purse, then reaches for her iPhone to check the time.

Oh, no—I should've been at work two hours ago!

Kicking herself for not placing a wake-up call, she telephones Hannah and explains the situation. The teenager promises her supervisor she will be in to work as soon as possible.

After a quick shower, MaryAna hustles downstairs to the lobby and has Leon hail her a taxi.

"Please hurry," she tells the driver after giving him her work address. "I'm runnin' really late."

MaryAna goes straight to Hannah's office. "I'm sorry I'm late. It won't happen again."

Her supervisor looks up from her desk. "Jacqueline is back from France and wants to meet you."

Of all days to be late!

"Does she know I've been on time every day since I started here?"

"You might mention it. She has your personnel file."

"What's in it?"

"Everything the company knows about you."

"Oh. Um . . . should I go to the bakery before I go see Jacqueline?"

"Kristen took care of it." Hannah points to the half-eaten doughnut on her desk. "She told me you two have become quite good friends."

"Yes. Kristen and her friend invited me and my girlfriend to the beach yesterday."

"Oh, I see." Her supervisor raises an eyebrow. "What you girls do on your own time is none of my business as long as you don't embarrass the company."

Does she think I'm a lesbian?

"Is there anything I should know before I meet Jacqueline?"

"Fix your makeup," Hannah says, picking up her phone. "I'll let her know you're here. Oh, and don't say anything derogatory about France."

After a stop at the lady's room to touch up her makeup, MaryAna taps on Jacqueline's office door.

"*Entrez.*"

She takes a deep breath and opens the door.

Jacqueline LeBlanc stands behind her desk, gazing out her office's plate-glass window. As tall as MaryAna, she has a slim figure, and her dark-brown hair is in a classic bob cut. She is wearing a stylish navy-blue dress with white trim. The teenager remembers a similar one in the samples room. She'd considered it for the concert but decided it was too conservative.

It looks great on her though. She could still be a model.

"Please have a seat, Miss Lindley."

MaryAna sits in the armchair, and her boss's boss takes the swivel chair behind the desk. For a long moment they stare at each other in an awkward silence.

"Do you know what time you're expected to be here in the morning?"

"Yes, Ms. LeBlanc. This is the first time I've been late since I started here. I forgot to put in—"

"I don't want excuses, young lady. In the future, make sure you adhere to our rules." Jacqueline glances at an open folder on her desk. "Your file indicates you have almost no work experience."

"I worked as a cocktail waitress at a club back home."

"You mean, like a disco?"

"Yeah, there was drinkin' and dancin'."

I'm not about to admit it was a strip club.

"The only recommendation here is from our CEO. Is that where you met him?"

"I met Mr. Rubenstein on a flight to Atlanta. He asked my opinion on some dress designs and liked my ideas. That's why he offered me this job."

"I see." Jacqueline places a finger under her chin as if deep in thought. "By any chance, would one of your ideas be for us to use brighter colors?"

MaryAna nods. "It was, yes."

Jacqueline leans forward. "Tell me about your fashion experience."

"I've designed several of my formals and some for friends, along with some weddin' dresses. I read all the fashion magazines and keep up with the latest trends. I sketch pretty good, and I've developed some unique design concepts."

"I'd like to hear more about them, especially the ones you mentioned to Mel. I've quite a lot on my plate right now, but we'll get back together soon."

It doesn't sound like she's going to fire me.

"One more thing, Miss Lindley. I see our company is putting you up at the Plaza. That's an expensive hotel."

"Mr. Rubenstein said the company would pay for my first month in town. That ends soon."

Jacqueline glances down at the folder. "It ends this Wednesday. Have you found another place to live?"

"I'm moving into an apartment with some friends soon. I'll stay at the Plaza until then, but I'll start payin' for it myself."

"Accounting tells me you've run up quite a hotel bill." Jacqueline glances at the folder once again. "You seem to be fond of room service."

"Mr. Rubenstein told me to charge everything."

"That was very thoughtful of him. We normally don't cover three-hundred-dollar facials or four-hundred-dollar massages. I hope you enjoyed them."

"You should try one. I could make you an appointment."

"I'm sure they're wonderful, Miss Lindley, but I'll pass. It also appears you like the minibar."

"Is that a problem?"

"You are not old enough to drink, young lady."

"I have an . . . a fake ID."

"You must learn to follow the rules."

"I can pay the hotel bill if you want."

"Mr. Rubenstein has already instructed accounting to cover the entire balance. He may be our CEO, but he doesn't own this company."

"Isn't he the big boss?"

Jacqueline closes the folder. "Mel certainly thinks so. He's very generous with my papa's money."

"You mean, your daddy owns the company?"

The woman nods. "If Mel wants to put you up in style, my husband should use his own funds."

MaryAna gulps. "He's your husband?"

***

After her meeting with Jacqueline, MaryAna is outraged. She fights the urge to march into Mel's office and tell him off.

He conveniently left out the fact that his "out-of-town" wife was the head of design.

But, upon further reflection and a few doughnuts later, MaryAna has second thoughts about confronting the CEO and wonders why neither Hannah nor any of her co-workers never mentioned the truth about the CEO. Before the meeting, she pictured his wife as some unattractive shrew who refused to give him a divorce, but now . . .

They all referred to her as Jacqueline LeBlanc. Why didn't she take her husband's last name?

And why would Mr. Rubenstein cheat on such an attractive, accomplished woman?

I thought I knew everything.

Turns out I don't know much of anything at all . . .

Chapter 30

A SAD STORY

On Tuesday morning, MaryAna distributes the usual Made Fresh goodies to her co-workers, including an espresso and jelly doughnut to Jacqueline LeBlanc.

"Is it OK?" MaryAna says. "Kristen told me you like it strong."

"It's fine." Jacqueline glances at the doughnut. "But no more of those for me. I'm officially watching my weight starting now."

"Ms. LeBlanc, you look awesome for a woman your age."

"Thank you. You're a very attractive young lady, Miss Lindley, but I'm sure you hear that all the time. You could probably eat doughnuts all day and not gain a pound."

"I have a high metabolism." MaryAna smiles. "Do you have time to discuss my design ideas?"

"A bit," Jacqueline says, before taking a bite of the last doughnut. "So, tell me about your obsession with certain colors."

"I like bold colors—and my friends do too. I believe younger women seek new and excitin' clothes. Bright colors reflect optimism and independent thinkin'."

"What kind of research have you conducted, Miss Lindley?"

"I've mostly just talked to a lot of girls."

"Have you reviewed national and international studies on color? How it influences mood and spending patterns?"

"No, can't say that I have."

"Do you know that very smart people research colors and their effects on the brain?"

MaryAna shakes her head.

"My husband seems quite taken with your ideas," she says, sipping her espresso. "Why do you think that is?"

"You need to ask him."

"Were you surprised he offered you a job?"

"Yes, and I appreciate the opportunity. It's a dream come true."

"This city can sometimes rip people's dreams into tiny pieces, Miss Lindley. We'll discuss your other ideas another time. That's all for now—please tell Hannah I wish to see her."

I don't think she likes me.

***

When MaryAna arrives at the diner for lunch, she spots Kristen and Heidi in their usual booth.

"Hey, y'all," she says, sliding in across from them. "Sorry I'm late."

Kristen waves her off. "No problem. I ordered you a Reuben. They don't have sweet tea on the menu, so I got you iced tea and some sugar packets."

"Thanks. I was finishin' up a blouse sketch that Jacqueline wants to see this afternoon. I'm tryin' to make a better impression today." She leans back in the booth. "By the way, you guys could've mentioned she's Rubenstein's wife."

"You were so down about him being married," Kristen says. "I didn't want to pile that on top. You'd already broken it off with him anyway."

MaryAna sighs. "Is it true her daddy owns the company?"

"Jacqueline Designs is a wholly owned subsidiary of LeBlanc International," Heidi explains. "It's headquartered in France. Her father is the chairman of the board and the majority stockholder. So, yeah, you could say her father owns the company."

MaryAna rips open a sugar packet and stirs in the contents. "What else don't I know about them? Do they have kids?"

"One son," Heidi says. "He's in his twenties and spends his summers in France."

Wonderful. Mel's got a son older than me.

"Izzy and I really enjoyed the beach," MaryAna says, changing the subject. "Thanks for invitin' us. By the way, I don't mean to pry, Kristen—but you really seemed scared of Brian and his loser buddy. They were annoying, but not that nuts."

Heidi turns to her girlfriend and pats her hand. "Tell MaryAna about Pittsburgh."

Kristen's eyes dart in all directions before she blinks and takes a breath. "When I was a junior in high school, I went on a date with Thomas, one of our star football players. We saw a movie, and afterwards, he drove to an isolated spot along the Allegheny River."

Kristen picks at her napkin. "We made out, which was cool with me, but he wanted to go further. When I refused, he threatened to throw me in the river even though he knew I couldn't swim. Then he . . ."

"He raped her," Heidi says.

"I reported it to the police. They did a physical exam and interrogated me." Kristen grits her teeth. "It was humiliating, but I wanted him to pay for what he did."

"My God. Was he arrested?" MaryAna asks.

"He claimed it was consensual and the charges were dropped. I complained to the district attorney's office, but they said it was a losing case. I found out the prosecutor was friends with the football coach."

MaryAna slams her fist on the table. "That's not right! What did your parents say?"

"My father said it was my fault for going parking in the first place. My mother was embarrassed and just wanted it to go away."

The waitress brings their sandwiches and refills their drinks. When she leaves, Heidi takes her girlfriend's hand. "Tell her the rest."

"A woman reporter at a local newspaper interviewed me. She'd heard other girls at my school had similar incidents. The next day, two guys in ski masks jumped me after a softball game and dragged me into a van." Kristen wipes her eyes with her napkin. "When they . . . when they were done, one of them said if the reporter kept nosing around, they'd kill me."

"Did you know who they were?"

"I'm pretty sure one of them was Thomas. They drove me to my house and basically dumped me onto my front lawn."

MaryAna can't believe what she is hearing. "You poor thing."

"My parents took me to the emergency room. I had a broken arm and several cracked ribs."

"What did they do about it?"

"I told them who I thought had kidnapped me, and they brought him in for questioning. The detective told me the guy had a solid alibi from several teammates."

"What about the reporter?" MaryAna asks.

"My father told her to drop her investigation. He was afraid those guys might make good on their threat. And the reporter did as my father asked, although she wasn't happy about it."

"Did the police ever arrest anyone?"

"As far as I know, the case is still open. Anyway, that's why I panicked at the beach. Brought it all back, you know?"

No wonder Kristen freaked out when Mr. Rubenstein tried to kiss her.

"I'm so sorry that happened to you," MaryAna says, putting her hand on Kristen's. "I know that wasn't easy to talk about. I've had some bad experiences with guys too. Maybe it affects how I see them sometimes."

Kristen picks up her sandwich and takes her first bite. "My therapist keeps telling me I need to face my past. It's easier now that I have someone who will stand up for me."

Heidi squeezes her girlfriend's arm and smiles. "Now you have MaryAna too."

***

That evening back at the Plaza, the eighteen-year-old gets a call while watching TV.

"Vladimir. I was hopin' to hear from you."

"Good news, Miss Lindley. The widow I told you about has agreed to sell the painting at my price. I wanted to make sure you were still interested."

"Definitely."

"I'm finalizing a price with the collector who will buy it from us. My commission will come out of the profits. You should still double your investment."

"Awesome. Where do I go to get the paintin'?"

"I'll handle that. All you'll need to do is provide the funds. I will finalize the details in a couple of days. Do you have the money readily available?"

"It's in my bank back home."

"You'll need to do a wire transfer."

"I don't know how to do that."

"Don't worry about it. I'll text you the instructions with the routing and account numbers when everything is finalized."

MaryAna tingles with excitement. "Would you like to come by tonight? We could have a couple of drinks to celebrate."

Vladimir clears his throat. "I am tied up this evening. Maybe another time."

"I'll wait to hear from you."

"Goodnight, Miss Lindley."

He's probably seeing some girl.

Chapter 31

ANDRE

Just after eight o'clock Wednesday morning, MaryAna delivers an espresso to Jacqueline's office. The door is open, but she knocks anyway.

"*Entrez.*" Jacqueline is seated at her desk and motions for MaryAna to come in.

From the chair in front of her desk, a dark-haired young man rises to his feet. His navy-blue blazer and white slacks hint he might have stepped off a golf course.

"MaryAna, this is my son Andre," Jacqueline informs her.

"Nice to meet you," MaryAna says as they shake hands. She then hands Jacqueline her espresso.

He's taller and more muscular than his daddy, but I see the resemblance.

"Would you like some coffee?" MaryAna says. "I could do another run . . .?"

Andre's eyes dart from Jacqueline's to hers. "Thank you, but I'm fine."

You sure are . . . whoa, is Jacqueline scowling at me?

"Miss Lindley is from out of state," Jacqueline tells her son. "She has no prior experience in the fashion industry, but your father saw fit to hire her nonetheless."

Andre's eyes bounce between the other two as if he were watching a tennis match. "Obviously, Dad saw that Miss Lindley has great potential."

Jacqueline huffs. "I simply expect an honest day's work from our employees. Miss Lindley is still learning to follow the rules."

His eyes swing back to MaryAna. "I'm sure she'll do just fine, mom."

Jacqueline takes a sip of her coffee. "I'll get with you and Hannah later on those blouse designs, Miss Lindley."

"I look forward to seein' you again," Andre says with none of his mother's French accent. "Welcome to the company."

MaryAna nods with a smile. "Thank you. Glad to be here."

As she turns to leave, she notes a definite frown on Jacqueline's face.

***

At noon, MaryAna heads over to the diner for lunch. Although she had not made plans with Kristen and Heidi, she expects them to be there, but when she does not see her friends, she starts to leave.

"Miss Lindley!"

She turns back and scans the diner, seeing a young man waving from a booth in the back. It is Andre. He is there with another guy about his age, and he motions for MaryAna to join them.

Well, I can't be rude, so . . .

"Nice to see you again," he says, stepping aside so she can slide into the booth.

Andre scoots in beside her. He is no longer wearing the blazer and his sleeves are rolled up to his elbows.

"Miss Lindley," he says, "this character is Wyatt Furman. He works in the marketing department. At least, he says he does."

Andre's friend has short black hair, matching eyes, and bronze skin. His other features indicate at least one of his parents is African-American.

Wyatt grins, "Oh yeah, massa Andy. I pick da cotton for all those purdy dresses."

MaryAna giggles.

"He also thinks he's a comedian," Andre adds.

"So, this is who you were telling me about," his friend says, shaking hands with MaryAna.

"How long have you worked there?"

"A couple years so far." Wyatt's eyes sweep over her. "Miss Lindley is even more attractive than you described."

"Y'all, please call me MaryAna."

Wyatt grins. "You were right, Andy. Her Southern accent is charming."

A blush passes in her cheeks as she turns to Andre. "So, is it Andy or Andre?"

"My friends call me Andy."

Wyatt laughs. "You've got friends? How'd that happen?"

"Don't mind him," Andre says. "The doctor dropped him on his head when he was born."

Wyatt grabs the sides of his mouth and makes a funny face.

"You're embarrassing me, man." Andy turns to MaryAna. "My mother and her family insist on calling me Andre. But to my father and his family, I'm Andrew. Pick one, I guess."

MaryAna waves her hands. "When we're at work, I'll use Andre. I don't want your mama upset with me."

He chuckles. "I don't spend much time at the office. Today, I mainly stopped by to see Wyatt. We're going to a Yankees game tonight."

"My ex-boyfriend is in the Yankees farm system. His name is Tyler Richardson. Have y'all heard of him?"

Before they can answer, a server arrives to take their orders.

"Richardson is the kid they picked up from the Braves," Wyatt says. "He had a slow start at Scranton, but he's tearing up the International League last I saw."

"Wyatt is the Yankees ultimate fan," Andre explains. "He can tell you what they have for breakfast. So, where'd you meet this ex-boyfriend?"

"High school. I just graduated in May." MaryAna says, before wishing she had not brought up the topic. "I'll be nineteen tomorrow."

"My mom mentioned you were young," Andre tells her. "I think she was trying to discourage me from asking you out."

"What else did she say about me?"

"That the company was paying for you to stay at the Plaza. I don't think she was happy about that. So, how did you end up in New York?"

167

"I was on my way to see Tyler in Pennsylvania when I met your daddy. He asked for my opinion on some dress designs, liked my ideas, and offered me a job."

"So, you only recently broke up with your boyfriend?"

"Yeah. Maybe that's why he's been hittin' better lately. How long have you two known each other?"

"Same high school," Wyatt answers. "A fancy one here in the city. None of the rich kids could catch Andy's passes, so they brought me in from the 'hood.'"

"You didn't exactly live in the projects, Wyatt."

"I didn't grow up in a mansion like you either."

"So, you were a quarterback?" MaryAna says.

"Just in high school. In college at Yale, I played defense."

An Ivy League school. I'm impressed.

"We have an extra ticket to the Yankees game on Friday," Andre says. "You wanna come too?"

"You're the son of my bosses. That doesn't sound like it would be a good idea."

"Don't worry about that. Wyatt's fiancée, Regina, will be with us."

"I don't know . . ."

"C'mon," he says. "Otherwise, Regina will fix me up with one of her uptown girlfriends. Nothing against her, but her friends don't know a damn thing about baseball."

"It'll be fun," Wyatt chimes in. "You'll like Regina."

Andre brandishes his best puppy-dog eyes at MaryAna. "Save me from a fate worse than death."

"Well, if it's a matter of life or death, sure. I'll meet you at the stadium, Andy, but under one condition."

"Name it."

"Don't tell your parents about me. I don't want them thinkin' I'm usin' you to get ahead at the company."

"I swear they'll never hear about it from my lips," Andy says, holding up his hand. "Scout's honor."

"Was Andy ever a scout, Wyatt?"

"Eagle Scout. I know my buddy here can keep secrets. He knows plenty of mine."

***

When MaryAna returns to the hotel after work, she notices a message light on the phone in her room. She contacts the front desk and is connected to the assistant manager.

"Jacqueline Designs will not be paying your bill after tonight," the man explains. "Will you be staying on with us?"

"Yes, for a while."

"Very well. Please come by the front desk either tonight or in the morning and make payment arrangements."

"Will I still get the corporate rate?" she asks.

"If your company requests it."

After hanging up, she calls Mel's cell. When he answers, she asks, "Can you talk a moment?"

"I'm still at the office. Go ahead."

"This is the last night the company is footin' the hotel bill. I'm gonna stay a little longer and I'd like to keep that corporate rate. Will you request it for me?"

"How much longer?"

"At least a couple of weeks. The apartment I'm gonna share with some friends is bein' renovated."

"I'll take care of it. They won't demand payment for another week. Do you have enough to cover the next bill?"

"I've got plenty, thanks. I'm sorry things didn't work out between us."

"I could set you up in your own apartment."

"We've been over this, sir."

"What if I stop by the Plaza tonight to discuss it further?"

"Are you and Jacqueline gettin' a divorce?"

"No."

"Then we have nothing more to talk about."

"But—"

"The situation at work is awkward enough. I'm worried Jacqueline

169

will find out about us."

"Our relationship can still be a secret," Mel says. "Let's at least get together for a drink. I want to see you."

"One drink, then another, then another. That could end up leading to my bedroom."

"Would that really be so bad?"

"Thanks again for your help, sir. Let's just be friends."

Not friends with benefits.

Chapter 32

BIRTHDAY WISH

MaryAna is awakened at 5:30 Thursday morning. It is a text from her twin brother wishing her a happy nineteenth birthday. She texts back the same message.

It's not even five in Mississippi. JoeE's up before the roosters.

As the now nineteen-year-old is wide awake, she decides to start the day with a hot shower. As the water pours over her, she makes a birthday wish.

Today, I want Prince Charming to take me on a carriage ride.

She has little confidence her fairy godmother will grant her wish, however. Her preferred prince, Vladimir, has shown little interest in her beyond business and sharing an apartment. Andy would be a prime candidate if he was not Mel's son. Samson also remains a possibility, but an unlikely one.

Maybe I should just cruise the bars tonight and find another Carson.

When MaryAna steps outside the hotel on her way to work, she finds her favorite doorman is on duty.

"Happy birthday, Miss Lindley."

"You remembered, Leon."

"How could I forget something so important? Here, I have a present for you."

The doorman steps inside the hotel and returns with a wrapped package."

"My son wanted you to have this. He painted it."

"How thoughtful," MaryAna says, removing the festive wrapping paper. "This is Central Park. I recognize the pond and the footbridge. Thank you so much."

In the painting, a blond girl is standing on the bridge, dressed in a sweatshirt, pink leggings, and a baseball cap. Behind her stands an angel, its wings spread wide as if to protect her.

MaryAna holds the framed illustration out at arm's length. "His imagery is very realistic. I can almost smell the wild flowers. One time when I was in the park, I stood in that exact spot."

"Look close at the girl's face."

"Oh my gosh," she says. "It's me!"

"It is indeed."

"Did you describe me to your son?"

Leon shakes his head. "I asked Max about it. He said he had a vision of you."

"I'd love to meet him. He's an excellent artist."

"Maybe we'll have you over for dinner one night. I'll talk to my wife."

"That would be awesome. I always name my paintings. Tell Max I'll call it 'Angel on a Bridge.'"

Leon grins. "He'll like that. Are you taking the subway this morning, Miss Lindley?"

"Hail me a cab, please. I don't want to damage the paintin'. I'll set it on my desk so everyone can see it."

As she waits for the taxi, MaryAna takes another look at the image. *The angel's face looks like my guardian angel!*

***

Throughout the day, MaryAna receives birthday wishes in texts from her family and friends. Her mother calls to let her know she deposited two thousand dollars in her daughter's checking account.

"Buy yourself a few nice things, dear. I miss you."

"Miss you too, Mama. My friend Isadora, and I plan to go shoppin' tonight. Did I tell you she's an interpreter at the UN?"

"I look forward to meetin' her. I might visit you next month— would you like that?"

She probably wants to check up on me.

"That would be awesome, Mama. I hope to be in an apartment by then. I'm gonna be sharing one with a brother and sister who are from Russia.

"How well do you know these people?"

"He's an art dealer, and she's a bookkeeper. I trust them. Why don't you wait until I move in, and you can help me decorate my room?"

"That sounds good, honey."

"Thanks for the money. Gotta go—need to get back to work."

***

During her lunch break, MaryAna calls Isadora to confirm their shopping plans. They decide to meet at Saks Fifth Avenue.

"I can't stay out late," Isadora tells her. "I'm bringing home some documents to translate."

"We can go out another night, Izzy."

"No, no. Today's your birthday. The translations will only take me a couple of hours. As long as I get home by nine, it'll be fine."

"We'll make it a quick trip, Izzy. I just need something to wear to the Yankees game tomorrow. I'm . . . I'm goin' with Mr. Rubenstein's son."

"You're going out with the son of that CEO you were seeing—are you kidding me?"

"I'll tell you all about it while we're shoppin'. See you then."

***

After the brief shopping adventure at Saks, MaryAna returns alone to the Plaza. She has three new outfits, two by Jacqueline Designs. One is a skirt and blouse combo she plans to wear to the baseball game, the others are dresses for work. She also purchased three pairs of shoes and assorted accessories.

Just after nine-thirty, MaryAna digs out the matchbook Vladimir gave her from her purse to light a scented candle while she has dinner, when her cell rings. The caller coincidentally is Vladimir.

"Miss Lindley?" His deep voice causes the hairs on her arms to come to attention.

"Vladimir, I'm so glad to hear from you—it's a nice holiday surprise."

"Ah, yes—today is your birthday."

"Yep, I hit nineteen today."

"I did not realize you were so young."

What does he mean by that?

"So, do you have some news?"

"I do, yes. The buyer has agreed to my terms. I'll be able to double your money, but we need to move fast. I sent you an email earlier with information about the wire transfer. We should review it tonight."

"Now, over the phone?"

"Actually, I'm downstairs in your hotel lobby."

He's in the lobby?!

Vladimir continues: "Would you like to have dinner? We could go over the information . . . and, of course, celebrate your birthday as well."

"Give me a few minutes to change. Meet me in the Champagne Bar. Order us a bottle and charge it to room 1819."

"As you wish, Miss Lindley. See you shortly."

MaryAna sticks the matches back in her purse.

I have a wish all right—my birthday wish!

Chapter 33

CINDERELLA

Twenty minutes later, MaryAna enters the Champagne Bar decked out in her pink satin dress with the slit up one side. The crystal chandeliers above bathe her in a soft, warm glow, accentuating her figure and long legs. She finds Vladimir at a table with an ice bucket stand and a bottle of Perrier-Jouët Grand Brut nestled within. The art dealer smiles and rises to greet her.

"Miss Lindley," he says, pulling out a chair. "You look fantastic. Is that dress one of your creations?"

"I wish. Do you like it?" She takes her seat and he slides the chair to the table before seating himself.

"It's quite striking."

"Thank you. I hope I didn't make you wait too long. Was this a special trip just to see me?"

"Actually, I was in Manhattan for a meeting earlier this evening. I took the chance you might be available."

So, I was just an afterthought?

A waiter in a red vest arrives and sets two champagne flutes on the table.

"Would you like me to serve you now?"

Vladimir nods, and the waiter pours a sampling of champagne into the Russian's glass. He takes a sip and nods a second time, and the waiter fills both glasses.

"To birthdays and profitable investments," Vladimir says as they clink their glasses. "Did you get my email?"

"I actually haven't read it yet. I was getting dressed."

He explains the procedure to wire money into his account as she finishes her glass.

"Any questions?" he says, giving her a refill.

"How much should I transfer?"

"One hundred thousand dollars."

MaryAna draws back. "That's almost my entire bank balance, includin' what my mama deposited for my birthday."

"You told me you had more than that available, Miss Lindley. Was I mistaken?"

"I've been shoppin' since we talked. If I transfer that much, I won't have enough left to pay my hotel bill next week. I don't get paid until a week from tomorrow, and that still might not be enough."

"After we sell the painting, you'll have doubled your investment. It'll be back in your account early next week. Tuesday latest."

"I don't know if I should do this," MaryAna says, taking a sip of her champagne. It's a great opportunity and all, but . . ."

"I've done dozens of transactions like this, Miss Lindley. If you are uncomfortable, I have other clients willing to jump at such a lucrative opportunity."

"Could I do, like half the amount?"

"That would entail far more paperwork, and we must act quickly." He fidgets with his tie. "I came to you first because we are going to be apartment mates. Either you do the whole amount, or I must offer this deal to another client."

"Please, don't," she says, and finishes the second glass. "I need time to think."

"Fine, but I require an answer before I leave this evening." He refills her glass once more. "Would you like to consider it while we get something to eat?"

"I was hungry but not anymore." She tries to think, but her thoughts are fuzzy. For a moment, the Russian seems to go out of focus.

Has that champagne already gone to my head?

"The other night, Miss Lindley, you mentioned a carriage ride.

How about I treat you to one for your birthday? It'll give you more time to consider your decision."

Thank you, fairy godmother!

She cocks her head. "What happened to not mixin' business with pleasure?"

"On the ride, business will be a taboo subject." The Russian's grin turns into a full smile. "I'm sure we can find something far more enjoyable to hold our attention."

MaryAna's goosebumps return, and she gulps down the champagne. She pours herself another glassful, eager to learn what he has in mind.

***

Once on Fifty-Ninth Street, MaryAna selects a carriage, and Vladimir helps her climb inside. The slit up one side of her dress provides an unobstructed view of her long legs. When she settles into the seat, his eyes are still on her.

"What?" she asks, noticing his weird expression.

"You look like a princess in her royal carriage. I am looking forward to seeing more of you."

"More of me?"

"You know, when we share an apartment. We'll see each other every day."

"Oh, right."

MaryAna shivers in the cool breeze, now a bit tipsy from the champagne.

This is so romantic.

The clip-clop of the horse's hooves mark the start of their excursion, and MaryAna takes her Prince Charming's hand.

"I've been wantin' to do this ever since I moved to New York." She looks into his eyes. "How old are you, Vladimir?"

"I am twenty-eight."

Perfect.

His phone buzzes, alerting him to a text. He reads it, turns the phone off, and stuffs it back into his shirt pocket.

"Was that your girlfriend?"

"Natasha. If I had a girlfriend, I wouldn't be here with you."

"Have you been, like, married before?"

"Why these questions?"

"I recently stopped seein' a guy when I learned he had a wife."

"You can trust me. Ask Natasha if you want."

"I believe you," she says, squeezing his hand.

"Are you cold?"

"A little."

He takes the woolen blanket from the seat across from them and spreads it over their laps.

MaryAna giggles. "I hope this isn't the horse's blanket."

The Russian smiles and puts his arm around her bare shoulders as the carriage turns into the park. She cuddles against him and lays her head on his chest. She notes his sandalwood-scented cologne and listens to his heartbeat.

What lies beneath his icy exterior?

While the art dealer enjoys a bird's eye view of her cleavage, she slips her hand beneath the blanket. Her fingers caress his thigh, and she feels his heart rate increase. He cups her chin in one hand, lifts her head, and plants a long, deep kiss.

MaryAna has achieved her Cinderella moment. Her prince has a Russian accent, an off-beat sense of humor, and a firm touch. Still, she fears that, like her fairytale counterpart, all will end at the stroke of midnight.

When the carriage returns to its starting point, Vladimir delicately removes the blanket from their laps, helps MaryAna down, and tips the driver. Hand-in-hand, they scurry back to the warmth of the Plaza.

In the lobby, MaryAna sees Samson and waves to him. The bell-man glances in her direction but looks away.

Samson is jealous.

She turns to the Russian art dealer. "I'm hungry now. Wanna get something to eat?"

"A steak sounds good."

"How about we go to my suite and order room service."

He licks his lips. "Outstanding idea."

"And maybe after we eat, maybe we could go dancing. I hear Paul's Casablanca in Soho is one of the best hot spots."

Vladimir smiles. "If you wish."

The nineteen-year-old pulls him toward the elevators. "And then, I'll give you an answer about the investment."

I hope he wants more than dinner and dancing.

Chapter 34

ON FIRE

Before MaryAna can slip off her shoes, Vladimir takes her in his arms and then dips, as if they are in the middle of a grand ball.

"Would you like to be nineteen and beautiful forever?"

"What? Well, *yeah*."

"Then give me your soul, MaryAna Lindley!"

White-hot lust gushes through every cell in her body. "It's yours for tonight!"

The Russian moves his hands to her hips, drawing her into a tight embrace. When he kisses the nineteen-year-old, his tongue teases hers, and her temperature rises even more.

If my guardian angel is in town tonight, I hope he's taking in a Broadway show.

Vladimir unzips and strips off MaryAna's dress, then her undergarments. To her, the clothes have simply melted away, leaving her naked in the middle of the floor, but for her shoes. He scoops her up and sets her gently onto the sofa. She is unconscious of her nakedness, wearing it as she might a summer frock.

He kneels beside her and his eyes sweep over her body as if praying at an altar where she is the sacrificial lamb. As his touch inflames her passion, her breathing quickens to the point she is almost panting.

"Is this tattoo your guardian or your demon?" he says, petting the kitten as if it were alive.

"I don't know . . . maybe both."

Her heart races as the Russian strips to his waist.

He doesn't have Tyler's muscles, but he's fine just the same.

When the art dealer drops his boxer shorts, MaryAna gulps. On the upper part of his thighs and his lower torso is a tattoo of a coiled snake. His erection forms its head.

"Oh, my. It's . . . your tattoo is very large."

The Russian smiles. "Time to party."

"Hey, did you bring a condom?"

***

The encounter leaves both spent. They now lie beside each other on the rug, gasping for air. MaryAna turns toward Vladimir, propping herself on one elbow.

"That was . . . like mind-blowing."

She gives him a quick kiss on the cheek. "Take a nap while I get a bath."

I knew he'd be fantastic.

MaryAna staggers to the bathroom, her back angry from the recent activity. She takes some Tylenol and runs a tub full of hot water.

After her bath, the teenager dons her pink bathrobe and tries to do something with her tangled hair. While brushing it out, she replays the evening's events in her mind.

I don't want to forget a thing from tonight.

The Russian appears in the bathroom doorway, still undressed. "That was a workout."

"You make it sound like we played racquetball," MaryAna says. "I didn't know we could make love in so many positions."

"You're very athletic, Miss Lindley—and quite flexible."

"I think you almost broke me in two a couple times." She gives him a devilish grin. "You're like the Energizer bunny or a being from another world."

"I am from another world."

"Isn't Russia part of this one, Vladdy? Can I call you that?"

"Call me whatever you wish. May I use the shower?"

"Be my guest." MaryAna turns back to the mirror. "Be careful. I've got it set to blazing hot."

"I like blazing hot," he says, stepping into the shower. "Cleanses the soul."

She giggles. "Did you steal my soul?"

"I didn't have to—you gave it to me." He pulls the curtain closed.

"Oh, guess I did." She giggles again.

MaryAna hands him a towel once he has finished his shower, and he watches her reapply her makeup as he dries himself.

"So, you hide behind a mask?" he says, wrapping the towel around his waist.

"I want to look my best when we go dancing. It's just foundation, eye liner, mascara, blush, and lipstick."

"Why use them? You're a natural beauty."

"That's sweet of you to say. They're like my warpaint in the battle of the sexes."

"So, we just did battle?"

"Yeah, kinda."

"Who won?"

"Ahh . . . I think we both did," she says. "Still hungry?"

"Famished."

"I'll order a couple steaks and baked potatoes from room service. How do you like yours?"

"Rare." The art dealer steps up behind her and nibbles on her earlobe. "Always."

"Quit!" She tries to push him away. "You're givin' me goosebumps."

He pulls up the back of her robe and smacks her bare bottom.

***

When they finish eating, Vladimir sits on the sofa and motions for MaryAna to join him.

"Hold your horses. I can't afford to be late for work again." She places a wake-up call, then stifles a yawn.

"Are you tired?"

"A little," she answers, still wearing only her bathrobe. "Maybe we should go dancing another night."

"If you prefer. Right now, I'm ready for dessert."

183

"I can order you something," MaryAna says, picking up the room-service menu.

He jumps up and grabs her around the waist. "You'll do just fine."

She grins. "By the way, I'll wire the entire amount to your bank tomorrow mornin'."

"Excellent. Now to more important business." He begins to play with her breasts through her robe.

"For the love of God, Vladdy. Haven't you had enough sex for one night?"

He grins, but MaryAna feels a chill pass through her as he does. "God has nothing to do with it."

"It's just an old sayin'."

"As is: 'Give the Devil his due.'"

She giggles. "So, do I have the Devil to thank for my birthday surprise?"

The Russian stares into her eyes. "Is it not more likely the Devil fulfilled your carnal desires?"

"It was you, Vladdy . . . right?"

"What do you think?"

"All I know is we both dress well, have good jobs, and love art. You're a fantastic lover, and I've got a hot bod you can't seem to get enough of. We could make the most awesome couple. I believe God put us together for a reason."

The Russian draws her to him once more. "So, your God approves of you surrendering yourself to someone you barely know?"

"But I do know you. We're doin' a business deal and will soon be apartment mates."

"You're correct, of course," he says as he loosens the belt of MaryAna's robe. "Now for dessert."

I sure hope after that show, my guardian angel flew out of town.

Chapter 35

YANKEE STADIUM

The next morning at work, MaryAna cannot get her mind off Vladimir. The previous night's adventure swirls through her brain like a tornado. Her emotions are an exhilarating mixture of excitement, anticipation, and lust.

Vladdy is my perfect Prince Charming.

She looks around to make sure no one is listening before calling him. When he answers, she hears someone speaking Russian in the background.

"Go to the other room, Natasha," Vladimir says. "It's Miss Lindley."

"I don't know what your sister was sayin', but it sounded like she was cussin' you out."

"She's upset because I stayed out so late and didn't answer her text."

"You're a naughty boy, Vladdy. In more ways than one."

"Did you wire the money, Miss Lindley?"

"As soon as my bank opened. They assured me it would be in your account by this afternoon."

"Outstanding. I'll contact the seller."

"I can't wait to tell my family what a good investor I am. When I get the money, I want to take you out to celebrate. You know, somewhere special."

"That isn't necessary."

"I want to, Vladdy. You made my birthday so memorable. I can't wait to go with you to museums, galleries, and concerts. I'm going to a Yankee game with some friends tonight . . . but, I can cancel if you want to do something this evening?"

"I'll be busy this evening, Miss Lindley."

"Maybe you could stop by the Plaza for a midnight supper?"

"Tonight I am going to meet with the widow who's selling us the painting, and I don't expect to be back until after midnight."

"I thought everything was settled."

"She needs to sign some paperwork when I give her the check."

"I could skip the ballgame and come with you?"

"I'm sorry, but I don't take clients to such meetings."

MaryAna is surprised by his abruptness. "After last night, I thought I was more than just a client."

"You are, but I don't want the widow to know we're turning a quick profit on her painting. She believes it's going to a private museum."

"I kinda feel bad, Vladdy. You know, trickin' someone whose husband just died."

"We're actually doing her a favor. She needs the cash."

"Yeah, but . . ."

"You want to make a lot of money, right?"

"I do."

"This is how it's done, Miss Lindley. It's perfectly legal, and the widow will never know."

"I suppose it's OK. By the way, thanks again for the carriage ride. You sure know how to show a girl a good time." MaryAna giggles. "I've got the rugburns to prove it."

For a few moments there is silence on the other end. "Is there anything else, Miss Lindley?"

"What's wrong, Vladdy?"

"Nothing. I just have much to accomplish today."

"Can we get together tomorrow? I'm free all day."

"If I'm in Manhattan, I'll stop by. Otherwise, I'll text you and arrange something."

"Please, tell your sister I'm sorry for keepin' you out so late. I don't want her mad at me."

"Natasha will be fine. I have to go."

Vladimir hangs up before MaryAna can say anything more.

I hope he's not upset with me.

***

That evening, MaryAna meets Andre outside Yankee Stadium. She is dressed in the mint-green blouse and tan skirt she purchased for the occasion.

"I didn't know this stadium was in the Bronx," she says as they go inside.

"One of the team's nicknames is the Bronx Bombers," Andre informs her as they weave their way to section sixteen behind the home team's dugout. "If you want more info, just ask Wyatt. But be careful—he's liable to give you their entire history."

The nineteen-year-old gives out a nervous giggle as thousands of other fans fill the stadium. "These seats are awesome. I feel like I could just reach out and touch the players."

"We're lucky to get them. They belong to a friend of my dad's who's a season ticket holder. He's out of town this week and gave them to my dad. Originally, my parents were going to come with Wyatt and me."

"What changed their plans?"

"They had a big blowup when my mother and I returned from France. Dad gave me the tickets and said to invite whoever I wanted."

I wonder if that argument was about him hiring me?

Wyatt and his fiancée soon join them. Regina is three inches shorter than MaryAna with a soft pixie hairstyle. She wears a stylish high-neck sleeveless summer dress, which shows off her toned arms and legs.

"This is the girl from Mississippi I told you about," Wyatt tells her. "MaryAna, this is Regina Kennedy, someday to be Regina Furman."

The teenager looks for something clever to say. "I hope you're not kin to those Massachusetts Kennedys. Back in the day, there was bad blood between them and my state."

Andre and Wyatt glance at each other.

"I'm Robert Kennedy's granddaughter." Regina's noticeable New England accent helps verify the fact.

Open mouth, insert foot.

187

Regina smiles. "At least you had the good sense to move out of Mississippi."

Touché.

They take their seats, with the girls sandwiched between the guys, but Wyatt jumps back up immediately. "Who wants a beer?"

MaryAna raises her hand. "I do."

"I'd prefer some wine, darling," Regina says. "A Chardonnay."

Andre hops up as well. "I'll go with you, Wyatt. Excuse us, ladies."

Oh great—some alone time with Miss Kennedy!

Chapter 36

REGINA

"It's a lovely night for a ballgame, Miss Lindley," Regina says after the guys have left for the concession stand.

"Yep, it certainly is."

Maybe we can stick to the weather, because I'm not getting good vibes from her . . .

"It's been hotter than usual. Is it terribly hot in Mississippi?"

"It is this time of year."

"Do you like New York, Miss Lindley?"

"I do, and please call me MaryAna."

"Of course. Where did you attend college?"

"I graduated from high school in May."

"High school? You look older."

"I turned nineteen yesterday. When I got the opportunity at Jacqueline Designs, I put college on hold."

"Oh." Regina seems surprised. "You know, it's illegal for you to be drinking. You could get the guys in trouble."

"I have a fake ID."

"I suppose Southern girls are more concerned with marrying well than obeying the law."

MaryAna fights to hold her temper. "What do you do, Regina?"

"I'm working on my PhD at Columbia. I plan to become a professor of sociology."

"Have you ever been to the South?"

"Yes, but not Mississippi. I know people there are poor, less educated, and racist—but not you, of course."

"Why not me?"

"You get along well with Wyatt who is biracial. If you were a racist, you couldn't do that."

"Wow, did you learn all that in sociology?"

"My impressions of Southern culture are mostly from television, movies, and the news."

"From those same sources, Regina, one might conclude that New York City is made up of the Mafia, bad cops, gangs, and greedy businessmen. Those people might exist, but I have yet to meet them."

"Well . . . I guess you have a point. Still, you cannot deny the racism of the South: the intimidation, the denial of human rights, the lynchings."

"You do know we're in the twenty-first century, right?"

"Don't those things still go on?"

"I doubt there has been a lynching in my lifetime. Murders make the news, so it looks more common than it is. Much of it is black on black as well as white on white crime."

"You seem to know quite a bit about this subject."

"We studied it in school as part of Mississippi history—the good, the bad, and the ugly. May I ask you something?"

"Of course."

"Most of the serious race riots take place in northern cities like Chicago, Detroit, Minneapolis, and here in New York. Doesn't that reflect racism in this part of the country?"

Regina considers the question. "Maybe I should look into this topic further and discuss it with my sociology professors."

"You do that." MaryAna decides to change the subject. "So, do you follow baseball?"

"I find it boring, frankly. Wyatt enjoys it, so I humor him. I prefer tennis and considered turning professional after high school, but my family frowned on the idea. Do you play?"

"Not very well. My twin brother is an awesome tennis player."

"Does he live in Mississippi?"

"He does now, but JoeE grew up near Syracuse, then moved to Mississippi three years ago.

"And he's your *twin* brother?"

"It's a long story. Our parents separated us when we were babies, each taking one of us."

"You might make an interesting sociology case study."

"No doubt." MaryAna looks around, praying for the conversation to end. "This stadium is something else. I'm glad Andy invited me."

"Is this your first date with him?"

"It's *not* a date. I'm just hangin' out with y'all."

"Yeah, right. Andy shows no interest in any of my girlfriends, yet you come along and he suddenly wants to double-date. It must be that cute accent of yours."

"I assure you there's nothin' between Andy and me. He just invited me to the game. That's all."

"Andy Rubenstein is one of the most handsome, wealthy, personable, and eligible bachelors in New York City. I find it hard to believe you just want to hang out with him."

MaryAna perks up in relief. "Here come the guys."

The young men return with beer, wine, hot dogs, and nachos just in time for the National Anthem. Once the crowd returns to their seats, the umpire yells, "Play ball," and the game gets underway.

Andre leans close and whispers in MaryAna's ear. "What did you and Regina talk about?"

"Just girl talk."

"Anything about me?"

"Regina thinks we're on a date."

"That's it?"

"Pretty much." MaryAna says.

Andy seems relieved and settles back in his seat.

Does he have some secret?

From then on, the conversation centers around the game. Wyatt adds color commentary and inside facts about the players. MaryAna learns Andy and Wyatt played baseball and football in high school.

"After we graduated college two years ago," Wyatt tells her, "I went to work for Jacqueline Designs. Andy went on to Harvard Business School."

"He graduated *summa cum laude*," Regina adds.

"I take it that's good?" MaryAna says.

Regina nods and smiles. "The very best. He's brilliant."

As the night rolls on, MaryAna finds both young men personable. Wyatt is the more outgoing of the two. If anyone wants more popcorn, peanuts, or drinks, he is on his feet, whistling to one of the roving vendors. Andre is reserved, yet friendly. He tells MaryAna about his summer in France, working in his grandfather's wine warehouses.

As the game comes to an end, Andre turns to MaryAna. "Do you like to sail?"

"You mean, like, in a boat? I was on one once, but the wind stopped and we just sat there. So, no, I haven't really been sailin'."

"This Sunday, the three of us are going out on Long Island Sound. I'd like you to join us. There should be plenty of wind."

If I keep seeing Andy, he might get the wrong idea.

"Can I get back to you on that tomorrow?"

"Sure."

"How about we all go to a club tonight," Wyatt suggests.

"I can't," Regina says. "I have an early morning meeting with my thesis advisor."

"Count me out too," MaryAna stifles a yawn. "It's been a long day, and this seat has my back aching."

Probably more from the acrobatics with Vladdy last night . . .

"That leaves only you and me, Andy," Wyatt says. "We could check out those Russian clubs over in Brighton Beach."

Andre claps his hands, grinning. "Hey, sounds like fun to me."

"Stay away from those clubs," Regina says, glaring at Wyatt. "I don't want you mixed up with other girls. Most of the ones in those places are hookers. And don't you dare take Andy there."

"Mr. Dudley Do Right wouldn't be caught dead in a joint like that," Wyatt proclaims, loud enough for the entire section of spectators to hear. "I, on the other hand . . ."

"You'd better be kidding," Regina says. "And hold it down. You're embarrassing me."

"I'll make sure he goes straight home, Mother Teresa," Andre assures her. "I'll even tuck him in for you."

Wyatt presses his palms together as if he were praying. "Will you read me a bedtime story too, Daddy?" he says in his best kid voice.

I really like these guys.

***

MaryAna sleeps until noon Saturday and checks her phone messages before getting out of bed, but none are from Vladimir.

Famished, she orders breakfast and calls Isadora.

"Last night, I went to a Yankee game with some friends."

"Did you enjoy the game?"

"I did, and that stadium is huge. Right now, I'm waitin' to hear from Vladimir, *Vladdy*—that's what I call him now. Isn't that cute?"

"I suppose. How is your business deal progressing?"

"He said everything is on track. For my birthday on Thursday, we went to the Champagne Bar here at the Plaza. Then he took me for a carriage ride around Central Park."

"You're keeping everything strictly business, right?"

"Not exactly."

"What do you mean?"

"After the carriage ride, we came up to my suite for dinner, and we kinda hooked up."

"MaryAna . . . you claimed it was a business arrangement, nothing more."

"I know, but Vladdy might be the perfect guy for me. He checks all the boxes—handsome, smart, well-dressed, loves art, and is an awesome lover. I think I'm in love."

"Oh, really? I'm happy for you, MaryAna."

"Thanks . . . what was that?"

"Just the TV. I'm kinda busy—got some documents to translate for work tomorrow."

"OK, but we need to go shoppin' soon. When I get the money from Vladdy, I want to buy y'all some really nice presents."

"I've really got to go, MaryAna."

After they hang up, the teenager stares at her phone.

Vladdy should've shown up or at least texted by now.

Chapter 37

SAM'S THE MAN

By the time breakfast arrives, MaryAna has lost her appetite. Her lower back is killing her, so she takes two Tylenols and runs a hot bath with extra Epsom salts. But, after soaking for twenty minutes, the pain does not let up.

She dries off and dons a T-shirt and shorts, then grabs a beer from the minibar before dialing the Bell Captain's desk.

"Is Samson workin' today?"

"You mean Sam? Yes, he is."

"Please have him contact Miss Lindley in Room 1819."

Five minutes later, she receives a call on the hotel phone.

"Hey, Mississippi. What's up?"

"Can you come by my suite? I want to talk to you about something."

"Be there in a few."

MaryAna is on her second beer by the time Samson arrives.

"Come on in. Wanna beer?"

"Thanks, but no," he says, closing the door. "I'm on the clock."

"How did your callback go?"

"I haven't heard anything yet. So, what's up?"

MaryAna takes a swig of beer. "You told me if I needed anything: 'Sam's the man.' Does that include hard-to-get items?"

"Hard to get like what?"

"Certain . . . substances."

He studies her for a moment. "You ain't a cop, are you?"

"Absolutely not."

"Had to ask. What do you want?"

"My back has been killing me, and the over-the-counter stuff isn't cuttin' it. Oxycodone has worked for me before, but I probably won't be able to get a doctor to prescribe it since I got hooked on it last year. I only need a few capsules, maybe a dozen."

"I can get it, but it ain't cheap."

"How much?"

"Don't know exactly. I'll have to find out the latest price."

"I'm kinda short on funds until next week," she says, handing him a twenty. "For your trouble."

He waves her off. "Keep it, Mississippi. Hey, do you like jazz? There's a place called the Black and Blues Jazz Bar up in Harlem. How about we go there tonight? There's a guy we can talk to who could hook us up with oxy."

"I'd love to, but I'm busy this evenin'."

Samson's smile fades. "I'll get you the price as soon as I can. Anything else?"

"Here's my cell," she says, writing her number on a piece of paper. "Use this instead of my room phone."

Samson enters the number into his cell and gives her his.

"So, who were the guys I saw you with in the lobby this past week—friends of yours?"

MaryAna sees no reason to lie, but no reason to tell the whole truth either. "The one Sunday night was here from Chicago for a seminar. He told me all about investin' in commercial real estate. The other guy's an art dealer. I'm investin' in a painting."

"So, it was just business stuff?"

"Yeah, pretty much."

"It looked friendlier than that."

"What can I say? I'm a friendly girl. Are you jealous?"

Sam pulls her into a tight embrace. His kiss is an obvious invitation to pick up where they left off last time. She considers the proposition while his hands explore her body like a blind man reading Braille.

When he attempts to lift up her T-shirt, MaryAna pulls away.

"Don't you have to get back to work?"

"I'm on my lunch break."

He kisses her again, slipping both hands inside the seat of her shorts. When he pulls her closer, she feels how aroused he has become.

"I can't do this right now, Samson. That art dealer might show up here at any moment."

"Don't answer the door."

"I can't do that."

"Why not?"

"Besides the business deal, I plan to share an apartment with him and his sister. You understand, right?"

"So, because he *might* show up, you want me to go?"

"He might see you leavin' my suite and mention it to someone at the hotel. I don't want you to get fired because of me."

Samson sighs and takes his hands back. "Can we get together again soon?"

"How about next week?" MaryAna says. "I'd love to go to that jazz bar."

Samson nods and opens the door. "I'll be in touch, Mississippi."

After the bellman leaves, MaryAna takes out another beer and plops back on the sofa. She tries to relax but is too keyed up. The abbreviated make-out session only serves to make her more desperate to see Vladimir.

The sweet earthiness of the Russian's cologne still resonates within her nostrils, the echo of his breath in her ears, his body against hers. The urgency to be back in his arms overwhelms her. She takes out her iPhone and calls his number.

"Vladimir Volkow. May I help you?"

"Hey, Vladdy. It's me."

MaryAna hears a voice in the background, speaking Russian.

"Quiet, Natasha. It's Miss Lindley."

The other voice falls silent.

"She sounds upset. What did you do this time?"

"I cannot seem to please her, no matter what I do."

"I should be upset with you, too. It's like you forgot all about little ole me."

"I meant to text you, but I've been extremely busy."

"I was hopin' we could go to an art museum or a gallery today."

"Maybe another time. I've got tons of paperwork to complete on your investment."

"Could you stop by tonight and hang out? Or I could meet you someplace?"

Vladimir clears his throat. "I can't promise anything, Miss Lindley."

"I bought a peppermint-scented massage oil. We could rub it all over each other."

". . . Go to the other room, Natasha," Vladimir says. "This is a business call."

"I get it—you don't want her knowin' about us yet."

He lowers his voice to a whisper. "I'll try to stop by this evening, around nine." Then, in a normal tone: "Everything is progressing well with your investment, Miss Lindley."

"Will the money be in my account on Monday?"

"Probably Tuesday."

"As long as I have it in time to pay my hotel bill. I don't want them to throw me out."

"No problem. I'll transfer the funds as soon as they are available."

"I can't wait to see you."

"I've got to go, Miss Lindley."

"Bye, Vladdy. Love you."

***

That evening and several beers and tiny bottles of gin later, MaryAna is slumped on the sofa in her suite. She is attired in lacey, peach-colored lingerie beneath a silk kimono.

Vladdy will love what I'm wearing.

When the Russian has not arrived by nine-thirty, she texts him: Where are you?

He replies: Can't make it.

She texts back: What about tomorrow?

198

His response: Tied up. Let's get together next week.

MaryAna slams her fist on the arm of the sofa.

She texts: I'll think about it.

I could call Sam, but he'll want to go to that jazz bar, and I'm not up for that tonight.

Or, I could just call him up to the suite and we could hook up . . .

No . . . he's too young to get serious about.

I could go to the hotel bar . . . no, I don't feel like changing clothes and trolling for some cute guy. Too much work.

What do I do then?

She picks up her phone again and dials a number.

"Andy, can I still go sailin' with y'all tomorrow?"

"Of course. How about I come by and pick you up around eight."

"Any chance I could bring a friend?"

"Sure."

"Isadora lives here in Manhattan. We could pick her up on the way."

"Bring swimsuits. We'll probably go in the water . . . I mean go swimming too."

MaryAna giggles. "So, you don't think the boat will sink with too many people?"

"Wyatt and I have been in sailing competitions since high school," he says with a chuckle. "You know, regattas and such. Pretty sure we won't have to worry about sinking."

"I'll text Isadora as soon as we get off the phone and let you know if she can go. See you in the mornin'."

I don't know why I did that. I can't get mixed up with Andy. Maybe Izzy's just insurance that I don't . . .

Chapter 38

MAID MARJORIE

At eight o'clock Sunday morning, MaryAna waits outside the Plaza for Andre. She is wearing a flowered summer blouse, a pair of Levi's Original 501 shorts, and her pink Air Jordans. Soon, a familiar silver limousine pulls up to the curb. When the chauffeur exits the vehicle, MaryAna sees it is Roger.

Oh no—is Mr. Rubenstein going with us?

Roger comes around to the passenger side and opens the door. MaryAna is relieved to see only Andre inside.

"Thanks," she tells Roger, afraid he will use her name.

It would be awkward explaining how he knows me.

Roger gives her a knowing smile. "You're welcome, Miss."

MaryAna slides into the rear-facing seat.

"What's your friend's address?" Andre says. She tells him, and he uses the intercom to inform Roger.

MaryAna takes out her phone. "I'll text Isadora to let her know we are on the way. I didn't expect a limo."

"It's my dad's. My Porsche is a two-seater."

So, Andy drives a fancy sports car. Why am I not surprised.

"Dad and my uncle Isaac visit my grandparents on Sundays for dinner. I usually go with them when I'm in New York, but yesterday I spent the day there."

"Do your grandparents live here in the city?"

"They live in the Hamptons. We're going to my cottage on the north shore of Long Island."

"So, you don't live with your parents?"

"I do for now. My grandparents gave me the cottage for my eighteenth birthday. Since they don't sail any more, they threw in their sailboat."

And everyone says I'm spoiled.

"I know what you're thinking," he says, grinning, "trust-fund kid with a silver spoon, et cetera."

"I was thinkin' how lucky you are to have grandparents who love you. Do they give all their grandchildren such nice presents?"

"I'm the only grandchild on either side of my family and also the peacekeeper. Uncle Isaac has never been married. He is a doctor and stays out of the feuds."

"And your family in France. What are they like?"

"Very traditional and very Catholic. When their only child became a model, they were not happy. Then when she married an American Jew, they threatened to disown her. But I came along and they reconciled."

"Have you always split your time between here and France?"

"For as long as I can remember. Most of the year, I'm Andrew Rubenstein from New York City. In the summers and during Christmas vacation, I'm Andre LeBlanc, resident of Paris. I've had both a Catholic confirmation and a Jewish bar mitzvah. I'm not sure that's even legal."

MaryAna giggles. "For sure, it's unusual. At least, you have people who love you."

"True. How about you, MaryAna? Much family?"

"There's my mama, a twin brother, a stepdaddy, and a stepbrother. Plus four half-brothers."

"Your father still around?"

"He's a no-good alcoholic who's in a jail cell. I didn't learn he was my daddy until I was sixteen. I wish I'd never found out."

Isadora is waiting outside when they get to her place. She slides in next to MaryAna, who makes the introductions.

"The limo belongs to his daddy," MaryAna tells her, "the CEO of my company."

"Do you also work at Jacqueline Designs?" Isadora asks.

"I'm currently unemployed," Andy admits. "My American grandfather wants me to work on Wall Street where he made his fortune."

"It sounds like that's not something you want to do," Isadora says.

"You are very perceptive. My grandfather in France wants me to go into the family wine business. I worked in their vineyards and warehouses for several summers. It kept me in good shape, but that's not my cup of tea either. My parents want me to work at Jacqueline Designs and take it over some day."

"And what do *you* want to do, Andy, if you don't mind my asking?" MaryAna says.

"You'll think me insane, but I want to coach football."

"Really? With all your education, that seems an odd choice."

"At Harvard, I was an assistant defensive coach for two years while I earned my MBA. I'd prefer a college coaching position, but I'll consider high school if I must. I've sent out résumés but no interest thus far."

"What about Harvard?" MaryAna asks. "Could you go back there?"

"Their coach filled my position before he knew I was interested. Besides, it'd be better to go to a different school—you know, to expand my knowledge."

"I have contacts at the University of Southern Mississippi. I don't know if they have an openin', but I could check."

"That's a big-time football program. They probably wouldn't be interested in someone like me."

MaryAna smiles. "You never know unless you ask."

***

They soon arrive at Andy's "cottage," which turns out to be a two-story colonial-style home. It is snuggled between wooded areas and looks like it popped out of a nineteenth-century English novel.

"This is awesome," MaryAna says as they pull into the circular drive. A ruby-red Jaguar and a light-blue Lincoln Continental are parked at the front of the house.

"Whose Jag is that?" she asks.

"Regina's. Wyatt drives the Lincoln."

"No use you waiting around," Andre tells Roger after they all get out. "We'll ride back with Wyatt."

The three stroll through the house to a backyard overlooking the water. Beside a boathouse is a dock where Wyatt and Regina are waiting in their swimsuits.

MaryAna introduces Isadora and they all board a roomy ski boat tied at the dock.

"Welcome to Northport Bay, girls," Wyatt says like a tour guide. "It's a perfect day to be on the water." When all are safely seated, they head out into the bay.

"I thought we were goin' sailin'," MaryAna says over the rumble of the inboard motor.

Andy chuckles and nods toward the water ahead. "The sailboat is anchored in the bay. We'll be there in a couple of minutes. Wyatt, you got the drinks and food on board?"

"I took a couple of coolers and some bags of snacks out to the Maid earlier."

MaryAna looks at Andre and Wyatt. "The Maid?"

"My sailboat. She's the Maid Marjorie," Andre explains. "I named her after my grandmother."

They soon glide up to a sixty-foot motorized sailboat. MaryAna is more than a little impressed. "It's like a giant yacht with poles stickin' up to put the sails on."

"Those are the masts," Andre says, helping her aboard. "You'll need to learn some sailing lingo if you want to be part of our crew."

After everyone is on board, he gives MaryAna and Isadora a tour below deck.

"Look, there's even a kitchen," MaryAna says when they step inside. "You could live here."

"It's called a galley," Andy explains. "The sleeping quarters are through there. It sleeps six comfortably, but we could handle more if necessary."

"This is bigger than my apartment," Izzy says.

"You girls can change into your swimsuits down here," he tells them.

"We've got our suits on under our clothes." MaryAna unbuttons her blouse to reveal the top of her silver bikini.

For several moments, Andre seems unable or unwilling to take his eyes off her chest. Finally, he blinks. "Let me change, and I'll meet you topside."

As the nineteen-year-old climbs back up the steps, she hears a rumbling and feels a vibration. Once on the deck, she watches Wyatt hoist the anchor.

"Do we put up the sails now?"

"We'll hoist them once we get out in the Sound," he explains. "More room to maneuver out there."

On the top deck, Regina takes the helm, ready to steer the boat out of the bay. She fills out her coral bikini almost as well as MaryAna does hers.

Wyatt opens a locker and hands out life jackets. "Everyone has to wear these at all times."

Andre returns to the main deck and helps MaryAna fasten the jacket across her bikini top. As he does, the boat jerks to one side, and they grab hold of the railing to steady themselves.

"Sorry," Regina yells from the helm. "My hand slipped."

MaryAna glances up at Wyatt's fiancée who smiles and looks away. *She did that on purpose.*

After motoring out of the bay and through a channel, the Maid Marjorie moves into the open waters of Long Island Sound, where a steady breeze blows out of the west.

Regina steers the boat while Captain Andy and First Mate Wyatt gather their newest crew members. After some hands-on instructions from the guys, MaryAna and Isadora unfurl and hoist the sails. The boat picks up speed as the wind whisks it along.

This is exhilarating—I can see why people love to sail.

Regina turns the helm over to Andre. She and Isadora find a spot to sit near the bow and make themselves comfortable. Soon, they are engaged in deep conversation like long-lost friends.

MaryAna ties her hair back and joins Andre on the upper deck. "Hey, Captain. What do we do now—swab the decks?"

Andre chuckles. "Maybe later. You want to take the helm?"

"You want *me* to steer the boat?"

He raises one arm so she can slip under it and take the wheel.

"Get a firm grip and hold a steady course." He lets go and steps back. "There you go—the Maid's all yours."

MaryAna giggles. "I feel like Captain Jack Sparrow. When we come back, do we have to wait for the wind to blow from the other direction—or do we just turn on the engines?"

"When we come about," Andre notes, "we'll *tack* against the wind. It's a technique developed by ancient mariners and still employed today."

"Who wants a beer?" Wyatt says.

MaryAna giggles. "Is it OK to drink and drive?"

"Get us a couple of cold ones and something to munch on," Andre tells him. "MaryAna's getting her sea legs."

"And pretty legs they are," Wyatt says before going to see what the other girls want to drink.

Andre stares at MaryAna and grins. "I like that kitten peeking out of your bikini bottom. It's rather provocative."

She grins. "It's supposed to be."

"You really seem to be enjoying this," Andre says.

"Maybe in a former life, maybe I was a pirate." MaryAna notices Regina intently watching them.

I don't think Miss Kennedy appreciates me moving in on her little threesome.

Chapter 39

MANIC MONDAY

The next morning on the way to work, MaryAna makes a phone call. A groggy voice answers.

"Hey, Vladdy. Did I wake you?"

"As a matter of fact, you did. What time is it?"

"A little after seven. I'm waitin' for the subway. Did you have a nice weekend?"

"It was busy."

"What's the status on my investment?"

"The transaction is almost complete. Please, stop worrying."

"I can't help it. Wanna know what I did yesterday? I went sailin'. The boat was gigantic, and the guy who owns it even let me steer it."

"What guy is this?"

Vladdy sounds jealous. Good!

"Someone I know from work. I'm not gonna just sit around and wait for you."

"I take it you're upset, Miss Lindley."

"Darn right I am. I can't believe you blew me off Saturday night."

"Sorry about that."

"I forgive you, but don't let it happen again."

"Do you want to get together this week, Miss Lindley?"

"I'll let you know. Got to go. The Four train is here."

Maybe now he'll stop taking me for granted.

***

Work keeps MaryAna's mind occupied the rest of the morning. At noon she takes a lunch break but is too keyed up to eat. She sits at her desk, closes her eyes, and cannot help but daydream about Vladimir.

Her thoughts are interrupted by Hannah. "At one o'clock, gather up all your original blouse sketches. Jacqueline wants to meet with you in her office."

MaryAna smiles for the first time today. "I've got some more besides the ones I've shown you."

"Take them all. Jacqueline also wants to hear about your conversations with Mel."

"Some of my comments about the company weren't very flatterin'."

"Jacqueline will give you a fair hearing. She can be open to new ideas—just don't get her upset."

"OK. I'll try."

***

At one o'clock, a nervous MaryAna enters Jacqueline's office. She relates everything she can remember about her first conversation with the CEO, and Jacqueline seems to accept it at face value.

MaryAna also shares her blouse sketches. Jacqueline looks them over, and pauses on one.

"This one's cute."

"I was goin' for a retro look. You know—1920's flapper—bold and sassy."

Jacqueline picks up a second sketch. "How about this one here?"

"It's also retro, an eighties off-the-shoulder *Flashdance* look. I have some other ideas along the same line using styles from the forties, fifties, and sixties."

"Very interesting, Miss Lindley. I find your approach unique."

"I also have some ideas about the fabrics. They should be made from less-common materials like chiffon, silk, nylon, and lace. They'll look even better in bolder and more daring colors."

"It sounds like you've given this much thought."

"Isn't that what you pay me for?"

"True." Jacqueline holds up another sketch. "This one is intriguing. Tell me about it."

"I was readin' about the history of women's fashion, and the idea popped into my head. Of course, it's super rad and maybe not appropriate for a company like this—I was just playin' around when I drew it."

"You have quite an imagination, young lady. I see why my husband was intrigued enough to hire you. How long have you been interested in fashion?"

"Since I was little. I've read everything I can get my hands on about design. When I met Mr. Rubenstein, it was like a dream come true."

"I bet it was. You're quite young, Miss Lindley and very attractive. Do you have a boyfriend?"

"I had one—we broke up just after I moved here."

"Oh, sorry to hear that. We want our employees to be happy. Are you seeing anyone now?"

"Kinda, but it's more a business relationship."

"Oh, OK. Have you moved into your own place yet?"

"I'm still at the Plaza, but I'm payin' for it now."

"Tomorrow, Miss Lindley, we're meeting with the marketing department. I'd like you to attend. I'll introduce your ideas and discuss your blouse designs."

"Hannah told me assistant designers don't attend those meetings."

"We'll make an exception in your case. May I hold on to your original sketches? I want to study them in detail."

"I'm so glad you like my ideas, Ms. LeBlanc."

"Call me Jacqueline."

Now that's what I'm talking about!

***

At the end of the workday, MaryAna calls Vladimir once again. "How's my investment?"

"I was just about to text you, Miss Lindley. The final details have been worked out. The money will be deposited into your bank account tomorrow."

"That's awesome. Just in time to pay my hotel bill."

"I told you not to worry."

"I never really doubted you, Vladdy. I shouldn't have gotten upset. I know you're really busy right now."

"The first investment of this type is always the most difficult. The next one will be a breeze."

"I hope so. You want to come over tonight?"

"I've got paperwork to finish. Government forms and such."

"Are you upset at me for goin' sailin' with another guy?"

"Should I be?"

"The truth is, I would've preferred to be with you. We had such a good time on my birthday. I miss you."

"Unlike you, Miss Lindley, I don't work eight to five. How about we get together tomorrow night and celebrate? I'll take you out to eat, say around eight. Maybe you can wear that pink dress again—the one with the slit up the side."

MaryAna giggles. "You mean the one that's so easy to take off."

"Yeah, that one."

"Will you spend the night with me, Vladdy?"

"If you want."

"Oh, I do. Have you told Natasha about us?"

"Not yet, but soon."

***

On her way to the hotel Monday evening, MaryAna receives a text from Andre: How about dinner tonight?

I shouldn't refuse without an explanation.

When and where?

He texts back: Seven at T.J. Morgan's Irish Pub. Dress casual.

Oh, great—his daddy's favorite restaurant . . .

I'll meet you there.

***

When MaryAna arrives at the pub, she looks around but does not see Andre.

"Are you looking for Mr. Rubenstein?" It is Sidney, the balding man who seated Maryana and Mel the first time she had been there.

"I'm meetin' his son, Andy."

"Come with me. Andrew is already at a table in the back. He told me to be on the lookout for a tall blonde with a Southern accent."

"That's me."

After MaryAna is seated, Sidney says, "Your waiter will be with you momentarily."

That could've been far more awkward.

The nineteen-year-old is relieved when a different waiter comes to their table. The dinner conversation is lively, with Andre telling her about his summers in France, his college days, and the two years in graduate school. MaryAna talks about her life in Mississippi, her family, and her new job. Neither mentions any romantic involvements.

After they eat, Andre drives her to the Plaza in his Porsche Carrera GT.

"How about dinner again tomorrow night?" he asks.

"Thanks, but I have plans."

"Wednesday then, or is your social calendar full?"

"Look, Andy, I like you, but maybe we shouldn't be seein' so much of each other."

"Why?"

"I work for your parents. They might not approve of you seein' one of their employees."

"Should I ask them?"

"Please, don't. Your mother is just beginnin' to warm up to me. I don't want to jeopardize that relationship. Besides, you promised you'd keep it a secret."

"I will, but you have to keep seeing me to make sure I don't spill the beans."

"Seriously," she says with a smirk. "Blackmail?"

"I'd call it an exchange of favors. My silence for your company."

"I'm sure there are plenty of girls in this city who could fill that role."

"Few with such a charming accent."

"So, you just want to hear me talk." She pushes her hair behind her ear. "OK, I'll call you tomorrow. Maybe we can get together later in the week, and I'll talk your ears off."

"Works for me."

Before she gets out of his car, Andre leans in for a goodnight kiss, but she pulls back.

"Come on," he begs. "One little kiss."

What the heck.

MaryAna obliges. "Thanks again for dinner."

"Remember to call me tomorrow," Andre says with a grin. "You wouldn't want me to spill your secrets."

If he knew about me and his daddy, he wouldn't be so cheerful.

Chapter 40

THE MEETING

Just before 10:00 Tuesday morning, Hannah stops by MaryAna's cubicle to pick her up for the meeting. Hannah introduces her to the three marketing supervisors gathered in the conference room.

The men are seated on the far side of a gleaming mahogany table. One of them is Wyatt Furman. When they are introduced, he does not give away the fact they are acquainted. She gives Andre's friend a thankful nod.

Hannah and MaryAna sit on the other side of the table, along with Sharree. Two minutes before ten, Mel enters the room. The CEO takes a seat at the far end and opens his laptop.

He looks up. "Hello, Miss Lindley. I didn't expect to see you here."

MaryAna gives him a nervous little smile.

"It was Jacqueline's idea," Hannah informs Mel. "MaryAna has some interesting ideas about our new blouse line."

The CEO nods and checks the time.

"Jacqueline called this special meeting," Mel says, his eyes roving around the table before landing on MaryAna. "We will wait to get started until she arrives."

At 10:00 exactly, Jacqueline saunters into the conference room. Mel's eyes shift to his wife.

"Nice you could make it to your meeting," he says with a touch of sarcasm.

"I'm always punctual, my dear—unlike some of our employees," she notes, turning to MaryAna.

The nineteen-year-old squirms in her chair but knows better than to say anything.

Mel looks around at the gathered group. "Let's get started."

Jacqueline takes a seat at the opposite end of the table from her husband and sets the folder with MaryAna's sketches in front of her.

Jacqueline looks up. "Have you all met Miss Lindley?"

Heads around the table nod.

She turns to the nineteen-year-old. "This young lady has some rather, let's say provocative, views about both our proposed and current designs."

Jacqueline's gaze shifts to her husband. "Yesterday, Miss Lindley was kind enough to share those ideas with me. It seems my husband agrees with her concepts. That is why you hired her. Isn't that correct, my dear?"

Mel swallows hard, like a man on trial. "Indeed, Miss Lindley has some innovative ideas."

Jacqueline turns to MaryAna. "Why don't you tell everyone what you think about our company and its products. You might start with our poor color choices—I believe you told my husband they were 'out of touch.' You may also want to explain how designing your homecoming and prom dresses qualifies you to make such judgments."

"Um, well . . ." MaryAna glances around at the expectant faces. "I . . . I'm a fan of Italian designers because of their extensive use of bright colors. It appeals to the younger generation. We need to be more . . . like more creative."

Jacqueline folds her arms. "So, you think we lack creativity?"

"Yeah . . . well, no. It's just . . ."

"Miss Lindley, yesterday you said we need to be bolder and more daring."

"Yeah, I said that, but I didn't mean to imply all your designs are boring."

"Thank God." Jacqueline turns toward her husband. "Is that what you are looking for, dear? A younger, more daring look?"

Mel's face has turned pale. "I'll admit, Miss Lindley has much to learn, but our industry is constantly evolving. We can't afford to fall behind."

Jacqueline glares at her husband and turns back to MaryAna. "Do you believe at eighteen you understand the fashion industry, young lady?"

"I'm nineteen. My birthday was last week."

"We should've had a party." Jacqueline chuckles. "Children love parties."

MaryAna feels her eyelids prickle as tears threaten to appear. "I'm not a child."

"Oh, I can see that." Jacqueline glances at the sketches she brought with her.

"Miss Lindley's age is not at issue here," Mel says. "She can provide our company with a youthful perspective."

"Is that what she provides? I suppose my perspective is too old and boring?"

"Of course not. You are our head of design—the rest of us are here to provide input. As always, the final decisions are yours."

"So, you only hired Miss Lindley to provide me with input?"

"I find her ideas interesting and hope you'll be open to them. You've always considered new concepts, no matter the source."

Jacqueline hands MaryAna the sketches. "Please explain these to everyone. Let's see what the team thinks of your innovative ideas."

MaryAna goes over the sketches one by one. A variety of comments is shared—some positive, some negative. Sharree is the most enthusiastic, declaring several of the designs "just fabulous."

Jacqueline half listens while monitoring her husband. He avoids looking at either his wife or MaryAna, focusing on his laptop.

After the teenager presents what she believes to be the last sketch, Jacqueline passes around one final drawing. Some eyebrows are raised, and Mel grimaces when he examines it.

When everyone has seen the sketch, Jacqueline says, "In my opinion, this one summarizes Miss Lindley's cutting-edge approach to blouse design."

"That was just a crazy idea," MaryAna says. "I was just messin' around."

"On company time?" Jacqueline huffs. "Even a Paris streetwalker wouldn't be caught dead in such a garment."

MaryAna feels her face burning. "There was a time a couple of centuries ago when bare breasts were all the rage in Europe—it was considered high fashion. I read about it on Wikipedia."

"Oh, really." Jacqueline snickers. "Maybe women all over the world will go around topless in your blouses."

Mel scowls. "Could we stick to the topic at hand?"

Jacqueline's eyes shift from her husband to MaryAna. "Some may think your designs innovative, but I find them more disruptive than creative. Do you have anything to add?"

MaryAna gulps. "Yesterday, you seemed to like my blouse designs, ma'am."

Jacqueline draws back. "What did you call me? The proper French term is madame. Are you making fun of my language?"

"Where I'm from, usin' ma'am shows respect for your elders."

"Oh, so I'm an elder?"

"Well, yeah."

"Is my husband an *elder* also?"

"He is."

"Do you respect both of us, young lady? Do you respect the fact we're married? Or is that some kind of foreign concept?"

Mel looks up from his laptop. "If there are no further comments on these designs, this meeting is adjourned."

Jacqueline stands up, glares at him, and walks out of the conference room.

What the hell just happened?

Chapter 41

WHAT NEXT?

Everyone files out of the conference room except for Mel and MaryAna, who sit in stunned silence. Once the room is quiet, she begins gathering up the sketches. The CEO gets up, closes the door, and takes a seat across the table from her.

"I'm so sorry about what Jacqueline just put you through."

"Maybe I deserved it."

"No, you didn't. You're an employee of our company, and as such, deserve to be treated better."

"I'm also the girl who fooled around with her husband."

"Even if Jacqueline knows, she was way out of line."

"Please, sir, just let it be. We shouldn't have done anything. Maybe we didn't sleep together, but we came close a couple times. It's our karma comin' back to haunt us."

"Nonsense. I'll have a talk with my wife this afternoon."

"And say what?"

"I'll tell Jacqueline the truth—that you had no idea I was married. I'll tell her it was my fault and take full blame."

"Do you really believe it would help? She'll hate me for sure and probably make you fire me. If we ignore the situation, maybe in time it'll blow over."

"Maybe," Mel says, closing his laptop. "What if I give you a call later—we could get together for a drink."

"Sir, we shouldn't have any contact outside of work."

Mel reaches out to her, but she does not take his hand.

217

"I need to get back to my desk. Hannah wants me to do some filing before lunch."

"It was nice seeing you again. I miss you."

MaryAna scurries from the conference room to her cubicle and sits there in silence, trying to figure out what happened.

Does Jacqueline know about Mel and me?

She finally pulls out her cell and sends a text to Vladimir: Can't wait to see you tonight.

Several minutes go by without a reply, so she sends another: Having a rough day at work. Need you to take my mind off everything.

After no response, MaryAna tries again: Maybe we could just hang out tonight and order room service?

She waits but still receives no answer.

Prince Charming doesn't communicate very well.

***

Early that evening after work, she receives a text from Vladimir: May be running a little late tonight.

She replies: OK can't wait to see you.

Recalling her promise to help Andre get a coaching job, the teenager calls her friend Coree. "Hey, girl, how's everything at USM?"

"It's so good to hear from you. Everything here is chaotic. Our season opener is this weekend. I'm tryin' to pack, catch up on schoolwork, and study for a test. And JoeE's nervous as heck about startin' Friday night. It's gonna be broadcast on national TV—you gonna be watchin'?"

"Of course. I'm sure y'all will do great. Oh hey, I almost forgot. I wanted to ask you something—does USM have an opening for another coach?"

"Well, since my daddy was promoted to defensive coordinator, his old position as linebacker coach hasn't been filled. He's been doin' both jobs."

"A friend of mine is lookin' for a coachin' position. He was an assistant at Harvard last year."

"Have him email me his résumé. I'll share it with Daddy and Coach Brown."

"Thanks so much. He's a great guy and really smart."

"How do you know him?"

"From work."

"What does he do there?"

"His mama is my boss lady, and his daddy is our company's CEO."

"You mean, the guy who you had the thing with?"

"It's complicated, like everything in my life."

Can you say understatement?

***

Just as MaryAna hangs up, she gets a text from Samson: HAVE INFO YOU REQUESTED.

She calls him and he tells her the price for the oxycodone. "Thanks for checkin', but I can't afford it at the moment. But I'll have plenty of money soon."

"I can't promise that price will be the same," Samson tells her. "Oxy is in high demand."

"I understand. I hear music—are you at that jazz place?"

"Want to join me, Mississippi?"

"I would, but I've got a date tonight. Maybe another time?"

"You're a popular girl."

"I know I've been puttin' you off, Samson, but I really do want to check out that place with you."

"Right. Text me when you can afford the merchandise."

"I really appreciate your help."

***

At 8:00, MaryAna sits on the sofa in her pink satin dress, waiting for Vladimir. When he has not shown up a half an hour later, she sends him another text: WHERE RU?

He responds: SOMETHING CAME UP. HOW ABOUT TOMORROW NITE?
Are you kidding me?

MaryAna checks her bank balance and texts back: WHAT ABOUT MY MONEY?

He replies: WILL HIT YOUR ACCOUNT DURING THE NITE. TRUST ME.

It dang well better be.

She replies: OK, TOMORROW THEN.

After a moment, she sends a text to Samson: DATE BAILED. YOU STILL AT JAZZ BAR?

He replies: YEP.

WANT SOME COMPANY?

SURE.

TEXT ADDRESS.

MaryAna chucks her cell into her purse, turns off the lights, and locks the door behind her as she marches toward the elevators.

I will have a good time tonight, Vladimir be damned.

He needs to know I will not be ignored.

Part 3

MATRYOSHKA

Chapter 42

RUFUS

Early Wednesday morning, MaryAna awakens with little memory of the night before. Her only clear recollection was arriving at the jazz bar and being the only white person in the place.

She lies in her suite's king-sized bed, naked under the covers, trying to recall the previous night's events. She notices her pink satin dress on the floor with her bra beside it, but she does not see her lace panties.

MaryAna rolls over to find a large black man asleep.

A man who is wearing no clothes.

Who—?

That's not Sam—who the hell is he?

Her unwelcome bedmate is pushing three-hundred pounds with black hair featuring several streaks of gray. Tattoos cover his upper body, with images ranging from barbed wire to the head of a dragon. She cannot even begin to guess his age.

Who is he—and what's he doing in my bed?

MaryAna sits up, pulls the covers around her, and shakes the man awake. His eyes pop open, and he blinks several times before rolling onto his side to face her.

"Good morning, Sunshine." He says with a grin. His breath reeks of cheap beer, and MaryAna nearly gags. "Who . . .?"

"I'm Rufus—now don't tell me you don't remember."

"Kinda," she says, blinking as images from the night before painfully come into focus.

"Samson introduced us. He said you were a good friend of his."

"You bought me a drink and wouldn't keep your hands to yourself."

"Guilty as charged, your honor. And that was several drinks, by the way. Martinis, to be more specific." Rufus tugs at MaryAna's bed covers.

"Stop that!" she says, pushing his hand away.

"You liked me playing with those twin peaks of yours last night."

"Samson took me to the jazz place to meet a guy who could get me something for my back pain."

Rufus chuckles, pointing to himself. "That would be me. I was out of opioids, so I gave you something that's supposed to be even better. After those martinis, you didn't know the difference. Or didn't care."

I must've been out of my mind.

"What did you give me?"

"A new drug my cousin brought from New Orleans. It's supposed to make you feel good and forget all your troubles—called a chill pill."

MaryAna shudders at the mention of the familiar drug.

"I've had it before. It makes you want sex and then wipes your memory."

Rufus grins. "I know that first part is true. In the elevator, you made me a present of your panties."

MaryAna is mortified by the thought. "What happened last night? Just the highlights."

"We blew off Samson, came to the hotel, hit the minibar, and ended up right here. We were just getting acquainted when you went out like a light. At first I was freaking because I thought you'd overdosed. I tried to wake you, but you were pulling a serious Rip Van Winkle."

"So, did we do it before I fell asleep?"

"What—have sex?"

"Yeah, and did you use a condom?"

"Seriously? I figured I made a better impression than that."

MaryAna shakes her head and swings her legs over the side of the bed, keeping the covers around her. "You need to leave. I gotta get dressed for work."

Rufus gets out of bed and gathers up his clothes from the floor. "So, you're a working girl."

"Yeah, for a company that makes women's apparel."

He slips on black boxer shorts and pulls his jeans over them. "I don't mean your day job."

"What? You think I'm a hooker?"

"That's usually why hot white chicks come to the bar." He takes out his wallet. "We never negotiated a price. How much I owe you?"

"I only went there to be with Samson and listen to jazz."

"Yeah, right—and to score oxy," Rufus reminds her. He lays three hundred-dollar bills on the bedside table. "That should cover what we did before you conked out. By the way, who's Tyler?"

"What?"

"You kept mumbling his name in your sleep."

"He's my ex-boyfriend."

From beneath his pillow, Rufus pulls out a large-caliber handgun and stuffs it into his waistband.

MaryAna gasps. "What the hell's that?"

"You afraid of guns, Sunshine?"

"Stop callin' me that. My name's MaryAna."

"How about we get together this weekend, MaryAna? I've got an apartment above the bar."

"What's the gun for?"

"Glock. For personal protection. I like to keep it close by." He slips on his shirt and pulls it down to conceal the weapon. "You know anything about guns, Sunshine?"

"A guy back home taught me how to shoot."

Rufus smiles. "I buy and sell guns, especially exotic military weapons. If you want to rob a bank, equip a small army, or run a black op, I'm the guy to talk to."

"What about the oxy?"

He kisses her on the forehead. "I'll have some for you real soon."

"How do I reach you?"

"Call the bar. I'm usually there since I own the joint."

***

After Rufus leaves, MaryAna takes a hot shower. As the water pours over her, she replays this morning's unexpected conversation.

I can't believe Rufus thought I was a prostitute. Did Carson think that too—is that why he left money?

How much cash will I need to buy the oxy? My checking account should have the funds transferred by now.

After putting on her makeup, MaryAna takes the cash Rufus left and sticks it inside the cover of the Gideon Bible in the desk drawer.

"I'm no hooker!" she says out loud. "I'll keep the money there until I can give it back to him."

MaryAna then gets dressed and heads out to the elevator. She hits the button, and as she waits for it to arrive, she whips her head around, sensing someone behind her. But no one is there.

She presses the down button again, anxious to get to work.

"You've changed since we talked in the park, MaryAna."

She jumps, startled by the stranger, who now stands behind her.

"What is it with you? Are you hiding in the air vents or something?"

"You've changed, MaryAna—and not for the better."

"I just had a birthday," she says with a shrug. "Maybe I look older."

"No, you have not followed the path of righteousness."

"You mean about me bein' with so many guys? I didn't plan all that—stuff just happens."

"Such behavior is worrisome, of course," he says, his eyes sad. "But there is more—you've chosen a dangerous road with many pitfalls. Your decisions can lead to severe consequences."

"What kind of consequences?"

"I do not pretend to know the future. I can only suggest you be careful regarding what you do and learn from your mistakes."

"Learn what—choose better boyfriends?"

The elevator arrives with a *ding* and the door opens. But when MaryAna turns back around, the man is gone.

OK, this is happening while I'm wide awake—is my guilty conscience messing with me?

She enters the elevator and presses the button for the lobby. As she descends, she pulls out her cell to check her bank balance. However, no funds have been transferred. MaryAna texts Vladimir, but the message fails to send. She then tries calling him, only to hear a message: "The number you have dialed has been disconnected or is no longer in service."

She redials but hears the same recording.

Did he forget to pay his phone bill or . . .?

As the elevator delivers her to the lobby, a disturbing revelation creeps into MaryAna's mind.

Is this what my guardian angel warned me about? Are these the consequences?

Did Vladdy rip me off?

Chapter 43

BARBIE

MaryAna checks her bank balance multiple times at the office, but no deposit has appeared.

My hotel bill is due today—I need my money!

After work, the nineteen-year-old returns to the Plaza and changes into a hot-pink, cut-off T-shirt and a matching pair of short-shorts. She then heads down to the lobby and saunters up to the front desk.

When you need a favor, it helps to look like a real-life Barbie doll.

"May I help you?" a middle-aged man with a thin mustache asks.

"I hope so." MaryAna turns on her most charming smile. "My bill is due today, but I'm a little short on funds. Can I get a bit more time—say until Friday?"

"Your room number, please?"

"1819." She juts out her chest, hoping it might help her cause. "I love your mustache."

The clerk clears his throat and brings up her account on his screen. "I'd love to give you more time, Miss Lindley, but your account is due in full. Do you have a credit or debit card we can charge?"

"I've got a debit card, but my checkin' account is kinda low and I don't get paid till Friday. I think I'll have enough then."

He glances back at his screen. "I see your account is guaranteed by Jacqueline Designs. We'll just bill them."

"No! I mean . . . before you do, I need to contact someone."

The clerk takes a long look at her. "I'll give you until nine o'clock tonight. Is that enough time?"

"I hope so." MaryAna steps away from the counter and makes a call. "Hey, Mr. Rubenstein?"

"I'm surprised to hear from you, Miss Lindley. Have you changed your mind about . . . us?"

"I've got a situation and don't know who else to turn to for help. I don't have enough money to pay my hotel bill, and I don't get paid till Friday. The hotel wants to bill the company, and I'm afraid your wife will find out. They gave me till nine o'clock tonight. What should I do?"

"Last week, you told me you had plenty of money. What happened?"

"I invested it with an art dealer. Now the guy's phone is disconnected."

"You gave him all of it?"

"Just about." She sniffs back tears. "He was supposed to double my money and deposit it in my bank account by today."

"You're way too trusting, Miss Lindley."

"If you don't want to help me, I understand."

"Where are you?"

"In the lobby at the hotel."

"I'm just leaving the office. Wait there."

It's nice to have someone I can count on.

***

When Mel arrives, MaryAna rushes over to give him a big hug.

"Thanks so much for comin'. I hate to ask you for another favor, but I've made a mess of things."

"We'll straighten it out."

MaryAna takes his arm and they stroll to the front desk. Mel hands his business card to the clerk with the pencil mustache.

"How may I help you, Mr. Rubenstein?"

Mel pulls out a personal credit card. "Please charge whatever Miss Lindley owes to this. Also, charge her suite on it for the next week in advance."

The clerk runs the credit card and returns it to the CEO. "She is all set for another week. Is there anything else I can do for you?"

"If my niece has another problem, please contact me. Do you understand?"

"Of course." The clerk gives MaryAna a little smirk. "Your niece is very lovely. Have a pleasant evening."

Mel nods, and they step away. She gives him another hug and whispers in his ear.

"Thanks so much, Uncle Mel."

"You are most welcome," he whispers back and kisses her on the forehead.

She giggles, impressed again by his generosity. "You didn't need to pay for an extra week. I should find someplace less expensive."

"Call it compensation for what Jacqueline put you through yesterday. I can't believe she did that."

"Do you think she knows about us, sir?"

"My wife might suspect, but she doesn't *know* anything. If she did, she'd have confronted me by now. Have you contacted the police about this so-called art dealer?"

"I'd rather not get them involved."

"I recommend you do, Miss Lindley, but it is your call."

She sighs. "I'll think about it."

Mel looks into her troubled eyes. "How about a drink? You look like you could use one."

MaryAna takes his arm. "Maybe more than one."

If I tell him everything, what will he think of me?

Chapter 44

FANTASY

In the hotel bar, MaryAna pours out everything about Vladimir—about meeting the so-called art dealer, their business arrangement, and the offer to share an apartment. Everything except the carriage ride and the Russian's visit to her hotel room.

Mr. Rubenstein sets down his glass. "Con men can be quite convincing."

"I thought Vladdy was perfect." MaryAna says, sipping her second martini. "He knows art, he was sophisticated, and he said he'd help me with investments."

"What do you know about him and his business?"

"Only what he told me."

"Does he have an office?"

"I don't know."

"Where does he live?"

"Somewhere in Brooklyn."

"That's a huge area, Miss Lindley. So, after knowing this fellow for only a short time, you gave him one hundred thousand dollars?"

It makes me sound really dumb—because I am.

"I didn't know you very long, sir, before we got involved. I tend to be impulsive, and it's gotten me into trouble before. I should learn from my mistakes, but . . ."

"I must ask you, Miss Lindley, were you romantically involved with this man?"

She does not answer, instead finishing her drink and ordering another. Once it is in front of her, she gathers her courage.

"On my birthday, Vladdy took me for a romantic carriage ride in Central Park. Afterwards, I invited him up to my suite. It's why I don't want to involve the police—they'll want to know everything, and it's too embarrassin'."

"Were you in love with this guy?"

"I thought I was."

She gulps downs half of her drink. "I want to believe this is all some sort of mix-up, but I know Vladdy ran off with my money."

Mel pats her arm. "You're not the first to fall for such a scam."

She finishes off her martini and wipes away a tear. "It hurts to know someone could be so mean."

The CEO points to her empty glass. "Want another?"

"Are you tryin' to get me drunk?"

"Not necessarily."

"At least, you're honest about it. I better get upstairs while I can still walk. I doubt you want to tote me up there."

"You mean *carry* you."

She nods.

Mel takes care of the bar bill, and they head to the elevators.

"Thanks for everything." She wipes away another tear. "Especially for listenin' to me ramble on about Vladdy. I hate him so much right now. I just want to . . ."

The elevator doors open, and MaryAna steps inside.

"Will you be all right, Miss Lindley?"

She shrugs. "I don't know."

"You look like you've lost your last friend."

"I've still got you, haven't I, sir?"

He steps into the elevator beside her. "A true friend wouldn't leave you alone tonight."

"If Jacqueline finds out we're together, she'll fire me in a heartbeat. I need my job so I can pay you back."

"Do not argue, Miss Lindley." He pushes the button for the eighteenth floor. "After all, I did just pay for your suite."

234

"Thank you, but I won't be very good company."

"Let me be the judge of that." Mel's phone rings. He glances at it and turns it off.

Once inside her suite, MaryAna goes to the minibar and takes out a beer. "Want anything?"

Mel shakes his head. "I thought you'd had enough."

He sits down on the sofa. She joins him and lays her head on his shoulder.

"I still have feelings for you, Miss Lindley," putting his arm around her, "but you know that."

She nods. "If you weren't married—" Her words die when his lips meet hers.

The CEO caresses her hair, her cheek, and her neck. She feels safe in his arms and yearns for intimacy, yet the teenager feels pangs of guilt for desiring it.

Mel senses her reluctance. "What's the matter?"

"Nothing, and everything," she says as tears form in her eyes. "I want to make love with you, but it's just not right."

"Jacqueline and I are married in name only. It's now more a business relationship than a marriage. We have separate bedrooms and rarely see each other even at work. She has her life, and I have mine."

"What if she finds out about us?"

"I'm sure my wife is seeing other men. Since she won't give me a divorce, I should have the same privilege. If we keep our affair secret, everything will be fine."

The passionate kissing and touching that follow chips away at MaryAna's resolve. Her own needs combined with the desire to please him are a potent combination, and the alcohol only makes the situation worse.

"You know, we're breakin' one of God's Commandments," she says, catching her breath. "We shouldn't go any further."

"If we've already sinned, Miss Lindley, why stop now?"

MaryAna pulls back. "Once we actually sleep together, I'm afraid everything will change. In the mornin', I'll regret what we did, and you might too. Is it worth it?"

"To me it is," he says and kisses her on the cheek.

"No matter the cost?"

"I can afford to put you up here at the Plaza or in a nice apartment."

"I'm not talkin' about money cost. Can you afford confrontations with your wife at work like yesterday? How about the looks the hotel clerk gave us? We'll get them at bars, restaurants—wherever we go. Do you really feel comfortable pretendin' to be my uncle?"

"I can handle it."

"I'm not sure I can. I don't want people thinkin' I'm your mistress or some sort of escort. The role of the *other* woman doesn't suit me—I want to be *the* woman."

Mel stares into her blue eyes as they again fill with tears. "Our chance meeting on the plane was a magical moment for me. Of course, I was attracted by your youthful beauty, but I hired you for your design ideas—nothing more. They're quite innovative, no matter what Jaqueline says."

"That's nice to know," MaryAna says with a sniffle.

"After you broke up with your boyfriend, I saw an opportunity to spend more time with you. I needed an escape from my loneliness, and I was thrilled when you accepted my invitations to the concert and musical."

"We did have a good time, didn't we?"

"We did indeed." Mel's eyes penetrate hers. "That weekend with you was like a bright shiny fantasy. After you broke it off, I was devastated."

"I didn't mean to hurt you."

"I know. The truth is, I desire my fantasy, even at the risk you will break my heart again. Can you see it in my eyes?"

She tries to look away but is drawn to his soulful gaze.

Would it really be that terrible if I slept with him?

"Believe it or not, sir, I'm not completely heartless or totally naïve. I know how the world works. I'll sleep with you, but it'll be a one-time thing—not an ongoin' affair."

"So, you'll commit adultery, just not on a regular basis."

"Sir, I owe you big time. The least I can do is fulfill your fantasy."

"You don't owe me anything, Miss Lindley."

If I do this, knowing he's married, my guardian angel will probably disown me.

But MaryAna has made her decision. She stands up and takes his hand. "Let's go to the bedroom."

"Will there be dancing?" the CEO asks, getting to his feet.

MaryAna shakes her head. "Do you have a condom?"

"I do not."

She reaches for her purse, but Mel grabs her arm to stop her.

"What's wrong, sir?"

"Upon further reflection, my dear, I've decided to leave my fantasy unfulfilled. It's enough knowing you'd go through with it."

"I don't understand . . ."

"The problem with fantasies, Miss Lindley, is that they rarely live up to expectations. Although making love to you might be the exception, I'd rather our relationship remain magical. At least, for now."

"Did I do something wrong?"

"I just don't want this to devolve into a sordid one-night stand. I do, however, hope you'll reconsider my offer of an apartment."

"And to be your mistress, right?"

He nods. "That's my fervent desire."

"Under my present circumstances, I won't deny it's more than a little temptin'. I'll think about it?"

"It could be an enjoyable arrangement for both of us. Get some sleep. The world will look brighter in the morning. If you need anything—"

"I've got your number."

He kisses her on the forehead. "Goodnight."

"Goodnight, sir. Thanks for everything."

I suppose Vladdy was my fantasy.

I wish he'd remained one.

Chapter 45

VENTING

Once Mel has left, MaryAna finishes her beer, then pulls out her cell to call Isadora.

"You sound down, MaryAna. Is something wrong?"

"You could say that."

MaryAna tells Isadora all about what happened with Vladimir, the fake investment, the fake apartment, as well as the apparently fake sister.

"I still think you should go to the police, MaryAna."

"I just don't know what they could do. All I have is Vladdy's description and that he has a Russian accent."

"Do you need to borrow some money? I've got a little extra."

"I'm OK for now. My boss paid my hotel bill through next week, and I get paid Friday. I don't want to go back home, but I might have to."

"I'd invite you to bunk in with me, but if Kira found out, she'd be upset."

"I don't want to cause you any trouble, Izzy. You've been such an awesome friend. Can we talk about something else?"

"Sure. I had fun Sunday. Thanks again for inviting me."

"You're welcome. You and Regina seemed to hit it off."

"We did. She asked me if I had a boyfriend. When I told her I liked girls, she kinda opened up. I got the feeling Regina doesn't have any close girlfriends."

"You're easy to talk to, Izzy."

"Regina isn't as self-assured as she first appears," Isadora explains. "She and Wyatt have been engaged for over three years. She claims she loves him but isn't sure she wants to get married."

"Why not?"

"Before Regina started dating Wyatt, she was seeing Andy. When they broke up, she went into a deep depression and tried to kill herself."

"Oh my goodness."

"I got the impression Regina still has a thing for Andy and is a bit jealous of you."

"That's why she kept watchin' me on the boat."

After MaryAna hangs up with Isadora, she turns on the television. After flipping through channels, she lands on the local news.

"The Manhattan Rapist has struck again," the female anchor reports. "NYPD announced a twelfth victim over the last three months. The unidentified female is a twenty-two-year-old resident of the Bronx. She was jogging alone in Central Park late last night when she was attacked."

Could that be the guy who stalked me in the park that night?

The anchor continues, "Although the assailant normally attacks his victims at night, some assaults have taken place in broad daylight. He is described as a white male over six feet tall with red hair, wearing a black hoodie and blue jeans. Police advise against females walking alone in the vicinity of Central Park."

I bet that was *him in the park.*

MaryAna shudders as she realizes how close she came to encountering the man.

She turns off the television and grabs another beer.

Oh, hey—I promised to call Andy.

"I didn't think I'd hear from you today, MaryAna."

"I try to keep my word. So, what are you up to this weekend?"

"If the weather cooperates, we're sailing to Nantucket. We plan to spend Saturday night on the boat. You and your friend are welcome to join us."

"Sounds awesome, but I'll have to get back to you tomorrow. Does the 'we' include Regina?"

"Yeah. Why?"

"I understand you two have a history."

"Where'd you hear that?"

"Regina told Isadora you and her were an item at Yale."

"Yeah, our freshman year."

"So, it was more than a fling."

"Considerably. Regina has some fine qualities, but I found her to be, let's say 'different.' A few months after we broke up, she began dating Wyatt."

"By the way, I talked to my friend at USM. They have an openin' for a coach. You should send her your résumé. I'll text you her email."

"Thank you so much."

"I can't promise anything, but I'm sure Coree will see that you're considered for the job."

"You can't imagine how much this means to me. You're so awesome."

If Andy finds out about his daddy and me, he might rethink that statement.

Chapter 46

NATHAN

The following day at work, MaryAna goes through the motions with a noticeable lack of enthusiasm. In mid-afternoon, she receives a call from Mr. Rubenstein's secretary, asking her to come to his office. Once there, she is ushered inside, and the door is closed behind her.

The CEO is seated behind his desk. "Please sit down, Miss Linley."

MaryAna settles into one of the two chairs across from him. "Thanks again for payin' my hotel bill. I'll pay you back as soon as I can."

"That won't be necessary." His shoulders slump as he leans forward. "I'm afraid I have to let you go."

". . . Are you firin' me?"

"You can resign. It'll look better on your résumé. We'll make it effective tomorrow."

MaryAna sits frozen, unable or unwilling to comprehend. "Why, sir? What did I do wrong?"

"My credit card's fraud department tried to contact me to verify the charge at the Plaza. My phone was off, so they were unable to reach me. Instead, they contacted Jacqueline, who's also on that account. She called the Plaza and learned the charge was for your suite."

"Did you explain to her that it was just a loan and that I'll pay you back?"

"I told Jacqueline the truth about us."

"The *whole* truth?"

Mel slumps back in his chair. "Yes."

"So, she's makin' you fire me?"

243

"I'm afraid so. I wish things had worked out differently."

"Can't you, like override her? You're the CEO."

"It doesn't work that way here. You're in the design department, and that's Jacqueline's turf. We agreed to that when we started the company. I shouldn't have hired you in the first place."

"So, it's hopeless?"

"I again asked Jacqueline for a divorce, but she refused. When I told her I would proceed anyway, she threatened to have me fired. Her father has the power to do that, and he isn't fond of me. I've put too much blood, sweat, and tears into this company to lose it now. So . . ."

MaryAna's life flashes before her eyes. "I understand. Could you help me get a similar job in another fashion company?"

"Because of the 'non-compete' agreement you signed, you can't work in fashion design at any competitor for five years."

"So, what do I do?" Crocodile-size tears begin to flow. "I can't go back home a failure."

Mel takes a box of tissues from his credenza and offers them to her. She takes one and wipes away the tears.

"I could still take care of you, Miss Lindley. I have bank accounts that Jacqueline knows nothing about. Of course, I'd still be married."

"Don't worry about the money. I intend to find Vladdy and get my money back."

"You should let the police handle that."

"It isn't their money. After I find him, maybe I'll turn him over to the cops."

"I'll have Roger give you a lift to the Plaza. It's the least I can do."

"Give me a few minutes to pack up my personal items and say goodbye to some people."

"Roger will meet you out front in thirty minutes. Is that enough time?"

MaryAna nods and stands up. "Do you need me to sign anything??"

"I'll take care of everything. Your check will be delivered to the hotel tomorrow. If you need anything, you have my number."

"Goodbye, sir."

"Good luck, Miss Lindley."

***

Once back at the Plaza, MaryAna calls her friend Nathan Hale in Mississippi. She hopes the former computer hacker can track down Vladimir.

"How's life in the big city, MaryAna.?"

"It's the pits. I just got fired."

"What happened?"

"It's a long story. Someday, I'll bore you with the details. Please, don't let anyone know I'm unemployed."

"I won't. So, what do you need from me?"

"Why do you think I need something, Nathan? I could've called just to see how you were doin'."

"It's always good to try something new."

MaryAna sighs. "OK, I need you to find someone." She tells him about Vladimir, Natasha, the wire transfer, and how she was ripped off. "A hacker like you should be able to locate them."

"Flattery from you, MaryAna? That's a new approach. Regardless, I'm not a hacker anymore."

"I need you to find these people, Nathan."

"What are you gonna do if I do find them?"

"Get my money back."

"And how do you plan to do that?"

"I'll figure that part out when I get to it. Are you gonna help me or not?"

"The last time I helped you, we almost landed in jail."

"Nathan . . . please."

"OK, give me his bank account number. It's always best to follow the money."

She provides the information. "I doubt I'm their first victim."

"It sounds like you ran into professionals. They always cover their tracks but may have left a few digital crumbs. I'll hack some databases and see what turns up."

"Don't take too many risks."

"I'll be careful. By the way, Happy Birthday a week late."

"I kinda wish I could go back to last year's birthday. Life was a lot simpler then."

"You mean when you moved in with me?"

"Yeah, I wish things had turned out differently. I really am sorry I cheated on you. It was because of the drugs, but I still feel bad about it."

"Water over the dam. Hey, I heard you broke up with Tyler."

"Another failed relationship. I'm gettin' good at it."

"Are you gonna move back here?"

"Maybe. If I get my money back, I won't feel like a failure. How could I trust a stranger like that?"

"You're a very trustin' person. It's one of your finer qualities."

"It hasn't served me that well. Now I need a place to live, a new job, and find Vladdy."

"You can do anything you set your mind to."

"You have more confidence in me than I have in myself. You're my ace-in-the-hole, Nathan."

"Let me get to work. If this guy is on the grid, I'll nail him—us aces always get the bad guys."

I hope we can.

Chapter 47

HONESTY

That evening, MaryAna receives a call from Andre. She is glad to hear from him, as he is one of the few bright spots in her chaotic life. However, she fears he may have learned about her relationship with his father.

"Have you decided about going sailing with us?"

"I'm sorry, Andy. I forgot all about it. Things have been hectic around here. I better not plan on goin'. Maybe another time."

"That's OK," he says. "By the way, I emailed my résumé to your friend Coree. Thanks for the help."

"All I did was make a phone call."

"It's important to me. Look, MaryAna, I don't often meet someone as charming as you who is also a nice person. You can't imagine some of the women I've been out with."

"Believe me, I'm not that nice, Andy. You just don't know me well."

"I'd like to know you better."

"I've got tons of baggage. Most of it I'm ashamed to admit."

"We all have secrets, MaryAna. Yours can't be any worse than mine."

"Wanna bet?"

"Come on. Share one of your secrets with me?"

"Andy, you really don't want to know."

"I thought we were friends. Don't friends share secrets?"

"OK," MaryAna says with a sigh. "Last year I was hooked on opioids. I was a cocktail waitress at a strip club and even went on stage one time. Nice girls don't do that."

"Are you off the drugs now?"

"Yeah, for over nine months. My psychiatrist is treatin' me for bipolar disorder, but I'm bad about not takin' my meds. I shouldn't drink, but I do. I'm addicted to shoppin' and have trouble with romantic relationships. You're a *nice* guy and need to keep lookin' for that nice girl."

"Hey, I've done things I shouldn't have, MaryAna. I had a cocaine problem in graduate school. I kicked the habit this summer, but while I was on drugs, I did some pretty stupid stuff. I'm not the Dudley Do Right Wyatt thinks I am."

"Why would you say that?"

"Friends don't sleep with their best friend's fiancée."

". . . Regina?"

"Whenever she visited her parents in Boston, we'd hook up, score some blow, and well, you know. I was under a lot of stress, what with graduate school, coachin', and family issues. It's no excuse, but it is what it is."

"I take it Wyatt doesn't know?"

"Not a clue. I don't know—you think I should tell him?"

"Hard call. Honesty may have its own rewards, but it also has its own punishments. Say, have you talked to your parents today?"

"No. I'm at the cottage—I cut down a couple trees and cleared some brush."

"I got fired today. Well, actually—your daddy let me resign."

"Why the hell did he do that?"

"Don't be mad at him. He's done plenty to help me. He hired me despite my lack of experience. He introduced my design concepts, even though they were controversial. I owe him a lot."

"Wyatt told me my mom wasn't pleased Dad challenged her design ideas. She have you fired because of that?"

"Well . . ."

"What's going on, MaryAna?"

"A guy who I thought was an art dealer conned me, and I couldn't pay my hotel bill. Your daddy came to my rescue, but Jacqueline found out and accused him of havin' an affair with me."

"Oh, I'm so sorry. My mom's bad about jumping to conclusions. When I get home, I'll talk to her and get your job back."

"Please, Andy—just let it be."

"What she did was wrong. I think she knows how much I like you. It wouldn't be the first time she'd try to run my love life."

"You don't know the whole story."

"Enlighten me."

MaryAna's hands begin trembling. "When I moved to New York, your daddy looked after me. He gave me rides to and from work. One weekend he took me to a concert and a musical to do market research."

"Market research?"

"We were checking out what the women were wearin'."

"I know what market research is, MaryAna. Who else went?"

"Just your daddy and me."

"What? You mean like a date?"

". . . Kinda. Your daddy doesn't wear a weddin' ring—I assumed he was single."

"What are you saying?"

"He's a good-lookin' guy and was so nice to me."

"Did you—?"

"Soon as I found out he was married, I broke it off. I didn't know about you and your mama—you believe me, right?"

". . . I need to go, MaryAna."

"Please, Andy. He and I just made out a few times, but never went all the way. It's over between us . . . Andy?"

The phone goes dead.

He hates me.

Everyone hates me.

249

Chapter 48

APOLOGY

At eleven o'clock Friday morning, MaryAna is still in bed when the hotel phone rings. A FedEx envelope has arrived for her from Jacqueline Designs. "Would you like it delivered to your suite, Miss Lindley?" the hotel clerk asks.

"Yes, thank you. Is Samson workin' today?"

"He is."

"Could you have him bring it up?"

"Right away."

MaryAna hops out of bed and throws on a silk dressing gown over her pajamas.

This is my chance to make it up to Sam for abandoning him at the jazz place.

The bellman soon arrives with the envelope, but his usual toothy grin is nowhere to be found. MaryAna gives him a quick hug and sets the envelope on the desk. "I want to apologize for the other night at the jazz place. I shouldn't have left with Rufus—it was rude of me."

Samson's face is hard. "You get your oxy?"

"Not yet, but he's supposed to get me some. Look, I want to make it up to you, Sam. You want to get together when you get off work? We could see a movie or go to a museum—maybe just take a stroll in the park. Then we could come here and hang out. What do you say?"

"I don't think so."

"Come on. I said I'm sorry. Did you know Rufus drugged me? He gave me a chill pill."

"I told you not to take it."

"You did?"

"Yeah, then you started making out with him right there. And then you just took off with him—left me high and dry."

"I'm sorry—I screwed up."

"Screwed is right. Rufus told me later what went down. You really give him your panties in the elevator?"

"That was the drug, not me."

"He said you're a hooker."

"That's not true!"

"He paid you."

"Well . . . yeah, he did, but I didn't ask him to. He put it on the nightstand—I couldn't just leave it there."

Samson chuckles but is not amused. "Did that dude from Chicago and the art dealer leave money too?"

"I did sleep with those guys, but it wasn't for money—I'm not a hooker."

"But you wouldn't sleep with me?"

"I thought you were too young for a serious relationship."

"Were those *serious* relationships with those other guys?"

"Well, no . . . look, that was then, but I want to get together with you now."

"Oh, really. Rumor is that some old guy's paying for this suite. You his mistress, or is he your pimp?"

"No. My *company* was payin' for this suite. I was gonna start payin', but that art dealer ripped me off. Our CEO helped me out, but his wife got me fired."

"You needed coins, so you figured you'd just spread your legs for your boss. Got it."

"That's not how it was!"

The bellman shakes his head. "Then you wanted drugs, so you got me to hook you up with Rufus. I know how you paid him."

"You don't know what you're talkin' about," she says, her anger rising to defcon 1.

Samson nods toward MaryAna's gown. "Are those your work clothes?"

"I can't believe you said that. You need to go."

"C'mon, Mississippi," he says with a sneer. "We can still have a good time if you want."

He tries to kiss her, but she pushes him away. "I told you to go."

He steps close and puts his hands on her chest. "You don't mean that."

"Stop it, Samson," she says, slapping his hands away. "I don't want to fool around."

"But I do." He reaches for his wallet. "I've got a few extra bucks. What do you charge for a quickie?"

MaryAna glares at him. "If I were a hooker, you couldn't afford me."

The bellman's nostrils flare, and he raises his hand as if to strike her.

MaryAna steps back and clinches her fists, her breaths shallow and quick.

The bellman lowers his hand but continues moving toward her. She retreats until her back is against the wall and his face inches from hers, his breath hot.

"You don't wanna do this, Samson."

"You've been teasing me since the day you got here, Mississippi. Every time I see you, you smile and act all nicey-nice. When I come up here, you want to make out, but won't go all the way—it ain't right."

He presses his body against hers, pinning MaryAna to the wall. "But it will be," he says, unzipping his jeans.

MaryAna can only speak in a whisper. "I'll call the cops . . . and then you can kiss your precious plans for Broadway goodbye."

The bellman freezes, then takes a step back. MaryAna's eyes lock onto his, and for several tense moments neither moves. A police siren somewhere in the distance filters in as if on cue.

Samson blinks, takes another step back, then zips himself up. "You ain't worth the trouble."

She finally takes a breath and steps away from the wall. "Get out."

The bellman turns and leaves the suite without looking back.

MaryAna realizes she is shaking once more and hugs herself tight, but she cannot stop it. After a moment she slumps to the floor, her muscles short-circuiting. Then she cries, silently at first, but soon her sobs fill the room.

I hate men . . . but I hate myself even more.

Chapter 49

TEDDY

Twenty minutes later, MaryAna takes the FedEx envelope from the table and settles on the sofa with a beer. The envelope contains her final paycheck and a note from Mel, wherein he apologizes once again and says to call if she needs anything. She crumples the note and chucks it into the wastebasket.

Men only want me for one thing.

She slams her fist onto the sofa, then a second time. Breath surges through gritted teeth and her face, now crimson, hardens.

No more.

Now it's my turn—time for me to be the bitch.

MaryAna dashes to the bathroom and grabs her ruby-red lipstick.

When she exits the elevator in the lobby twenty minutes later, every male head—as well as a few females'—turns in her direction. She is decked out in a red cocktail dress, its hemline well above the knee, and a scoop neckline that screams *wardrobe malfunction ahead*. Red six-inch pumps, silver earrings, and a matching necklace round out the outfit.

MaryAna is ready for battle.

"Good afternoon, Miss Lindley," Leon says as he opens the door for her.

"I'm afraid there's nothing good about it for me."

"What's wrong?"

"I got conned out of my money and lost my job."

"I'm so sorry. Will you be staying on here at the Plaza?"

"My room is paid for till Wednesday. After that, I don't know what I'm gonna do. I don't want to go back home, but I might have to do just that."

"I'll miss you around here Miss Lindley. You always brighten my day."

"Please, call me MaryAna."

"We're not supposed to use first names," he says, then grins. "But sometimes, you gotta make a exception, MaryAna."

She reaches out and gives him a big hug. "I know we're probably not supposed to do that either, but I'm gettin' kinda tired of what I'm not supposed to do."

Leon frowns. "Now, it's probably not my place to say, but I hope you're not going to do anything detrimental to your well-being, Miss Lindley."

"MaryAna."

He smiles again. "MaryAna."

"Oh, don't you worry about me," she says, sauntering off.

What I want is simple: world domination.

***

MaryAna cashes her check at a nearby Citibank, then finds the nearest bar. It is a small neighborhood place with a handful of patrons this Friday afternoon. She glances around and smiles at the men before landing on a stool near the end of the bar.

A husky man in his mid-thirties rises from his table and approaches MaryAna, bringing his bottle with him. He has slicked-back dark hair and bushy sideburns, and his gray work shirt is spattered with yellow and green paint.

"I'm Ted," he says, settling on the barstool beside MaryAna. "Can I buy you a drink, gorgeous?"

That was quick—the first casualty of the day.

"I was just fixin' to order a martini, but you can buy me one if you want."

"Get the pretty lady a martini, Carl," he tells the bartender.

Gorgeous and pretty. I suppose "beautiful" is next.

"Ain't seen you in here before, beautiful. What's your name?"

Bingo.

"Jolene. You know, like the Dolly Parton song?"

He nods at her chest. "You and Dolly have at least two things in common."

She giggles. "And what would that be, Teddy?"

His eyes rise to meet hers. "You're both blondes."

"What else?"

Before he can answer, the bartender sets down MaryAna's drink. She shows her ID, then he leaves to help another customer.

MaryAna points to the paint stains on Ted's shirt. "Are you an artist?"

He laughs. "Hell no. I'm a painter in Local union 582. You a tourist, Jolene?"

"How'd you guess?"

"I caught your accent. Somewhere down South, right?"

"You're very observant."

He takes a swig from his bottle. "Before the divorce, I drove my kids and the old lady through the South on the way to Disney World."

MaryAna slips the olive off the toothpick in her glass, pops it into her mouth, and rolls it around before swallowing it. She takes a sip of her martini, then downs half of it.

"You really like those fancy drinks." Ted takes another swig of his beer.

"They help me forget my troubles."

"You got troubles, honey?" He puts his hand on her knee. "I'm a good listener."

"I don't want to bother you with my problems, but maybe we could hang out. You know, get to know each other."

"Sounds good to me." He moves his hand farther up her leg. "I love that dress. Looks good on you. Probably looks good offa you too," he says laughing.

MaryAna smiles. "I'm lookin' to have an awesome time while I'm in town. Any ideas?"

"I could show you around. I know all the best places—including my place."

She finishes the rest of her drink. "So, you looking to hook up?"

"Sure am." His hand inches up her thigh. "Want a refill?"

"Are you tryin' to get me drunk?"

"Just wanna help you chase those blues away."

"Are you good in bed, Teddy?"

"The ladies seem to like me."

MaryAna leans closer, making sure he has an unobstructed view down the top of her dress. "How far is your place from here?"

He swallows hard. "Not far."

MaryAna holds up a finger. "Choice number one: We take a romantic carriage ride, then go to your apartment and have mind-blowin' sex. What do you say?"

Ted grins from ear to ear. "Hell yeah—but what say we skip the carriage part."

She adds another finger. "Then there's choice number two: I leave this bar and you never see me again."

"I'll take door number one!" Ted says, reaching for his wallet. "Carl, how much I owe you?"

MaryAna snatches her purse from the bar and stands up.

"Hold on, Jolene. I need to pay the man."

She locks eyes with him. "The choices were mine, *Teddy*, not yours. "Have a nice life." She waves goodbye and heads for the door.

"You bitch," he yells after her. "Go to hell."

MaryAna cackles. "Been there, done that." The door closes behind her.

Should I feel bad that that felt so damn good?

Chapter 50

RODNEY

In half a dozen bars on the back streets of Manhattan, MaryAna repeats her revenge game, flirting with men anxious to buy her drinks. As with Ted, she offers them a false choice, then leaves them to foot the bill as she moves on to the next victim. As the afternoon winds down, MaryAna finds herself in a rundown commercial area away from the main thoroughfares, where the sidewalks are mostly deserted.

While the bar encounters went off exactly as MaryAna had anticipated, the pleasure she received from screwing the male half of the population suffered from diminishing returns. She basically walked through the last two would-be trysts. Revenge had lost its luster, but the alcohol MaryAna had amassed throughout the last several hours was swirling inside her head, making her mind and focus fuzzy.

Thus, she was at first unaware that the last guy she hoodwinked was now following close behind as her stilettos took her down the sidewalk in search of yet another bar. But, despite the multiple martinis she had consumed, her spider sense was still online, warning her that danger was near.

Is my guardian angel nearby? Someone's—

Before MaryAna can look behind her, she is grabbed by a large man in a black hoodie, who drags her into the alleyway between two warehouses. She kicks out wildly but succeeds only in losing her right shoe. The man tosses her against a dumpster and she falls to her knees, dropping her purse in the process.

She scrambles to her feet and kicks him in the stomach, breaking the heel of her other shoe. The man's hood falls away, revealing his red hair.

It's Rodney from the last bar!

He grabs her arm and heaves her into the concrete wall of the warehouse, knocking the wind out of her. An SUV passes by and MaryAna cries out, but her screams go unheard.

Rodney punches her in the stomach, and she staggers backward, hitting her head on the dumpster. He then snatches up her purse and dumps the contents onto the ground.

"No, stop!"

"What, you gonna give me another *choice*, Jolene?" He picks up the Citibank envelope and yanks out the cash, flashing it in MaryAna's face. "This all you got?"

"Please . . ."

He rifles through MaryAna's wallet before pausing on her ID. "Well, hello, MaryAna. Another lie, *Jolene*," he says, slipping the ID into his pocket. "It's all you girls do is lie."

"Please, it's all I've got." Adrenaline surges through her, but so does terror, thus preventing her from fighting or running. "I'm sorry I lied to you, I didn't mean it," she says, her voice indistinct.

"Too late for apologies, bitch. I'm gonna teach you a lesson you won't forget."

MaryAna tries to dash past him, but he is too quick. He grabs a fistful of her hair and drags her farther into the alley.

Oh my God, he might be the Manhattan Rapist!

He punches her in her midsection a second time and she collapses onto a wooden crate next to the dumpster. He flips her onto her stomach and unzips his jeans.

MaryAna's mind races through any and all possibilities that might save her—including more deception. "Rodney, wait—look, we don't have to do this here. I've got a suite at the Plaza with a big bed and minibar. We can go there and do whatever you want."

"You're full of choices, aren't you?" he says, grabbing her neck from behind. "We can do whatever I want right *here*." As he unbuckles his belt, she tries to kick him in his groin but misses, hitting his thigh instead.

"Try that again, and I'll break your legs." He pries them apart and gets down on his knees.

"Stop, you bastard," is all MaryAna can get out before he chokes her into silence. She senses someone else in the alley . . . *Help me!* . . . but the feeling abruptly ends.

Rodney pulls MaryAna's dress up around her waist and rips off her thong. He gets in close, his hand around her neck once more. "Now, it's my choice, and I choose door number two."

MaryAna flails, trying to scramble away from him, but he yanks her back onto the crate. Then his weight is on her, and she feels his hand maneuvering his penis toward its target.

"Please, I beg you . . ."

God, don't let him do this!

Rodney grabs another fistful of her hair. "Shut up and don't move if you wanna leave this alley alive."

She stops squirming, every ounce of resistance gone.

MaryAna has been raped more than once in her young life. Each time, she was given a chill pill, and most of what happened was erased from her memory. This time is different—although under the influence of alcohol, the nineteen-year-old is all too aware of what is happening.

***

After Rodney is done, he collapses onto MaryAna, his breath hot and stale on her neck.

When the man finally slides off, he rips away her silver necklace. "Those earrings look expensive. Take 'em off and give 'em to me," he says, zipping up his jeans.

MaryAna does as she is told. "Don't kill me," she mutters and begins to sob. Still sprawled out on the broken crate, she holds her breath, wondering if it will be her last.

Rodney leans close, his sweaty hand on her neck. "Go to the cops, and so help me—I'll find you and kill you."

MaryAna forces herself not to look at him and continues crying.

Moments later, his footsteps fade into the distance. She lies unmoving for several minutes, her sobs echoing softly off the uncaring walls around her. When she finally staggers to her feet, she realizes her knees are bleeding and picks splinters from her thighs and hips. She hurts everywhere, and Kristen's assault in Pittsburgh suddenly flashes through her head.

I hate men—all of them!

After locating her purse, MaryAna gathers up everything Rodney did not take. The only money she has left is a fifty-dollar bill stashed in a hidden pocket of her wallet.

The battered teenager hobbles around on one damaged shoe, looking for the other. She finds it several feet away, along with the broken-off heel. When she is unable to reattach it, she tosses the pair into the dumpster.

I begged God for help . . .

Where was my guardian angel?

I hate men—I hate everybody!

The barefoot young woman steps tentatively out of the alley, noticing that the streetlamps are now lit. A few vehicles pass by while she tries to decide which direction to go.

I should tell the police . . .

But I can't—I'd have to tell them what I did this afternoon, what led up to this—and they'll blame me!

Dammit . . .

As much ashamed as she is traumatized, MaryAna wanders aimlessly for blocks until she spots a taxi.

"Where to, Miss?"

She pulls the fifty dollar bill from her purse and gives the driver Isadora's address.

I need a friendly face . . .

Chapter 51
FLIPPING A SWITCH

"MaryAna!"

The nineteen-year-old's eyes pop open. She is on the floor, slumped against the door of Isadora's apartment.

"Izzy . . ." MaryAna blinks and looks up at her friend. "I guess I fell asleep."

Isadora kneels down, putting a hand on MaryAna's shoulder. "How long have you been waiting out here?"

"I don't know."

"Are you drunk?"

"No. Yes. I don't know. Maybe."

"What happened? You look terrible—did you get hit by a car or something?"

MaryAna grabs her purse from the floor and tries to stand but slumps back down. "Hey, you wanna go shoppin'? I need shoes."

"Let me help you up." Isadora unlocks the door and pulls her friend to her feet.

"I've had a horrible week, Izzy. Vladdy stole all my money, and Jacqueline got me fired."

"Let's get you inside so we can talk." Isadora opens the door and maneuvers her friend into the apartment.

MaryAna babbles on. "I told Andy I'd been with his daddy, and now he hates me. I woke up to find a drug dealer in my bed. And now the bellman thinks I'm a hooker."

"And today was the worst of all. A guy I met in a bar robbed me and . . ." MaryAna begins to sob.

"Let's see if we can get you sobered up."

Before Isadora can get her to the sofa, MaryAna turns and kisses her on the lips.

Taken by surprise, her friend pulls away. MaryAna staggers backward and bumps against the wall.

"How much have you had to drink?"

"That's right, officer. The bottle just jumped right into my hand . . ." MaryAna leans against the wall for support. "There are a lotta bars in New York and guys wantin' to buy you drinks. You have to be careful though—some of them are really mean."

"Sit down, and I'll fix some coffee. What's this about you being robbed?"

"The guy from the bar. He dragged me into the alley. He took my cash, my jewelry, and my ID. Why would he want my ID?"

"Why didn't you use your karate?"

"He was too big. I couldn't get away . . . and then he was on top of me and . . ."

Isadora puts her hands on MaryAna's shoulders. "Wait, what?"

"He . . . he . . ." MaryAna's face bunches up and suddenly she is back in the warehouse alley. She grabs Isadora and hugs her tight, her tears back in full force.

"Oh, you poor thing," Isadora says, patting her back. "Did you report it to the police?"

"I don't wanna deal with them. I just wanna forget about it—like it never happened."

Isadora rises and goes the kitchenette. "OK. We don't have to talk about it right now."

MaryAna steadies herself and brushes her hair off her face. "Let's go to Boots 'n Heels. I wanna dance. Maybe McKenzie will be there—you think she'll like the way I'm dressed?"

"You need to get yourself cleaned up, MaryAna. You've been through a lot."

The nineteen-year-old gets to her feet and staggers over to Isadora.

"McKenzie said she could blow my world apart, Izzy. What do you think about that?"

"I think you need to sober up."

"You wouldn't believe how many guys tried to pick me up today," MaryAna says, now animated. "I want all the guys to go to hell. I'm done with them, like forever!"

"You've said that before."

"This time I mean it. I'm gonna become a lesbian like you and Kristen. How about I move in, and you teach me everything?"

Isadora places a cup of water in the microwave and sets the time. "I told you: I don't sleep with straight girls. And you don't just 'become' lesbian."

"Don't you get it?" MaryAna says. "I'm not straight anymore. Men just wanna screw me, one way or the other." She rushes over to the sofa and tries to pull it out into a bed.

"What are you doing?"

"I kissed you when we came in like Kira did." The teenager continues struggling with the sofa. "Is she back from Europe yet?"

"Soon, yeah."

"In the meantime, we can be lovers." MaryAna finally gets the bed to cooperate and plops down on the edge. "If you don't wanna be my girlfriend, I'll find someone who does. You said McKenzie wanted to take me home, right?"

"MaryAna! There's a big difference between giving up men and being with women. You can't just flip a switch."

"Just watch me." The teenager wiggles out of her dress and tosses it to the floor. Her cherry-red bra quickly follows.

The microwave beeps and Isadora retrieves the cup. She then grabs a packet from a box on the countertop and rips it open, pouring its contents into the cup.

She takes a container of creamer from the refrigerater and stirs it in. "You're welcome to spend the night, MaryAna, but no hanky-panky. Understand?"

A naked MaryAna lies back on the bed and props her head up

on one hand. "You'll change your mind, trust me."

"No, I won't." Isadora says, bringing MaryAna the coffee. "How can you even think about sex anyway after what happened to you?"

MaryAna waves dismissively. "It's all gone, like a bad dream."

***

The next morning MaryAna wakes in Isadora's bed to find herself alone. She is as naked as she was the night before.

The nineteen-year-old sits up and glances around the apartment. She spots her purse on a table, but her clothes are nowhere to be seen. Her bruised body is sore, her head pounds, and her stomach is doing back flips.

She drops back onto the pillow, hoping to fall back asleep. Then her eyes snap open to the sound of a key in the lock. The door swings open and a young woman with purple hair enters.

It is Kira.

The teenager draws the sheet around her and forces herself to sit up once again.

"What you doing here?" Kira says. "Where Isadora?"

"I don't know. When did you get back?"

"This morning. I want surprise her."

MaryAna cannot read the expression on her face.

"She'll be happy to see you. So, you have a key, huh?"

"Um . . . Isadora gave me key when we met."

"That means Izzy *really* likes you."

"Yes." The purple-haired young woman's eyes dance around the room.

"I just came by for a visit," MaryAna tells her. "I'll text Izzy and find out where she is."

"That OK. I go."

How do I get myself into these situations?

"It was nice seein' you again, Kira. I'll tell Izzy you stopped by."

"You do that."

Without another word, Kira leaves. MaryAna collapses back onto the bed.

266

What happened last night? I don't remember.

In Mississippi, the teenager had attended AA meetings for several months. Each time, she admitted to being an alcoholic, although never truly embracing the idea. Her ability to quit drinking for long stretches had reinforced her disbelief.

I'm out of control again.

Her drinking has led MaryAna down a path where casual sex is standard operating procedure. Her latest incident proves she is powerless against alcohol, and it once again rules her life.

Although this recognition is the first of the twelve-step AA program, MaryAna only now admits the brutal truth to herself.

I really am an alcoholic.

I drove Tyler away, tempted Mel, had a one-night stand with Carson, and teased Samson. Then I seduced Vladdy, let Rufus drug me, and I scared off Andy.

The teenager begins to sob.

I acted the fool with Teddy and the others and practically invited Rodney to rape me. To top it off, I threw myself at Isadora. What's wrong with me?

MaryAna pounds the pillows with angry fists.

Lord, please help me.

Men aren't the problem.

I am.

***

Fifteen minutes later, Isadora returns to the apartment with breakfast.

A naked MaryAna is finishing a cup of instant coffee. "Where'd you go?"

"I got us something to eat." Isadora pulls two small white boxes from a bag and hands one to her friend. "I hope you like ham and cheese croissants."

"Awesome. Want some coffee?"

"Sure." Isadora says, folding the bed back into a sofa. "I hung your dress up in the bathroom. You should get dressed."

MaryAna fixes a second cup and hands it to her. "So, what

happened last night?"

"You don't remember?"

"Pretty much everything after I got here last night is a blank."

"You remember wanting to have sex?"

"Kinda. So, did we?"

Isadora shakes her head. "We slept in the same bed after you passed out, but that's all."

"Oh, thank God."

"You change your mind about becoming a lesbian?"

"It was a stupid idea, Izzy. I'm sorry I came on to you."

"Forget it."

"I should tell you something else," MaryAna says. "Kira probably thinks we did a lot more than sleep in the same bed."

Isadora takes a sip of her coffee. "What are you talking about?"

"She stopped by."

"What? What did she say?"

"She wanted to surprise you and seemed shocked I was here. I don't think she was happy about it.

"I'll . . . talk to her, no problem. How're you feeling, by the way?"

"Sore all over—worse in some places."

"You should see a doctor. Those bruises on your chest and stomach look really bad."

When I close my eyes, all I see is Rodney and that red hair and hoodie. I can still smell the stink from the alley, from him.

"Izzy, I don't want anyone to know what happened."

"If that's what you want. Say, why don't you get a hot shower—it might make you feel better."

MaryAna grabs her purse from the small table. Once in the bathroom, the teenager hears her friend on the phone through the thin door.

"She told me you stopped by." Isadora listens a few moments, then adds, "I'll meet you there later and explain."

Soon MaryAna exits the bathroom, still drying her hair. "Everything OK with Kira?"

"We just need to talk face to face," Isadora says, her face somber.

"I didn't mean to cause problems, Izzy."

"I uh . . . I think it'd be better if you stay away from me in the future, MaryAna."

"But we're friends, Izzy . . . shoppin' buddies."

"You can always call in an emergency . . ."

MaryAna's lower lip trembles. "If that's what you want."

I've done it again.

Chapter 52

FRIENDS AGAIN

It is raining late Saturday morning when a shoeless MaryAna returns to the Plaza. Leon greets her with an umbrella and escorts the hungover young woman to the hotel entrance.

"Miss Lindley, what happened to your shoes?"

"I broke a heel and trashed them. It's OK. Mississippi girls love to go barefoot."

"That's not a good idea in this city. And . . . it looks like you hurt your knees."

"Clumsy me," she says, waving him off. "Slipped and fell—no biggie. So, where's the sunshine the weatherman promised for today?"

"It appears they weren't quite on the money. By the way, my daughter Jasmine is here from Boston this weekend. My wife and I want to invite you to dinner."

MaryAna's face brightens up for the first time today. "That's so sweet of y'all. I'd love to."

"How about tomorrow, around four?"

"Four's good for me."

Leon gives her his Brooklyn address, and MaryAna puts it into her phone along with his cell number.

"May I bring something—maybe dessert?"

"Just bring yourself. My wife likes to cook, and I love to eat," he says, rubbing his belly. Max is working on another painting for you, but he won't let us see it."

"Why not?"

"He won't say, and it's not like my son to keep secrets."

***

Back at her suite, MaryAna retrieves the three hundred-dollar bills she had stashed in the Gideon Bible.

I was going to give these back to Rufus, but now I need this money.

The nineteen-year-old starts to put the Bible back in the drawer but stops. She suddenly feels very far from home and her religious upbringing. Sarah made sure her daughter's life was filled with Sunday school lessons, weekly services, Wednesday night prayer meetings, revivals, and vacation Bible schools.

I haven't thought much about church since I got here.

It's been great to be on my own, doing whatever I want, but . . .

Just about everything I've done has led to one disaster after another.

Why do I keep messing everything up?

Is my guardian angel still around . . . or did he give up on me?

MaryAna sits on her bed and turns to Genesis, chapter one. She leans back on the pillows and begins reading, finding the familiar words soothing. Soon, she is absorbed into the stories she has loved since childhood.

I need to forget about everything that's happened and renew my faith in God.

***

Three hours later, MaryAna is still engrossed in the Bible when her cell rings. It is Andre.

"Hey. I'm surprised to hear from you since . . . since the other day."

"I'm really sorry I hung up on you, MaryAna."

"I deserved it."

"No, you were just telling the truth. I'd heard rumors about my dad and the women at the company, but I didn't believe it. So, when you basically confirmed what I'd heard, I couldn't handle it."

"Do you hate me, Andy?"

"On the contrary, I admire your honesty, even though it was a lot to swallow. Can we just start over?"

MaryAna brightens for the second time today. "I'd love for us to be friends again. Where are you, by the way—it doesn't sound like you're on your sailboat."

"The weather didn't cooperate, so we decided to reschedule. Are you gonna watch the Southern Miss game tonight?"

"Oh my gosh, I totally forgot about it."

"I'd invite you over to watch it, but my parents will be home, which could be awkward."

MaryAna chuckles. "You think?"

"It kicks off around eight our time," Andre says. "How about we watch it at a sports bar?"

"I want to stay away from bars for a while, if that's okay."

"Really? I thought you were a party animal."

"Not anymore. Why don't you come here? We can have our own tailgate party."

"Awesome. I'll pick up some drinks—are you a Coke or Pepsi girl?"

"I'll leave it up to you."

"I can bring chips and dip too."

"I'll order wings from room service and we can pig out. Do you want to invite Wyatt?"

"He'll want to bring Regina, so . . . let's not."

"See you tonight!"

***

Andy arrives that evening loaded down with snacks and drinks. MaryAna greets him in her USM sweatshirt and gold shorts.

He sets everything down, then starts to give her a hug, but she freezes and jumps back.

Why did I do that?

"Sorry," she says, grabbing the remote. "What channel is the game on?"

"You seem jumpy, MaryAna. You OK?"

"I'm just anxious about my brother playing college ball for the first time."

They settle onto the sofa with plenty of personal space between them. Before the game gets underway, MaryAna tells Andre about the USM players and coaches whom she knows.

"There's JoeE!" she squeals when his team takes the field. "He's number ten."

"Whoa, he's one of the tallest players out there."

"Yeah, he's like six-seven."

"Then again, you are not exactly a midget, MaryAna."

She stretches out her long legs, which show off her toenails. They, like her fingernails, are painted alternately black and gold.

"Cool, that's their school colors, right? Say, what happened to your knees?"

"I slipped on some wet asphalt when it was raining."

"Looks like it was a bad fall—you okay?"

She waves dismissively. "Oh yeah. I'm good."

From the opening kickoff, JoeE shreds Nebraska's defense. His brilliant performance combined with the stellar defensive play of MaryAna's half-brothers, Mason Calhoun and Kane Robinson, keep her mind occupied.

"There's Coree," MaryAna says, when the camera shifts to the USM sideline.

"She's pretty cute. Are all Mississippi girls drop-dead gorgeous?"

"People say Coree and I look a lot alike. Of course, not so much since she dyed her hair that hideous dark-brown. She thinks it makes people take her more seriously."

"I think her hair looks awesome," Andre says. "It's the same color as mine."

MaryAna turns to him. "Oh, yeah. But guys can get away with a color like that."

"Gee, thanks." Andy chuckles. "Your twin is having a monster game."

"JoeE is destined for greatness. I'm glad one of us has a bright future."

"What? You giving up on being a famous designer?"

She shrugs. "For the time bein'."

"You have incredible talent and could still have an awesome career."

"Did your daddy tell you that?"

"Wyatt said your blouse designs were the most innovative he's ever seen. He was shocked when they fired you."

"Thank Wyatt for me. Maybe someday you and I could start our own fashion company."

"Sounds like a good investment," Andy scoots closer. "I could use some of my trust fund money."

"I've got one of those, too."

"Seriously?"

MaryAna nods. "I don't get it until I'm twenty-one. We could have an arrangement like your parents—I could handle design while you take care of everything else."

"You never know," he says smiling. He reaches out to put his arm around MaryAna's shoulder, but she pulls away and jumps to her feet.

"Whoa, what's wrong? I was just hoping we could—"

"We're talkin' business here. Not romance."

"But—"

"You think I invited you so we could make out . . . or—"

"No . . . well, OK, yeah—I won't deny I like you."

When he touched me, Rodney and the alley flashed back into my head. But I can't tell him . . .

"It's just . . . my feelings for your daddy haven't completely gone," she says, mentally crossing her fingers. Until then, a romantic relationship with you is out of the question."

Andre blinks. "You still want to be with my dad?"

"That's not what I'm sayin'." She sits back down, caught in her own lie.

"My mom will never agree to a divorce," he says. "Plus, they work together. I don't see them parting ways any time soon."

"Your daddy's made that perfectly clear."

"Why can't you just forget about him and start dating me?"

"I don't believe either of your parents would approve of that. And I couldn't blame them."

"To hell with them. They don't run my life."

"Oh, Andy, can't we just be friends and hang out? I like being with you."

He sighs. "I suppose we can keep it G-rated—at least for now."

They watch the second half of the game in relative silence. "I hope we can do this again soon," he says as he gets up to leave.

MaryAna walks him to the door. "You're an awesome guy. If things were different . . . well, who knows?"

"When I want something, I don't give up easily."

As he opens the door, MaryAna extends her hand, but he ignores it and leans in to give her a peck—first on one cheek, then the other. Her body stiffens, but she does not pull away.

"That's a proper French goodbye," he says, smiling. "I'll call you."

He leaves, closing the door behind him.

MaryAna takes a deep breath then slowly lets it out.

Maybe this's my first step in starting over . . .

Chapter 53

REPENTANCE

On Sunday morning, MaryAna takes a taxi to Guardian Baptist Church, even though it is only a few blocks from the Plaza. Her body is stiff and sore, every muscle screaming to get back in bed. Each time she breathes, the pain reminds the nineteen-year-old of Rodney and what happened in the alley.

I've got to get that bastard out of my head.

The cab lets her out in front of the ornate building she saw in the flight magazine article, "The Churches of New York." She spends a minute studying the statue of Gabriel near the entrance. Its face is identical to that of the mysterious stranger.

The service is about to get underway when the teenager slides into a pew near the back of the half-filled church. The singing and prayers soon take her mind off her problems. The inspiring sermon is about angels and how they often walk among us. The pastor makes the point that the spiritual world sometimes intersects with the physical one.

After the service, MaryAna decides to walk the several blocks back to her hotel. It is another warm day in Manhattan, and the sun feels soothing to her battered body. Before long, she is lost in her own thoughts.

As the nineteen-year-old strolls along, she senses someone behind her, but a glance over her shoulder proves she is alone. MaryAna picks up the pace, and she crosses the next intersection just before the light goes to red. As she reaches the opposite curb, a sharp honk startles her and as she whips around, a man hops up onto the sidewalk.

"Hello, MaryAna," says the man with the face of a statue.

She nearly smiles. "I thought I'd lost you . . . or that you'd given me up for dead."

"No."

"I need to apologize. I didn't heed your warning about choosin' my friends carefully. I did some stupid things that led to . . . well, very bad other things."

"What do you see yourself doing now, MaryAna?"

"I've stopped drinkin'. That's a good start, isn't it? I just went to church and asked for forgiveness."

"So, you wish to turn your life around?" he says, and they start walking down the block.

"I do."

"You must prove the sincerity of your repentance."

"I was assaulted—isn't that punishment enough?"

"I know it was a horrible experience and you suffered greatly."

"Do you know what Rodney did to me?"

"Yes."

"I begged for help—why didn't you do anything?"

"I never left your side, but I could not intervene."

"Why not?"

"Your own choices put you in harm's way. A sinful lifestyle is like dancing with the devil."

"So, what happened to me was because of my sins?"

"They led to you losing your money, your job, and being in that alley. You must now repent if you want to change your life."

"I've already suffered so much. I don't know if I can take any more."

"Repentance is not suffering for your sins, but sorrow for them. Are you truly remorseful?"

"Yes. I had no idea everything could go so wrong."

"In that case, God has a task for you. Lucifer has once again aligned himself with powerful allies here on earth. Our Lord has chosen you to disrupt their operations."

"Me? I have trouble dealin' with my own demons. How can I . . .?"

"You have shown uncommon courage and determination in stressful times. This task will be your repentance."

MaryAna gasps for breath. "What if I fail?"

"The true measure of success is in the effort put forth, not necessarily in the results."

"What do I get to do all this—do I get a magic sword or something? My own superpowers?"

"Your friends are your superpower. Your faith is your weapon."

"I don't have a lot of friends left."

"You still have some—and you have not lost your faith."

"The Lord's askin' a lot from a country girl like me."

"More than he asked of Moses in facing the Pharaoh? More than David when he fought Goliath? More than Joan of Arc or Mother Teresa?"

"When you put it that way—so, who am I going to fight?"

"You already know some of them."

"I bet Vladimir is part of all this. So, what is the thing . . . the task I'm supposed to do?"

"All will be revealed in time."

"Talkin' to you is like wanting to know what happened on *Lost*. I've got like a zillion questions."

"You can always talk to me, MaryAna. Or with our Lord."

"You mean I should pray." She sighs. "I've kinda gotten out of the habit."

They stop at the next corner, and the teenager glances up at the traffic light. When she turns back to the stranger, he is gone.

How does he do that? Unless he ducked into that pizza place . . .

***

By the time MaryAna reaches the Plaza, her lower back is killing her. She draws a hot bath, but it does little to relieve the pain.

As she soaks, she mulls over the stranger's words. The more she tries to recall them, the more dreamlike they seem. Not sure what to believe, MaryAna fears the conversation was a product of her overactive imagination.

Maybe it was prompted by that sermon.

While the teenager relaxes on her bed after her bath, her iPhone rings. It is her friend Nathan in Mississippi.

"Hey, you found Vladimir yet?"

"Good afternoon to you too."

"Sorry. So, what did you find out?"

"I'm almost certain your con man's real name isn't Vladimir Volkow. He used that name to open the account where you wired the money. The money's gone, and the account's closed."

"Any idea where he or his sister might be?"

"No, but I hacked the Russian Embassy in Washington and—"

"Nathan, you didn't."

"Then I piggybacked a secure communication to the Kremlin. From there, I pretty much had access to a whole bunch of Russian databases."

"You better hope the KGB doesn't come after you."

"The KGB is long gone, MaryAna. Now they have something called the Federal Security Service."

"And?"

"I couldn't access the security service's files, but the Russian military's cyber-security isn't as impressive."

"What'd you learn?"

"A Vladimir Volkow was born in Moscow and joined the Russian military ten years ago. His younger sister, Natasha, still lives there."

"Could that be them?"

"Accordin' to the records, Vladimir was sent to Chechnya where he was an interrogation officer. The Russians have been accused of human rights violations in that region."

"What kind of violations?"

"Mostly torture."

"So, you think Vladimir tortured people?"

"More than likely. That is, until he was murdered five years ago. Rebel dissidents were suspected in his death, but nothing was ever proven."

"He can't be dead."

"His wife, Delaura, sure thought he was. Two months after her husband's murder, she married his friend, Dimitri Sokolov. This *friend* was also an interrogation officer in Chechnya. Dimitri and Delaura came to the U.S. on their honeymoon, but there's no record of them returning to Russia—they just dropped off the grid. He has an uncle, Ivan Sokolov, in New York City."

"Vladdy mentioned an uncle. Could Vladimir and Natasha be Dimitri and Delaura?"

"Maybe. Dimitri probably killed her first husband so he could marry her. I couldn't find much info on them, so I focused on his uncle. Unfortunately, I was blocked at every turn."

"By who—the Russians?"

"I don't think so—too sophisticated. I took a quick peek into the NYPD computers. They have an extensive file on Uncle Ivan's illegal activities but have never arrested him."

"Why not?"

"It's not clear. I could try to take a deeper dive into their system, but you know what happened the last time I hacked a police department."

"Yeah, we almost landed in jail. I don't want us to get in trouble again, Nathan. Whatever you do, be careful."

"You're the one who needs to be careful, MaryAna. These are dangerous people."

"I'll bet that's who my guardian angel was warnin' me about."

"Your what?"

"Nothing." MaryAna catches herself eyeing the minibar. "I can take care of myself, Nathan."

If I can stop drinking . . .

Chapter 54

MAX

Late that afternoon, MaryAna takes a taxi to Leon's address in Brooklyn, a two-story colonial-style home in a middle-class Brooklyn neighborhood.

"I like your place," she says when he answers the door.

Leon shows her in. "I grew up in this house. My father died a few years ago, and my mom is in a nursing home, so I more or less inherited this place. What's in the bag?"

"Just some art supplies for Max," MaryAna says, handing them to him.

"Thanks. Max will be tickled."

They are joined in the hallway by a slender young black woman in jeans and a T-shirt. Her ebony eyes sparkle and match the color of her neatly done locks.

"You must be MaryAna. I'm Jasmine. Leon tells me you're from Mississippi."

"That's right. He told me you live in Boston."

"I come back to visit when I can. Come meet my mother."

MaryAna goes along as Leon trails behind the two young women.

"Mom," Jasmine says as they enter the kitchen, "MaryAna's here."

A woman in her mid-forties turns from the stove. She is a slightly heavier version of her daughter. She smiles and wipes her hands on her apron.

"I'm Victoria, but everyone except my husband calls me Vee."

"Thank you so much for invitin' me to your home. It's been a while since I've had a home-cooked meal."

"Mom's an awesome cook." Her daughter gives her mother a hug. "Me, not so much."

"You're still learning, dear," Victoria says. "Now help me set the table while Leon gets Max."

"May I help you, Vee?" MaryAna asks.

As her husband heads off to perform his task, Victoria says, "Why don't you help set the table while I finish up here." She turns to her daughter. "Make sure you use the good china, dear."

Jasmine leads MaryAna into the dining room to a cherry dining table with six chairs. Against the far wall is a matching china cabinet.

Jasmine opens the top drawer of the cabinet to reveal a shiny set of silverware. "Will you put those out while I take down the china?"

"Looks like someone just polished these."

"Mom and I did when Dad said you were coming to dinner. We don't get many visitors—you know, with Max and all."

"You have some beautiful antiques in this house. Your parents have great taste in furniture."

Her new friend chuckles. "These aren't really antiques, just old. My stepfather's family has lived here for well over a century. Much of the furniture is original."

Leon soon returns with his son, who is holding the bag of art supplies MaryAna brought. Max has wavy black hair and matching eyes and is a couple inches taller than his sister.

Leon introduces his son to MaryAna, but he does not make eye contact.

"Thank MaryAna for the present," Leon instructs.

Max glances up, mumbles "Thanks," and returns his stare to the floor.

"You're welcome. Thank you for the lovely birthday present. The angel on the bridge looks a lot like me."

"It is you," he replies, still looking down.

"How did you know what I looked like?"

Max sits down at the table without responding.

"Our boy is still working on his social skills," Leon explains, also taking a chair.

Victoria enters from the kitchen with a large white bowl of mashed potatoes and places it on the center of the table. Jasmine and MaryAna help her retrieve the remainder of the meal, including a pot roast.

When everyone is seated, Leon says a short prayer, then they all dig in.

"Leon tells me you've been staying at the Plaza," his wife says as she passes a bowl of carrots to her husband. "How do you like it there?"

"It's wonderful," MaryAna tells her. "But I'll be movin' out this comin' week."

"Where will you go?" Jasmine asks, helping herself to the green beans.

"I'm not sure yet. I was gonna share an apartment, but that fell through. Then I lost my job. I need to find another, and an inexpensive place to live. Otherwise, I'll have to go back home."

"That's unfortunate." Victoria glances at her husband. "Honey, you didn't tell me about her problems. You know this city. You should help her."

Before Leon can answer, MaryAna says, "Thanks, ma'am, but I got myself into this mess, and I gotta be the one to get myself out of it."

"Well, dear, if you think of any way we can be of assistance, please let Leon know."

Although Max remains silent throughout dinner, the others engage in lively conversation. As they finish their apple pie, the boy leans over and whispers something to his mother.

Victoria turns to MaryAna. "Max has another painting for you. It's in his room."

"I'd love to see it," MaryAna tells him.

Max scoots his chair back and rises from the table. "Just you."

MaryAna looks at everyone and then also rises. "I guess I'll be back shortly."

He leads her upstairs to his bedroom. The rest of his family gathers at the bottom of the stairway. The young man ushers her inside the room and shuts the door.

Max's room is sparsely furnished with a single bed and a dresser. There is also a small table with various art supplies. The walls are covered in posters of famous paintings, including the Mona Lisa. Near one of the walls is an easel with a canvas sitting on it, facing the bedroom's only window. Max picks it up and hands it to MaryAna.

"For you," he says, still not making eye contact.

"Thank you, Max."

The painting portrays several men seated at tables across from scantily clad young women with creamy-colored skin. Each girl has a small pair of angel wings, but their attire is more suited for a bedroom than a barroom. The dark colors of the men's dingy work clothes contrast with the bright hues of the angels' attire.

In the middle of the scene, a blond beauty has spread her wings as if she is about to take flight, but a woman in black is grabbing her wrist and attempting to drag her away.

Whoa, quite a difference from the painting of me in the park.

"This is really unique, Max. What inspired you to paint this one?"

Without answering, Max picks up a pillow from his bed, removes the pillowcase, and slides the painting inside.

Max hands it back to her. "Only for you."

"I always name my paintings. I'll call this one 'Angels in the Big Apple.' Is that all right with you?"

MaryAna nearly jumps when Max looks directly at her and speaks up for the first time since she arrived. "They need you."

"Who needs me?"

"They're in trouble."

"What kind of trouble?"

He looks away again. "It's a secret," he says, mumbling once more.

"I can't help them if I don't know what's going on—"

"They need you."

"Yeah, I get that, Max. Where are they?"

The boy shrugs.

"How will I find them?"

286

He does not respond, opens the door, and leaves the bedroom. A bewildered MaryAna follows him downstairs.

"What's with the pillowcase?" Leon asks when they reach the bottom of the stairs.

"Max put my paintin' in there to protect it. I'll make sure you get the pillowcase back."

"No need," Victoria says. "It's an old one."

MaryAna starts to slide the painting out to show them, but Max speaks up once again.

"Only for you. Not them!"

"Max!" his mother snaps. "Behave yourself. MaryAna just wants to share it with us."

"No. Only for her."

Victoria turns to MaryAna. "I don't know what has gotten into him. This is the first time he's been so particular about one of his paintings."

"Has Max ever had art lessons where they used models?"

Leon answers. "He just paints from memory, like the one of Central Park. Do you like this one?"

"I do." MaryAna chooses her words carefully. "It's very unique. Your son has a vivid imagination."

***

That night at the hotel, MaryAna removes the painting from the pillowcase and props it up at one end of the sofa. She settles on the other end and studies the image in detail.

What in the world would inspire him to paint this?

She checks out each of the men, then the angels. The nineteen-year-old does not recognize any of their faces, and although some are blondes, none resemble her. The woman in black is clearly the most dynamic character, reminding MaryAna of evil witches and fairy tales. She stares as the image for nearly ten minutes, but finally gives up, concluding that if there is a meaning or some sort of secret message within the painting, she cannot find it.

Max's desire for secrecy and his message that the girls "need her help" is more than a little weird, she thinks. She suddenly flashes on her old Sunday school Bible studies.

Noah, Moses, Joshua, and David all had clear instructions of what God expected of them, but I don't remember them ever getting a weird painting or someone telling them about some unknown cosmic plot.

Without thinking, she hops off the sofa and reaches for the door to the minibar, but once again stops herself from opening it.

If Max and his painting are telling me to be some kind of a holy warrior, I should be a sober one.

Chapter 55

HELGA

After breakfast at a nearby diner Monday morning, MaryAna returns to her suite. With just two more nights at the Plaza, she has a decision to make.

The nineteen-year-old sits down at the desk with a pen and paper and jots down all her possibilities:

- Return to Mississippi, share the house with Carleigh, and get a job.
- Live with Mama and Coach Brown and go to college.
- Stay in New York and ask Mama for money while looking for a job and a place to live.
- Become Mr. Rubenstein's mistress while I look for Vladdy.

MaryAna wracks her brain for more choices, but nothing else comes to mind. One by one, she crosses out the first three.

She reconsiders Mel's offer of an apartment, but she refuses to be with a married man, so scratch that one too.

Frustrated, MaryAna goes to the bedroom and gathers up her purses and handbags. She has a habit of stuffing change into them— both the jingling and folding kind.

Right now, every cent counts.

She dumps the contents of the first handbag onto the bedspread. No money, but she finds Elton's business card, which she immediately tosses into the wastebasket.

I should've put my money in his bank.

She finds $2.73 in change in the next handbag, along with Carson's business card, then bingo—two one hundred-dollar bills he had left for her.

By the time she has checked them all, she has recovered $211.76, and a book of matches with the word MATRYOSHKA on it.

Hey, this's the matchbook Vladdy gave me!

She flips it over and her heart flutters when she sees a phone number on the other side.

She calls the number and gets a recorded message in both Russian and English—Matryoshka is the name of a club open 6:00 pm till midnight Monday through Saturday, and the address is in the Brighton Beach area of Brooklyn.

Does Vladdy hang out at this place? Right now it's the only clue I've got.

***

Just before seven that evening, a taxi pulls up to the address from the recording, a nondescript windowless red-brick building, save for the sign spelling out Matryoshka in neon above the door. MaryAna, wearing a sleeveless aquamarine evening dress and fishnet stockings, pays the cabbie and steps inside the club.

Though the place looks nothing like Boots 'n Heels or any of the night spots she had frequented in Mississippi, she has a moment of déjà vu nonetheless, which persists as she steps into the dark entranceway.

A hostess in her mid-thirties stands behind a wooden podium, which is situated in front of a wall that blocks MaryAna's view of the club's interior. The woman looks up and says something that MaryAna figures is Russian.

"I'm sorry, ma'am. I don't understand—do you speak English?"

"Are you here for waitress job?" the hostess says without expression.

"I . . . yes, that's right—I'm here for the waitress job."

"You must talk to manager. I tell Helga you here." She picks up a phone, punches in two digits, then nods toward the main room. "Go wait by bar."

MaryAna winds her way around the podium and the wall to the club's interior. But instead of a bustling disco with drinking, dancing, and boisterous conversation, she finds a rather subdued scene. The dimly lit main room has a dark-brown tile floor and paneled walls, which only lends to the dingy, cave-like feel of the club.

To MaryAna's left is a short bar with no barstools. Nearly two-dozen smallish tables are spread throughout the room, each with two chairs. There is no dance floor—or music, for that matter. The only sounds are muffled conversation and the occasional tinkling of glasses.

A dozen or so young women are seated at the tables, each attired in brightly colored, lacey undergarments, covered only with see-through dressing gowns, which brings back MaryAna's feeling of déjà vu.

Oh my gosh, feels almost like Max's painting.

At some of the tables, men are conversing with the women. They are drinking, but the women are not. MaryAna scans the room as she heads toward the bar, but Vladimir does not appear to be present. The middle-aged bartender looks her up and down as she approaches but says nothing.

"The lady at the front told me to wait here for Helga," she tells him. "I'm MaryAna. I'm here for the waitress job."

"Oh, OK." The bartender smiles and offers his hand. "I'm Charlie. Nice to meet you."

"Same," she says, as they shake hands. "I'm surprised at your accent."

"My accent?"

"Oh, sorry. I mean, I thought you'd have a Russian accent. But you sound like a New Yorker."

"Local boy, born and bred," Charlie says, as he wipes down the bar. "By the way, don't let her scare you off."

"Don't let who scare me off?"

"Helga. She's not the warm, fuzzy type. If I had to make a guess, I'd say she's ex-military."

"I'm not intimidated easily."

He winks. "Good for you, honey."

MaryAna nods toward two doors beyond the bar to the left, each with a sign she cannot read. "Are those the restrooms?"

"Yeah. The one on the right is ladies."

"Thanks. I need to freshen up. Be right back."

When she returns several minutes later, the hostess is at the bar talking with Charlie.

"Helga will see you in about ten minutes," she says.

Charlie smiles at them. "Something to drink while you're waiting, ladies?"

"Maybe some water?" MaryAna says.

The hostess frowns. "We no supposed to drink at work."

Charlie sighs, then scoops ice into a glass and fills it with water, before placing it on the bar for MaryAna.

Olga huffs and returns to her hostess station.

As the nineteen-year-old sips her water, she watches as one of the young women gets up from her table and leads the man with her to a red door on the back wall, where she presses what looks like a doorbell. A moment later there is a buzzer sound, and the door pops open. The man and woman proceed through it.

These girls are selling something—and I don't think it's Girl Scout cookies.

MaryAna turns to Charlie. "Do I need to speak Russian to work here?"

"Actually, Helga would prefer that you don't."

"Why not?"

"She doesn't want you listening in on the conversations."

"Do you speak Russian, Charlie?"

"Enough to get by."

"So, what's beyond the red door?"

Charlie clears his throat. "I . . . um, don't know—or care to know. It's above my pay grade."

A few minutes later, another buzzer sounds and the red door flies open. A tall lanky woman with no makeup enters the room, holding a single sheet of paper. With her high-collared black dress and dour expression, she approaches the bar.

Whoa, I think there's a Disney movie missing its wicked witch.

"My name Helga. You want waitress job?"

"I do, yes."

"You got experience?"

"Last year, I was a cocktail waitress at a club back home."

"You look nice. You speak Russian?"

"I only know a couple of words."

Helga says something to her in Russian, but MaryAna does not understand.

"Sorry, I said I only know a couple words."

Helga chuckles and hands MaryAna the application form. "Fill out and leave with Charlie. I call you tomorrow."

Before MaryAna can respond, Helga turns and walks away to one of the tables, where she says something to the girl seated there. Then she leaves back through the red door.

MaryAna digs out a pen from her purse and fills out the form. When she has finished, she hands it to the bartender. "That was a quick interview. I'm surprised she wanted me to fill out the application."

"The Russians can be unpredictable, but you should get the job."

"Does it pay well?"

"It's the only reason I work here," he says. "And they don't report to the IRS, so it's tax free, if you're OK with that."

"Isn't that illegal?"

He grins. "They get away with a lot more than tax evasion. Don't worry, you won't get in trouble. The authorities don't hassle them or seem to care what goes on here."

"What, they pay off the cops or something?"

Charlie shrugs. "Don't know. Don't care."

"What was that that Helga said to me in Russian?"

"She insulted you to see if you understood the language. The fact that you didn't react told her all she needed to know."

"Can I ask—what did she say?"

"She more or less called you a stupid slut with questionable ancestry."

Maybe I should memorize one or two good ones when I run into Vladdy . . .

Chapter 56

ELENA

MaryAna's cell rings at 9:00 Tuesday morning, waking her from a sound sleep. She does not recognize the caller ID and almost lets it go to voicemail before realizing it could be Helga from the Russian bar—so she sits up and answers the call. It is indeed Helga calling to let MaryAna know she got the job and how much it will pay. "Also," Helga says, "you keep tips, but no give girls drinks. And they do not talk to you."

"I understand, ma'am."

"We open at six. Charlie give you instructions. We close midnight and not open Sundays."

"OK, got it."

"Application say you live at Plaza Hotel. It is expensive place."

"It's temporary. I'm lookin' for an apartment."

"When move, tell me address. You start tonight, OK?"

"I'll be there."

After getting off the phone, MaryAna decides to take a bath. The scent of lavender bath beads relaxes her as she soaks in the oversized tub. The silence is refreshing to her, as if she has slid into a dream world, one free of decisions and responsibility.

Maybe Andy will let me live at his cottage.

She soon steps out of the tub and dries herself off, armed with a new option. She texts Andre, asking him to call. While MaryAna waits to hear from him, she decides to take a walk in Central Park. In the lobby, she sees Leon manning the front doors as usual.

"Miss Lindley. I was going to contact you."

"What's up?"

"My wife and I are worried about you. Have you found a place to live?"

"Not yet."

"Would you like to stay with us until you find something more suitable?"

"That's so sweet, but—"

"Jasmine won't be back in town until at least Thanksgiving, so her room is available."

"I wouldn't want to intrude . . ."

Leon waves his hand. "I insist. With our daughter in Boston, Victoria could use some female companionship."

"When you put it that way, how can I refuse? I got a job, so I can pay rent."

"Save your money. You'll need it to get a place of your own."

"Are you sure Jasmine won't mind me takin' her room?"

"She's the one who suggested it."

MaryAna wipes away a tear. "I can't believe you and your family."

***

After making arrangements with Leon to move her belongings to his house the following day, MaryAna heads over to the park. As she approaches the pond, she receives a call from Andre. No longer needing a place to stay, she makes up a quick excuse for calling him.

"Hey, Andy. I was hopin' we could get together again."

"I'd love to, MaryAna, but I'm in Atlanta, waiting for my flight to Mississippi. I have an interview with Coach Brown."

"That's awesome. I hope you get to meet JoeE and Coree—and my stepbrother Clay."

"I'll make a point of it. You wouldn't believe how nervous I am."

"You'll be fine. Coach Brown is a good guy even though we've had our differences."

"What happened?"

"He thought I was a bad influence on my stepbrother. So,

mentioning me to my stepfather might do more harm than good."

"Before I meet with him, I have an interview with USM's defensive coordinator, JJ Butler. Do you know him?"

"He's Coree's father, was a teacher at my high school, and also my karate instructor. You'll like him."

"So, you know karate?"

She giggles. "That's right. Don't mess with me, mister, or I'll go Chuck Norris on you."

He laughs. "I took karate lessons when I was young. We'll have to spar sometime."

"As long as you're ready to be knocked on your butt."

"I know a gym where we can settle this. You found a job yet?"

"I start at a club tonight."

Andy chuckles. "As a bouncer?"

"Funny. No, I'll tell you all about it when you get back. Good luck with the interviews, Andy."

"Thanks, I'll need it."

***

MaryAna makes sure to arrive at the Matryoshka Club before six that evening. Once there, she enters and goes to the bar.

"Hey, Charlie. Helga told me to see you for instructions."

"Not much to it. Customers pay a cover to Olga at the door. For that, the men get to talk with the girls and receive a coupon for a drink of their choice. You collect the coupon when they order."

"Sounds easy enough."

Charlie wipes down the bar. "After the men finish their drink, they either leave the club or go with a girl through the red door. Few of them leave."

"Have you ever been through that door yourself?"

"I've taken drinks to an office back there. There are usually a couple guys in the hallway with guns. Security, I suppose. There are also several closed doors, each with a number on it. I can only guess what goes on there," he says, using air quotes.

MaryAna leans closer. "The girls are all prostitutes, right?"

"Remember what I told you about asking too many questions? Helga runs a tight ship, and Olga passes on what she hears."

MaryAna smiles. "Sometimes, I'm too curious for my own good."

"Be careful about that." Charlie points to an area behind the bar. "You can put your purse in one of those cubbies."

More than a dozen young women come through the red door, each finding their own table. Like the night before, they are scantily clad and do not make eye contact.

"I'm goin' to the lady's room," MaryAna tells the bartender. "Be right back."

"Better hurry, it's almost six. You don't want Helga upset with you."

MaryAna is surprised at how busy the club is for a Tuesday night. Nearly all the customers speak English, most with thick Eastern European accents. She becomes used to vodka pronounced as "wod-ka."

Around ten o'clock, one of the young women sitting alone has a dry coughing fit. Like MaryAna, she has long blond hair. MaryAna catches Charlie's attention. "Give me some water, please."

The bartender complies, and she takes a glassful to the young woman's table.

Helga said the girls can't talk to me, but she didn't say I couldn't talk to them. This girl looks a lot like the angel in the middle of Max's painting.

"Here," MaryAna says, setting the glass down. "This should help that cough."

The blonde looks up, her eyes wide.

MaryAna nods toward the glass and points to her throat. "For your cough."

The young woman takes a sip. "Spasiba," she says in a hushed voice.

MaryAna smiles. *The third Russian word I've learned tonight.*

"Do you speak English?"

The young lady looks up again, nods, and holds her thumb and forefinger apart slightly.

"Oh, I get it. Just a little?"

The blonde nods again.

"If you need more water, let me know."

The young woman glances around and whispers. "My name Elena Shevchenko, from Ukraine."

Olga comes out of the ladies room and spots MaryAna at Elena's table. She immediately heads over to them.

"Do you talk to her?" the hostess asks.

"I just brought her some water. She was coughing."

Olga gives her a stern look and returns to her station.

Less than a minute later, Helga barges through the red door. Dressed in black as before, she walks directly to Elena's table, picks up the glass, then heads to the bar. She steps in front of MaryAna.

"Did you give girl drink?"

"It's just water. She was coughin'."

"I told you, no give girls drink."

"I thought you meant alcohol."

Helga grits her teeth. "Did she talk to you?"

"She said 'Spasiba.'"

"That all?"

MaryAna nods.

"No talk to girls, or I let you go."

"Sorry. It won't happen again."

Helga turns and marches over to Elena's table, grabs her wrist, and takes her through the red door.

OK, that was just like Max's painting—except for the angel wings.

MaryAna turns to Charlie. "What was that about? Is she gonna get in trouble?"

The bartender shrugs. "Probably, yeah."

"All I did was get her some water."

Charlie pats MaryAna on the shoulder. "These folks live in a different world, honey. Don't try to figure it out."

Does this have to do with what my task is supposed to be?

Chapter 57

MOVING DAY

Early Wednesday afternoon, Leon helps MaryAna gather up her belongings at the hotel. On the way out, she sees Samson by himself at the bellman's desk. When she waves to him, he glances at her, then turns away.

MaryAna marches over to the bellman and taps him on the shoulder. He turns to face her, tenses up, and grits his teeth.

"You can hate me, Samson, but don't you dare ignore me."

He steps back as if surprised. "I hear you're checking out, Miss Lindley. Do you need assistance?"

"Look," she says, her voice soft, "it was my fault things got weird between us. Can we just forget what happened and be friends again?"

The bellman looks around as if to make sure no one is listening. "You want to be friends?" His toothy grin reappears. "Yeah, sure. Why not?"

"I really do like you. Good luck on Broadway."

"Are you going back home?"

"I'm movin' to Brooklyn. Got a job there. I'll remember one thing for sure about the Plaza."

"What's that?"

"That Sam's the man."

He smiles. "Be safe, Mississippi."

***

"So, tell me about your new job," Leon says as he drives MaryAna to his address in Brooklyn.

"Not much to tell. I'm workin' evenings as a cocktail waitress at a Russian club in Brighton Beach."

"Oh, OK." He pulls to a stop for a red light. "Don't mean to be nosy, but some of those places have bad reputations."

"It's temporary. I believe the guy who ripped me off might show up there. After I find him and get my money back, I'll decide whether or not to stay in New York."

Leon turns to her as the light goes to green. "Shouldn't that be a matter for the police?"

"I doubt the cops will be able to find the guy. I hope I can."

"Just be careful, MaryAna. That part of Brooklyn is dangerous."

It is not long before they have arrived at Leon's house. "You're welcome to stay with us as long as you want," he says, opening the trunk.

"That's so nice of you and your family. You have no idea how much I appreciate it."

The nineteen-year-old pulls a suitcase from the backseat. Leon takes two others from the trunk.

"After we get these to your room, you should start unpacking. I'll bring up the rest of your belongings."

"Sounds like a plan, Leon."

Once they are in the house, Victoria greets the teenager with a hug. "I was so glad when Leon told me you accepted our invitation."

"It's so sweet of you, Vee."

"Let's get you settled in." Victoria leads them upstairs to Jasmine's bedroom.

Leon sets a suitcase on the bed. "Be right back," he says, heading back down to the car.

MaryAna opens the suitcase, which contains several of her dresses. As she takes them out, Victoria puts them on hangers.

"You certainly have wonderful taste in clothes, young lady."

MaryAna grins. "I love to shop." MaryAna lifts a second suitcase onto the bed. "Did Leon tell you how I got ripped off?"

"He did. I'm so sorry." Victoria holds up one of the crumpled dresses. "This is cute." She glances at the label. "Oh my! It's a Chanel, but it needs a good dry cleaning."

MaryAna recalls how she tossed that dress to the floor the night she danced on her bed.

My gosh, that wasn't even a month ago.

"Several of these are really wrinkled. Is there a dry cleaners close by?"

Victoria picks up another dress to hang up. "There's a shop just a few blocks away."

"I'll show her."

MaryAna and Victoria turn to see Max standing in the doorway, his head pointed downward, as usual.

"Max," Victoria says. "What do you mean?"

His head tilts up slightly. "I'll show her where the store is."

"Hey, great," MaryAna says. "We can go as soon as I unpack."

Victoria steps over to her son and puts her hand on his arm. "The shop isn't far, but I'm not sure Max knows the way—"

"I'll show her," he says louder, his arms by his side, but his hands now fists.

"Max . . ."

For a microsecond, her son looks directly into Victoria's eyes, before his gaze once again drops to the floor. "I'll show her."

MaryAna hangs up another dress. "It's OK with me if he comes along. I could use the company."

Victoria shakes her head. "I don't know what's gotten into him. He's been anxious since we told him you were going to stay with us. Maybe teenage hormones kicking in or something."

"I have to go."

Victoria faces her son, her arms crossed. "Why, Max—why do you have to go?"

"I need to show her something."

"Can't you show her here?"

He shakes his head in two definite motions. "It's a secret. Can I go, Mom? Please?"

"I'm sure we'll be fine," MaryAna says.

"I don't know, MaryAna. I've never let him go off with someone new like this before."

MaryAna puts her hand on Victoria's arm. "We won't be long. I promise I'll keep an eye on him."

***

Half an hour later, MaryAna and Max are on their way to the dry cleaners. She carries a garment bag over her shoulder, which contains several of her designer dresses. Max walks with his arms at his sides. They stroll past homes similar to Leon and Victoria's, many of which are over a century old.

"I think I've found the angels," MaryAna tells Max. "They work at a club in Brighton Beach called Matryoshka." She stops and turns to him. "It's called Matryoshka. Do you know of that place?"

He stops a couple steps ahead. "What angels?" he says, his gaze downward.

"The ones in your paintin'. Don't you remember?"

"Painting?"

"The painting you did for me. The painting you gave me the last time I was at your house. You remember that, don't you?"

He glances up and then back toward the sidewalk.

"Max, the girls in your painting who are in trouble. You said they needed me to help them?"

Max turns and continues walking.

MaryAna sighs and hurries to catch up. "Max, I'm pretty sure you've never been to that club before—how do you know about those girls?"

He says nothing and continues on until he reaches the intersection. He waits until the light changes and the WALK sign comes on. MaryAna takes his hand and they cross to the other side. They step onto the curb, but Max does not let go. Instead, he squeezes her hand tight.

A tingling, then a rush of something surges through her arm, her shoulder, then her. MaryAna's stomach drops and the world goes black.

***

I thought I was gonna throw up . . . what's—I can't see.

I can't move. I'm . . . tied up. To a chair. Why can't I see any—wait, I'm blindfolded . . . and there's something in my mouth—I'm gagged! Oh my God—my clothes—I'm naked!

It hurts all over—like I got beat up . . .

I gotta wake up I gotta wake up I gotta wake up oh God let me wake up.

Somewhere a door opens and closes, and then . . . footsteps.

A whisper of sandalwood tickles her nose and MaryAna freezes.

Vladimir.

"This isn't the first time you've broken the rules, Elena. But it will be the last."

Elena? Is she tied up too?

The blindfold is yanked off and MaryAna blinks in the dim glow of the lightbulb dangling from the ceiling of the dingy storeroom. She whips her head around, but Elena is nowhere to be seen. Vladimir, in a black T-shirt and jeans, towers over MaryAna with a greasy smirk—reminescent of Rodney's in the warehouse alley—that makes her stomach heave.

"I went easy on you last go-round, Elena." He slips the gag off MaryAna's mouth and slaps her.

She lets out a hoarse scream that echoes throughout the dank storeroom.

"Heh, that never gets old."

Before MaryAna can speak, Vladimir punches her square in her mid-section. Bile fills her throat and she retches. Another punch, this time to the chest. There is a sickening crack from somewhere inside her, and white-hot lava fills her lungs.

A third punch—to the jaw, breaking her nose. MaryAna screams again, but she cannot muster the same volume as before. She floats in and out of consciousness, hanging on to a vague hope that somehow, it will all be over soon.

Vladimir grabs a fistful of MaryAna's hair and jerks her head close. "Don't you dare pass out on me, bitch—I'm just getting started."

He reaches over to a shelf and grabs a stainless-steel knife, brandishing it in front of her.

"Say hello to my little friend."

This is it . . .

***

MaryAna and Max stand in front of the dry cleaners. Several cars drive by in the late afternoon traffic. She blinks and looks around, as Max lets go of her hand.

"Max, what the hell was that . . . look at me!"

He tilts his head up. "He wanted you to see."

"Who?"

"The angel."

"Is that what I'm supposed to do—save Elena? Is she the one they're hurting? Max?"

He lowers his gaze away from her once more.

Am I losing my freaking mind?

Chapter 58

THE NOTE

About a dozen young women pass through the red door at the club Wednesday evening, but Elena is not among them.

Was what I saw real? Did Vladdy torture her?

As the night wears on, MaryAna takes a closer look at the girls, noting that several have bruises.

They're probably illegals who can't go to the police.

And still no sign of Vladimir—when is he gonna show up?

What do I do when he does?

I'll just cross that bridge—when and if.

***

The next morning, MaryAna calls her friend Nathan in Mississippi.

"I need you to check on a Ukrainian girl named Elena Shevchenko."

"Who? I'm still at work, by the way."

"Please, Nathan—it's important. I might have gotten her into serious trouble."

"What do you know about her?"

"Early twenties, blond hair, blue eyes. She works at a club called Matryoshka in Brooklyn and speaks some English. Oh, and like I said, she's from Ukraine."

"What does she do at the club?"

"She's a prostitute. There's about twelve or so girls who work there."

"How do you know her?"

"I, um, I work there too."

"So . . . you're a *hooker?*"

"Heavens no! I know that Vladimir goes there, so I went lookin' for him, and they hired me as a cocktail waitress. It's the perfect cover—I can hang around without causing suspicion until he shows up."

"You're unbelievable, MaryAna. First you work at a strip club and now this place. Why the interest in this girl?"

"I think Elena's in the U.S. illegally. The manager got all upset at me for talkin' to her."

"What are you gonna do if Vladimir shows?"

"I'll have him arrested. Of course, I might have to rough him up a bit before I deliver him to the police."

"What? Can't you just let it go before someone gets hurt—like you."

"I want my money back, and Vladdy has it."

"It's not worth you workin' in a place like that. Just come back home."

"I can't, Nathan. These girls need my help."

"You're in over your head, MaryAna."

"It's nice you're worried about me, but I can take care of myself."

"I'm not so sure about that. Please be careful."

"That's the plan."

***

Thursday is a busy night at the club with men in and out of the red door every few minutes. But again, Elena is not among the girls working this night.

"That western shirt and jeans look good on you," Charlie tells her as she waits for the next customer.

"So, you like my American-girl look? This lets the customers know I'm off limits. I've had several ask me to go through the door with them."

"I thought you were curious about what goes on back there."

"Not that curious, Charlie."

"I'm pretty sure you're safe—Helga has her rules. Of course, I like cowgirls. How about you go back there with me?"

MaryAna glares at him.

He holds up his hands in surrender. "Just kidding."

As the evening progresses, the nineteen-year-old notices the girls periodically making eye contact with her. They do not smile, but neither do they ignore her presence. Like they want to say something to her but for whatever reason cannot do it.

Soon another customer arrives, and after a brief browse around the room, joins a brunette at her table. MaryAna collects his coupon and returns to the bar with his order.

"Another Vodka Collins, Charlie. That seems to be the go-to drink tonight."

"You OK, MaryAna? You seem kinda jumpy."

"I actually don't feel well," she says.

Could part of it be withdrawal from alcohol?

"I may need to go home early."

Charlie finishes the drink and sets it on the bar for her. "Do you want some water or something?"

"No, thanks." MaryAna leans on the bar and whispers. "You're my friend, right?"

"Of course."

She nods toward the tables. "Are these girls forced to work here?"

"You really don't want to know the answer to that," he says. "Better to just let it be."

"I can't work here anymore. This is gonna be my last night."

The bartender frowns. "Sorry to hear that. You've been a breath of fresh air around here. You going to tell Helga, or shall I?"

"I'll tell her after we close," MaryAna says, picking up the drink for the customer.

I'll have to find Vladdy some other way.

Several minutes later another customer enters the club and sits at a table with a girl with dark-brown, shoulder-length hair. MaryAna hurries over to take the man's order, and as she does so, the girl quickly slips something into MaryAna's palm. MaryAna is momentarily confused, as the girl barely made eye contact, but she does not say anything. Back at the bar, she slips the object, a tightly folded paper towel, into her jeans pocket.

After serving the customer his drink, she goes to the ladies room and into a stall, where she unfolds the towel. On it are six words written in lipstick.

That girl risked a lot to give me this.

MaryAna stuffs it back into her pocket and heads back out to the main room. She eases over to the bar and whispers to Charlie.

"Don't mention anything to Helga about me quittin'. I've decided to stay."

"What changed your mind?"

"I think God wants me here."

Charlie chuckles and returns to his work.

MaryAna takes out her phone and holds it up like she is checking a message, but instead takes a quick photo of the girl who gave her the note.

I'm sure that's against Helga's rules too, but it might come in handy down the road.

Chapter 59

THE POLICE

Unable to sleep, MaryAna tosses and turns, going over the words in the note again and again. Before dawn Friday morning, she calls Nathan.

"Please tell me you found out something about Elena."

"Geez, MaryAna, you know what time it is?"

"It's almost six."

"Try four-forty-five my time." Nathan yawns. "I only got to bed a couple hours ago. I was up trackin' down your mystery girl."

"What'd you find?"

"You know the Russians invaded eastern Ukraine last year, right?"

"What does that have to do with Elena?"

"She probably got caught up in the turmoil. I found a Ukrainian police report about a young woman by the same name who went missin' several months ago."

"You think it's her?"

"Well, Shevchenko is a common name in Ukraine. Your blond friend fits the description."

"Poor Elena."

"Quite a few girls have disappeared from that region of Ukraine. The authorities suspect they've been trafficked outside the country."

"So, the girls at the club have been forced into prostitution?"

"Could be. Have you talked to her again?"

"She hasn't been at work the last two nights. Something's happened to her. One of the other girls slipped me a note last night."

"What did it say?"

"It said, 'Elena need doctor. Please help us.'"

"You have to go to the cops, MaryAna."

"It might make things worse for Elena."

"How can it get any worse? And you could be in danger yourself. Promise me you'll contact the police."

"OK, OK," she says with a sigh. "I'll go this mornin'. There's a police station not far from where I'm stayin'."

"I worry about you."

It's nice to know he still cares about me.

***

After MaryAna hangs up, she puts on a robe and slips into the hallway to visit the bathroom. She notices light from under the door to Max's bedroom. Pausing outside the door, she hears voices from within the room.

She knocks softly. "Max? It's MaryAna—may I come in?"

The voices stop, but there is no response.

"Max?"

MaryAna tries the doorknob, but it is locked.

She raps on the door again, this time harder.

"Are you okay in there, Max . . . *Max*?"

She is about to knock again, when the door is unlocked and opened. Max stands there in his pajamas, his gaze aimed at the floor as usual.

She looks around the room but sees no one else. "Max. I . . . I thought I heard voices. Did you have the radio on?"

Max trembles, as if he is trying to say something while also trying to keep it in.

"You can tell me, Max. You know I can keep a secret—I haven't told anyone about the paintin'. You can trust me."

He glances up at her. "It was the angel."

MaryAna puts her hand on his arm. "What? What was the angel, Max?"

"I was talking to him. And he talked to me."

"Excuse me?"

"He visits me and tells me what to paint."

MaryAna sees a painting on the easel and steps over to get a look at it. The illustration is of a man in a white tailored suit standing on a flight of stairs. She studies the image a moment before looking up at Max, her eyes wide.

"Max, who is this?"

"I told you, the angel."

"I know, but who is the angel?"

Max glances up once more. "Gabriel."

***

Later that morning, MaryAna arrives at the nearby police station. She sits on one of several wooden benches along with eleven other individuals waiting to be called, her arms crossed and her foot tapping nonstop.

The husky sergeant on duty eventually signals for her to come to the counter.

"Name?"

"MaryAna Lindley."

The sergeant enters it into his computer terminal and without looking up, asks, "How may I help you?"

"I want to make a report about . . . um, well, I'm not exactly sure."

The sergeant sighs and turns to MaryAna. "I'm not a mind reader, Miss."

"Sorry, it's kinda like a missin' person."

"Who's missing?"

"Elena Shevchenko."

"Spell that for me."

MaryAna takes her best guess, and he enters the name.

"I'm not sure Elena is actually missin', but she's definitely in trouble and needs a doctor."

"In trouble how?"

"Two nights ago, Helga—that's our manager at the club—got mad at her for talkin' to me. Then last night, one of the girls handed me a note that said Elena needed a doctor. I'm pretty sure that they've all been sex-trafficked."

"Whoa! Slow down. How do you know these girls?"

"We all work at a club called *Matryoshka*."

"That the Russian joint over in Little Odessa?"

MaryAna nods.

"I'm afraid that's a different precinct, Miss Lindley. You need to report all this to the department there."

"Look, I've already waited for almost an hour. Can't you forward it to whoever needs to see it? It's a matter of life and death."

The sergeant glances at the room of people waiting to see him. "Let me get someone who can help you. Please take a seat."

Ten minutes later, a middle-aged man in a well-worn suit comes into the room holding a printout. He scans the crowd, then calls out MaryAna's name.

"That's me," she says, raising her hand.

"I'm Detective Esposito. Please come with me."

The teenager follows the balding detective through a labyrinth of hallways to his cubicle. As he indicates for MaryAna to sit down, his phone rings.

"Esposito," the detective says, answering the call. "I've got someone with me. I'll call you back soon as I'm done." He hangs up and turns to her. "Sorry." His eyes shift to the printout. "It says here you work at the Matryoshka Club and have been sex-trafficked."

"No, not me. I'm a cocktail waitress at the club. It's the other girls who have been trafficked."

"How long have you worked at this club?"

"This is my first week."

He glances at the printout again. "Who's Elena?"

"She's one of the . . . well, one of the other workers at the club."

He sets the printout on the desk. "She a waitress too?"

"No. I think . . . well, I'm pretty sure she's a prostitute."

"You think? She tell you this?"

"The girls dress in really sexy outfits and talk to the men who come into the club and then take them through a red door to the back of

314

the club. Why else would they go back there?"

"These girls tell you what they do?"

"No. They mostly speak Russian."

"Did you witness any exchange of money?"

MaryAna shakes her head. "I think they do that in the back."

"Have you overheard the girls proposition the men?"

"Like I said, they speak Russian. You need to send someone under-cover who understands Russian. That way you'd have proof."

Esposito rolls his eyes. "Thanks for the advice. Have you witnessed these girls having sex with the men?"

"I haven't been in the back area. Charlie, he's our bartender, told me there are men with guns back there."

"Have any of the girls told you they were sex-trafficked?"

"They're not supposed to talk to me."

"What makes you believe they've been trafficked?"

"Last night, one of them handed me this," she says, unfolding the note and handing it to the detective. "My friend Nathan learned from the internet that a girl named Elena Shevchenko is missin' in eastern Ukraine."

Esposito glances at the note. "Why do you think she needs a doctor?"

"Probably because they beat her up for talkin' to me."

"Or maybe she has the flu? Or she could've had an accident. This note is ambiguous at best."

"But I know they've done something to her."

"How do you know that?"

"I . . . had a vision."

He falls back in his chair. "A vision? Who do you think you are, Kreskin?"

"I'm not makin' this up. I saw through Elena's eyes that someone was torturing her."

"And who was that?"

"A Russian named Vladimir—or maybe Dimitri."

"He work at this club too?"

"No. I don't know where he is."

Esposito sighs. "It is OK with you if I make a copy of this note, Miss Lindley?"

MaryAna nods.

The detective scans the note into his computer, then hands it back to her. "Unfortunately, your club is in another precinct. I'll forward this to the vice squad over there. May I get your phone number in case they need to contact you?"

MaryAna gives it to him. "Do you think they'll look into this right away?"

"Your story doesn't really give us much to go on. Other than the note, it's basically guesswork."

"Tonight, I'll try to learn more."

The detective rises from his chair. "We handle a buttload of cases 24/7, Miss Lindley. It may be a while before they can fully investigate this."

"So, basically," MaryAna notes as she stands up, "Elena's pretty far down on the list."

"I didn't say that," he says, his eyes softening. "If this Matryoshka club was in this precinct, I'd take a closer look myself. I'll recommend the other precinct do the same."

Her face softens as well. "Thanks."

In the hallway, he stops and turns to her. "By the way, you may want to consider working someplace else. Some of those Russian clubs have bad reps."

"I won't be there much longer—just long enough to save those girls."

Esposito cocks an eyebrow. "You can't take the law into your own hands, Miss Lindley.'

Someone has to . . . and Someone picked me.

Part 4

DIVINE INTERVENTION

Chapter 60

SOFIA

Back in her room at Leon's house, MaryAna sits on the bed lost in thought regarding Elena and the other women at the club.

I think Detective Esposito wants to help, but even he doesn't know when the other department will get around to investigating the club.

Will it be this week, this month? This fall?

Esposito said to not get involved, that the cops will handle it.

But what if by the time they do, it could be too late to do anything to help Elena?

I have to do something.

I need someone who speaks Russian to go to the club, but it's too dangerous for Izzy.

So, who else do I know who—

MaryAna whips out her phone and selects a number in her contacts.

"Tony, hi."

"Hey. I didn't expect to hear from you again after our last conversation—"

"You once told me you speak multiple languages. By any chance, is one of them Russian?"

"It might be a little rusty, but yeah. Why?"

"I need your help."

"I'm listening."

MaryAna tells him about Vladimir ripping her off, the club, the girls, and the note. She relates what Nathan found on the internet and describes her visit with the detective.

"That's quite a story, but what does it have to do with me speaking Russian?"

"You need to talk to the girl who gave me the note and find out what's goin' on."

"So, you want me to infiltrate a club run by Russian mobsters, make contact with a prostitute, and find out if she and the other girls have been sex-trafficked?"

"And find out what happened to Elena."

"Oh, is that all?"

"Then you back up my story with the police. You've done black ops stuff for the government, so this should be a piece of cake."

"Successful ops start with good intel, MaryAna. I have a buddy in the FBI here in the city. Maybe he can give me the lowdown on this club and the people running it."

"So, you'll help me save the girls?"

"I can't promise anything."

"Elena may be runnin' out of time."

"OK, I'll . . . um, get back to you after I talk to my friend . . ."

"What?"

"Not long ago, you said just talking to me might be misconstrued. Now you want me to go to a club full of call girls. Could that be misconstrued?"

"Tony, I need your help."

"Should I tell Dori what we're doing?"

"Probably not."

***

Less than an hour later, Tony calls back. "The FBI is well aware of the Matryoshka Club, the Russian mobsters who run it, and the sex trafficking."

"So, your buddy will help us?"

"Unfortunately, no. The whole operation is under the protection of the NSA."

"The what?"

"The intelligence arm of the Defense Department. Along with

320

the CIA and FBI, they're responsible for national security. I've done ops for them before."

"What does the club have to do with national security?"

"My friend doesn't know and suggests we steer clear of the whole situation."

"If they won't step in, I doubt the police will either. Those girls are depending on me. Maybe I should go to the newspapers or a TV station."

"Are you insane, MaryAna? You do that, and the Russian mob, the NSA, and heaven knows who else will be after you."

"I've got to do something. Are you going to help me or what?"

"MaryAna . . ."

"Please, Tony. I can't do this by myself."

"OK, will you do exactly what I say and follow my instructions to the letter—no exceptions?"

"Yes, yes, I promise. So, what do we do?"

"Give me the address and I'll go to the club tonight and talk to the girl who gave you the note. What does she look like?"

"I can text you a photo. If you get there soon as we open, she will be alone at one of the tables."

***

That evening, Tony arrives at the club at 6:15. MaryAna, who is taking a drink order from a customer, sees him enter but pays no particular attention to him. Tony scans the room, "considers" the girls at the various tables, and then strolls over to the young woman matching the photo MaryAna sent him. Other than his limp, he looks like any other patron of the club.

"*Privet*," he says, as he seats himself at her table.

After MaryAna delivers the drink to the other customer, she hustles over to Tony's table. "What would you like to drink, sir?"

"Wodka on the rocks," Tony says with a distinct Russian accent.

"May I have your coupon?" As Tony pulls out the ticket, MaryAna catches the eye of the girl, then winks and gives a slight nod toward Tony. The girl's eyes light up and she returns the nod.

321

By the time MaryAna brings his drink, Tony is in a hushed conversation with the young woman. As MaryAna sets down the glass, Helga appears through the red door and marches over to the table. MaryAna's heart freezes, but she does not outwardly react.

"*Privet*," Helga says to Tony.

MaryAna eases away to the bar. She hears them talking in Russian, but the only other word she picks up on is "spasiba."

A moment later, Tony and the girl rise from the table and follow Helga through the red door.

Please watch over them.

Nearly 30 minutes later Tony re-emerges through the door and leaves the club. Twenty minutes after that, the girl who gave MaryAna the note is back at her table, waiting for her next customer.

***

When MaryAna leaves the club that night, Tony is waiting nearby at a prearranged spot in his Mercedes S-550.

Once she is in the car, Tony drives one block, makes a U-turn, then parks in front of a darkened building and cuts the lights and the engine.

"We need to wait here a few minutes."

"What for?"

Tony points down the street. "See the alley next to the club? A black panel van with the girls in the back will pull out onto the street. It will take them to a building where the Russians keep them when they're not working. We're gonna follow them there."

"Then what?"

"We'll watch. You were right, by the way. These girls were forced into prostitution."

"So, you'll help me save them?"

Tony nods. "I'm working on a rescue plan."

"What changed your mind?"

"I realized how I'd feel if you or Dori were sex-trafficked. These girls have families, friends, and sweethearts who want justice—I can't just look away."

"Thank you. You don't know how much this means to me. By the way, I thought we were dead when Helga went to your table. What did she say?"

"She offered me a discount since it was my first time at the club: one girl for half off or pay full price and be with two of them."

"Geez, it's like the early bird special at the cafeteria."

"But a lot pricier," he says. "Even the discount took most of my cash."

"Tony! You didn't have sex with that girl . . . did you?"

He chuckles. "You jealous?"

"Don't tease me. Did she open up to you about everything?"

"Yep, she told me plenty. Her name is Sofia, by the way."

"What about Elena—where is she?"

"She's at the location where they keep the girls."

"Is she OK?"

"Beaten up pretty bad, but alive."

"Why won't they get her a doctor?"

"They're making an example of her to keep the others in line."

"Oh, I can't believe they're doing that—they deserve what's coming to them. How did the girls get here from the Ukraine?"

"Sofia said she and about thirty other girls were captured by Russian soldiers earlier this year. They were sold to some men who threatened their families if they didn't cooperate. The prettiest of them were shipped to Cuba, then smuggled into the States."

"Have any of them tried to escape? I mean, they could just run out the front door of the club, couldn't they?"

"And go where? Sofia told me one girl ran off when they first got here. The Russians found her and killed her. They showed the others what was left of her body, and since then no one else has tried to escape."

MaryAna shudders. "Are we gonna go to the police now?"

"NYPD is an option, but it'll take time for them to investigate, even if they believe us. To save Elena, we have to move now."

"Can we do something tonight?"

"There it is." Tony nods toward the alley. A black van pulls out

323

onto the street and drives off. "We need more intel," he says, starting the engine.

MaryAna fastens her seatbelt. "How do we get the girls away from the Russians? And where do we take them?"

"I'm working on that." He puts the car in gear and, with the headlights off, starts after the van.

Maybe this thing is gonna turn out all right after all.

Chapter 61

THE PLAN

MaryAna and Tony follow the van to a rundown industrial neighborhood a couple miles from the club, where it pulls up to a dilapidated red-brick building illuminated from a streetlight in front. Tony parks along the street just over a block away.

Two armed men exit the front of the vehicle. The taller man unlocks the rear doors and the women, now in jeans and sweatshirts, exit the van. The shorter man stands guard with an AK-47 while his partner unlocks the building's front door and ushers the girls inside.

"I counted fourteen," Tony says, looking through a mini-binoculars. "Elena makes it fifteen total."

He tilts the binoculars upward slightly, and MaryAna looks at the van, then back to Tony.

"What are you looking at?"

"Checking for security cameras," he says. "Don't see any offhand, but I'd be surprised if they don't have them. If they don't, it'll make things easier."

"What if there are more guards inside?"

"Sofia says there's only those two at night. Any girl they don't take to the club is locked in her room. That's where Elena is now."

"Tony, are you going to kill those guards?"

He turns to her. "I'll do what I have to to free those girls and keep us safe."

"I don't want anyone to die."

"Neither do I. Look, it may not come to that. I've helped plan

325

and execute far more complicated missions."

"I'm sorry I got you into this. I had no right to disrupt your life."

"It's OK, MaryAna. I'm your friend, and these girls look like they need our help."

She leans back in her seat. "So, what all happened when you went with Sofia through the red door?"

"She took me to a small room with a bed and a bathroom. While we got undressed, I checked the room for bugs with my phone."

"I didn't know there was an app for that."

"It's not something you get at Best Buy. The room was clean, so we got into bed and spoke in whispers. When I got all the info I needed, I got dressed and left."

"So, you didn't . . ."

"No, I didn't have sex with her."

"I'm glad."

Tony chuckles. "That's what you're worried about—if I got laid? Let's get back to the rescue—we'll need help to pull this off. You remember my friend upstate, the ex-Marine sniper guy?"

MaryAna nods.

"I talked to him and Fred volunteered to be a part of our little rescue mission. He's driving down tomorrow morning."

"Where do we take the girls when we get them out?"

"We need a place to stash them until we figure out how to get them back to Ukraine."

"Any ideas yet?"

"My parents own a cabin in the Catskills, three hours north of the city, but it's smaller and farther away than I would like. We should talk to the Ukrainian government, but doing it without the NSA finding out could be tricky. Unfortunately, I don't have any contacts in Ukraine."

"Do you think they'll help us?"

"They'd never sanction an armed action on American soil, so we'll contact them after the rescue. They should take the girls off our hands—after all, they're Ukrainian citizens."

"I have a friend who works at the UN. Maybe Izzy could contact someone there."

"Can she be trusted?"

"Absolutely. And she speaks Russian."

For the next hour, the two discuss his plan, looking for ways to eliminate flaws and minimize risks. Tony then drives MaryAna to Leon's house.

"You've been a big help with this, MaryAna. I always knew you had a good head on your shoulders. It's just sometimes you forget to use it."

"Like when I get wasted? So, what are you gonna tell your wife about tonight?"

"My mother took Dori to my grandparents' in the Hamptons for a few days. I told them I volunteered to help out in the emergency room at Columbia Presbyterian Hospital this weekend—which I've done before."

"So, now I have you lyin' to your wife."

Rather than responding, Tonly leans over to kiss MaryAna, but she pulls back. "Whoa, what are you doing?"

"I still love you, MaryAna."

"No you don't."

"I've wanted you since that night I saw you in Syracuse. Let's go to my place—"

"No," she says, keeping him at arm's length. "As long as you're married, that's not gonna happen. Please don't make this any harder than it already is. I appreciate you helpin' me, but it can't lead to anything between us."

He relents and turns back in his seat. "All right, you win for now. Get some rest. Tomorrow's a busy day, because we're gonna rescue some folks from bad guys."

MaryAna smiles and opens her door. "See you tomorrow."

She waves as he backs out of the driveway and drives off.

My angel would be proud of me tonight.

Chapter 62
LAST-MINUTE DETAILS

After her late night, MaryAna sleeps until ten o'clock Saturday morning. As she gets dressed, she gets a call from Andre in Mississippi.

"Great news, MaryAna. I might get the linebacker coach job. Coach Brown seemed impressed with me."

"I knew they'd like you, Andy. When will you know for sure?"

"They want me to stick around this weekend and be on the sidelines during the Auburn game. A final decision will be made next week."

"Have you met Coree and my brothers?"

"Yeah, and they introduced me to all the coaches and a bunch of the players."

"So, if you get the job, you won't be comin' back to New York any time soon?"

"Not until after the season. Coree said she would help me find an apartment and pick out clothes more suited to Mississippi weather."

"It sounds like you two are gettin' along," she says. "By the way, I've got a favor to ask."

"Shoot."

"Could I use your cottage for a few days, startin' tonight?"

"Of course, but I thought you found a place."

"I'll only need it for a short time. A bunch of my girlfriends will be with me."

"You having a party?"

"Something like that. They're girls from where I work."

"Have fun. I'll have Wyatt drop you off a key this afternoon.

Where are you staying?"

MaryAna gives him Leon's address.

"There's some sleeping bags in the upstairs hall closet. If you need more room, you can always use the sailboat."

"You don't know how much this means to me."

"I only wish I could be there. A cottage full of girls sounds intriguing."

MaryAna giggles. "I bet it does."

When MaryAna hangs up, she calls Tony.

"I've got us a cottage where we can take the girls. Actually, it's more like a small mansion. A friend of mine who's out of town owns it. It's on the north shore of Long Island, less than an hour from the city. There's even a big sailboat if we need more room."

"Sounds perfect. Fred's here, and we've gone over the plan. After we rescue the girls, we'll need to dump the Russian's van. They may be able to track it. "

"Could we rent another one?"

"I don't want a paper trail. We have my car and Fred has an SUV, but we'd have to make multiple trips, which increases the risk of the Russians catching up to us."

"The guy bringin' me the key to the cottage might help us. He has a Lincoln Continental. I also know someone with a limo."

"We should keep the number of people involved to a minimum. Do they have any ties to the Russians?"

"None that I know of. If I tell these guys what we're doin', I'm sure they'll help us and keep our secrets."

"I don't know, MaryAna. We don't want to blow the whole operation by bringing in too many people."

"These guys are my friends. They wouldn't betray us."

"OK. Talk to them."

"Thanks. Where do we meet to transfer the girls?"

"There's an area in South Brooklyn where Coney Island Avenue dead ends. My parents used to park there when they took my brothers and me to the beach. Tell your friends to rendezvous there thirty minutes past midnight tonight. You got all that?"

She repeats everything back to him.

"Good. I'm going to take Fred by the building now to reconnoiter the area."

"To what?"

"It means to observe, inspect, and survey an enemy position. We are now soldiers at war against these Russian mobsters. I'll pick you up outside the club at midnight."

"Do I really need to go to the buildin' with you? I have to admit I'm kinda scared—"

"Those girls will be scared and need a familiar face, MaryAna. So . . . you good?"

"I'm good."

After MaryAna hangs up, she texts Isadora: PLEASE CALL FIRST CHANGE YOU GET.

The nineteen-year-old goes down to the kitchen to get something to drink. Victoria is there, hard at work at the stove.

"Good morning, MaryAna. I'm making vegetable soup, but it won't be ready for a while. Would you like some breakfast?"

"Thanks, but I'll just have orange juice. By the way. I won't be home after work tonight. I'm stayin' at a friend's place on Long Island for a couple days."

The less Vee and her family know about the rescue, the better.

"I'll tell Leon. He's working today because another doorman called in sick."

MaryAna grabs the orange juice from the refrigerator. "Where's Max?"

"In his room. He showed me his latest painting. It's some movie star—Bruce Lee, he said."

"He's a martial arts legend," MaryAna tells her. "His movie *Enter the Dragon* is a classic."

"Max and Leon like to watch movies together. I suppose that's how my son knows about him."

"The paintings Max did for me were quite unusual."

331

"He used to paint only cartoon characters and superheroes. I suppose he won't stay a child forever."

"Your son may be quiet, but the gears are workin' in that brain of his."

Victoria smiles. "Thank you for taking an interest in our boy. It means a lot to my husband and me."

I hate to keep secrets from these nice people.

Chapter 63

PREPARATIONS

A few minutes past noon, MaryAna is in her room when she receives a call from Wyatt wanting to know when she needs the key to the cottage.

"Did Andy tell you why I need it?"

"He mentioned a party with some of your girlfriends."

If I'm going to ask Wyatt to help, he needs to know what he's getting into.

MaryAna tells him about the girls and the rescue plan. "We could use your help, but I'll understand if you don't want to get involved."

"Are you kidding? Sex-trafficked girls, Russian mobsters, and the NSA—sign me up."

"It could be dangerous, Wyatt. These people don't play around."

"Sure, but how often do you get the chance to rescue people in trouble—much less a bunch of hot girls. They are hot, right?"

"Yes, but do I need to remind you you're engaged?"

"It doesn't keep me from looking. Count me in."

"Tonight, after we rescue the girls, we'll need your Lincoln to transport some of them. We'll follow you to the cottage in the other vehicles."

"Where and when do I meet you?"

MaryAna gives him the information. "Thanks, Wyatt."

"Just call me 007. How long will they be at the cottage?"

"At least a couple of days."

"I'll pick up some food and see you tonight. Secret agents don't let hot girls starve."

MaryAna knows who she needs to contact next, but she hesitates. *This is more than a little awkward.*

"Can you talk?" she says, when her former boss answers the phone.

"I'm in my office here at home," Mel says. "Let me close the door." A moment later he is back on the line.

"I need to borrow your limo, sir."

"Whatever for?"

There's no point in lying. He needs to be fully aware of the situation.

MaryAna tells the CEO about the plan to rescue the Ukrainians, the urgency, and the unlikelihood of help from either the police or the FBI.

"You still there, sir?"

"Let me see if I have this right. You're wanting to rescue 15 sex-trafficked prostitutes from Russian mobsters who are under the protection of the NSA and you need my limo to transport them. You can't be serious."

"I am. If you don't want to help, I—"

"Where are you taking these women."

"To your son's cottage on Long Island."

"*What?* Is Andrew a part of this? He said he was on a job interview, but wouldn't say where."

"I talked to Andy earlier today. He said we could use the cottage, but he thinks it's for a party. Wyatt knows all about it. He's bringin' me the key and is helpin' us too."

"This is insane. And how do you know my son?"

"Jacqueline introduced us at work. He and I have been hangin' out. But we're not datin' or anything, just friends."

"Did you tell my son about us?"

"Andy wanted to know why you fired me—I wasn't gonna lie. At first, he was upset, but he's accepted that it's over between you and me."

"You had no right to reveal our secret, Miss Lindley."

"What secret? You told your wife. Your chauffeur knew, as well as half the office. I had every right to tell Andy the truth. If you had been up front with me from the beginning about being married, this whole thing could've been avoided."

Mel huffs. "I suppose it's time for a father and son talk."

"If you're honest with Andy, it might improve your relationship."

"My relationship with my son is just fine. We're grooming him to take over the company."

"Don't bet on it."

"What do you mean?"

"I mean your communication with your son is far from perfect. Just be honest with Andy, and maybe he'll open up to you. So, what about the limo?"

"You are putting me in a dilemma, here. I want to help, but it could be extremely dangerous."

"I know, but these girls need our help."

"I can't ask Roger to get involved in something like this."

"We can get someone else to drive the limo."

"So, saving these girls is that important to you?"

"Yes, sir—it is."

"I'll drive the limo then. It is my car."

"Thank you, sir. You don't know how much this means to me."

"What time should I meet you and where?"

"Tonight at twelve-thirty," she says, then gives him the location.

After hanging up with Mel, MaryAna calls Tony to let him know she has solved their transportation problem.

"You did good, MaryAna."

"What else do we need?"

"What about your friend at the UN?"

"I'm waiting for Isadora to get back to me. How is everything goin'?"

"Still need to acquire a certain rifle that Fred requested. So far, I've come up empty."

"I know someone who buys and sells military weapons."

"Excuse me—you know an arms dealer?"

"I suppose that's what he is. Maybe he can help."

"You never fail to surprise me." Tony gives her the model number of the weapon. "If your friend has one, I need to pick it up this afternoon."

MaryAna then calls Rufus at his club.

"Nice to hear from you, Sunshine. Sam told me you moved out of the Plaza. Why don't you come to my apartment, and we can finish our business. I've got your oxy, by the way."

"I called because I need a gun."

"For protection?"

"No, a special rifle for a friend of mine." She gives Rufus the specifications Tony gave her.

"You're lucky. I happen to have one in stock. It comes with special ammo. Why would you need a weapon like that?"

"I can't tell you."

"You don't trust me, Sunshine? I'm hurt. That particular item isn't cheap."

"We only need it for a day or two. Can I rent it?"

Rufus chuckles. "Are you serious?"

"Please. It's important."

"How important?"

"I know some girls who have been sex-trafficked, and we're gonna rescue them. That's how important."

"Tell you what, I'll make you a deal. Say, five hundred bucks for two days and another fifty for the ammo."

"That's highway robbery, Rufus. I just started workin' again, and my funds are limited."

"You could always ask Steven Seagal if you can borrow one. Take it or leave it—it's all the same to me."

"OK, I'll take it. I also need a dozen oxy for my back. Can you cut me a deal on them?"

"This ain't Walmart, Sunshine." Rufus chuckles. "That'll be another two-fifty. And remember, cash only."

"I don't think I've got that much."

"Come by the bar in about an hour. If you don't have enough cash, I'm sure we can work something out."

God, please help me out here.

Chapter 64

NEGOTIATIONS

Just before three o'clock that afternoon, MaryAna takes a taxi to Harlem where Tony is waiting in his car outside the Black and Blues Jazz Bar. The business appears closed.

He joins her and peers through one of the darkened windows. "How do you know this Rufus guy?"

"I met him here one night."

Tony knocks on the front door. "Have you told him our plans?"

"All Rufus knows is that we are rentin' the rifle for a couple of days to rescue some sex-trafficked girls. Why does Fred need this particular gun?"

"In the hands of a marksman, it can be quite effective. I used up my cash last night at the club, so I hope this guy takes a check."

"He won't. I'll take care of it."

Rufus soon comes to the door, unlocks it, and ushers them inside. MaryAna introduces the two men.

"I don't get many calls for this particular item," the arms dealer tells Tony.

"Look, we're on a tight schedule. Can we move this along?"

Rufus hands him a piece of paper with a name, address, and short message scribbled on it.

"Go to that flower shop in Queens and hand Squeaky the note," he says. "She'll have a package for you. They close in an hour. When you are done with the item, call me here, and I'll let you know where to drop it off."

Tony turns to MaryAna. "Pay the man and let's get going."

"Sunshine and I have unfinished business."

Tony scowls. "'Sunshine'? What unfinished business we talking about?"

"What are you, her daddy?"

"She's leaving with me."

MaryAna steps between them. "You go on ahead, Tony. Rufus will make sure I get back to Brooklyn, won't you?" she says, turning to the arms dealer.

Rufus nods. "She's in safe hands. You better get going if you want that weapon."

"What's going on here?"

MaryAna puts her hand on Tony's arm. "I'll see you at midnight outside Matryoshka."

"I don't feel right leaving you here."

"I'll be fine. You need to go."

Tony stares down Rufus. "If anything happens to her, bro . . ."

"I can take care of myself," MaryAna assures him. "Now, get goin'."

With a frustrated sigh, he heads to the door. "See you tonight."

After he leaves, Rufus says, "Lover boy seems a little jealous."

"We're just friends. So, do you have something for me?"

"Let's go upstairs where it's more private."

Inside the arms dealer's apartment, pizza boxes and beer cans litter the living room. The place has minimal furniture but does boast a gigantic wall-mounted flat-screen TV.

"Want something?" Rufus takes a beer from a cooler next to the sofa.

"No thanks," MaryAna says, looking around the room. "You need someone to pick up after you."

"Want the job?"

"I'll pass."

"You want some weed? Just got in some Columbian. It'll curl your toes."

"No. Let's get down to business."

He points to a coat rack. "Just hang your clothes there."

"Is that what you say to all your female guests?"

He chuckles. "As a matter of fact, it is."

He reaches in his pocket and pulls out a baggie.

"That better be the oxy," she tells him.

"It is." He hands it to her. "I'll keep some in stock for you."

"I only need these for my back."

"Yeah, right."

MaryAna takes out a capsule, examines it, and pops it into her mouth. "I don't want Tony to know about this. He'll think I'm hooked again."

"So, you care what Tony thinks, but not me?"

"I know you don't care, Rufus. You just sold them to me."

"Not *sold*, Sunshine. We're making a trade. You get the gun and the oxy, and I get you."

MaryAna takes an envelope from her purse and hands it to him. He counts the bills inside.

"It's all there," she tells him.

"I see that. Thought you were strapped for cash."

"With the money I earned this week and what was left on my bedside table, I had enough. You need to keep all this a secret, by the way."

Rufus smiles. "You mean from the Russians?"

MaryAna freezes. "How do you know about them?"

"You mentioned one of their clubs. The Russians are my most reliable supplier of weapons. They smuggle them in from Eastern Europe. You planning a smash-and-grab?"

"No."

"Over the phone, you mentioned rescuing sex-trafficked girls. I assume you were talking about the whores at that club."

If he squeals to the Russians, our goose is cooked.

"So, you've been to the Matryoshka Club, Rufus?"

"I've sampled their hospitality a time or two. Are you sure those hookers are forced to work there?"

"They've tortured them and even killed one girl. You're not gonna tell the Russians what we're planning, are you?"

"My silence comes at a price, Sunshine." He points to the coat rack again.

"I'm not sleepin' with you." MaryAna reaches in her purse and takes out a few bills. "This is all I've got left. Here, take it."

Rufus smiles and takes a swig of his beer. "Keep your money. I'll keep your secret."

"You won't say anything to the Russians?"

"No. That is, if you tell me everything that's going down—and I mean everything."

"Why?"

"Let's just say I'm curious. The Russkies would pay a bundle for what I already know. You might as well trust me."

I suppose I have to.

***

MaryAna takes a taxi back to Brooklyn after telling Rufus about the rescue.

Tony wouldn't be happy about yet another person knowing our plans— but if I don't tell him, he won't worry about it.

Now running late for work, she showers and hurries to get ready. As she hustles to the subway station in her pink blouse and white miniskirt, her cell rings.

"Hey, Izzy. Thanks for callin' back."

"I thought we decided not to contact each other."

"It's an emergency." MaryAna tells her friend about the Matryoshka Club and the Ukrainian girls.

"How long have you worked there?"

"Just a week. At first, I was just tryin' to find Vladdy. We're gonna rescue these girls tonight."

"What?"

"They've tortured one of them, Izzy, and she needs a doctor." MaryAna explains about the note. "It's a matter of life and death."

"That's horrible. How can I help?"

"After we rescue them, I need you to contact the Ukrainians at the UN. We think they could make arrangements to get all the girls

340

back to their country."

"Who's 'we'?"

"Some friends of mine. A couple of them are ex-military."

"I've done some translating for the Ukrainian delegation, but I don't know them that well."

"All you have to do is relay a message to them."

"I could do that."

"We don't want the U.S. authorities to get wind of our plans—especially the NSA."

"Why not?"

"It's a long story, Izzy. I'll tell you later. If you're up to it, there's something else you could help us with."

"What's that?"

"The girls don't speak much English. Tony speaks Russian, but we could use another translator."

"You want me to be part of this rescue?"

"It would be a big help but could be dangerous."

". . . Sure, OK."

"Thanks so much. I'll give Tony your address. He'll pick you up around eleven tonight."

"You're rescuing them tonight?"

"It's complicated. I'm at the subway station and running late for work. Tony can fill you in on the details. Thanks for your help. See you around midnight."

I can't believe I'm putting so many of my friends in danger.

Chapter 65

THE RESCUE

At midnight, MaryAna leaves the Matryoshka Club and slips into Tony's Mercedes, which is waiting outside. Isadora, in a black hoodie and jeans, sits in the backseat.

"You ready?" Tony says, hitting the ignition.

MaryAna fastens her seatbelt. "Let's do it. Izzy, did Tony fill you in on the details?"

"Yep. Do any of the girls speak English?"

"Sofia seems to understand English better than she speaks it," Tony says, pulling out into the street. "The others probably do as well. If any of them don't want to come with us, we'll leave them behind."

Isadora leans forward in her seat. "We're taking the girls to Andy's place, right? What's the address? The Ukrainians at the UN will need it to pick them up."

"Wyatt will give it to you, Izzy," MaryAna says.

"I understand Andy's father is helping us—isn't that the CEO you had the fling with?"

Tony glances in MaryAna's direction.

Geez. Thanks, Izzy.

MaryAna turns her gaze out her passenger-side window. "Mr. Rubenstein and I are just friends now."

***

They drive past the building, make a U-turn, and park on the other side of the street, where they will have a clear view of the area where the van will unload the women.

343

"Look in that duffel on the back seat, Izzy," Tony says. "Take out the three pairs of latex gloves."

She hands out a pair to Tony and MaryAna, then puts on the remaining pair.

"I don't want to leave anything behind," he adds as he slips them on, "including fingerprints."

Tony clicks open the glove compartment and takes out a pistol. He makes sure it is loaded, then sets it on the dashboard.

"You told me what kind of gun that was before," MaryAna says. "But I forgot."

"Sig Sauer P226. Like I used in the military."

"I learned to shoot a couple of years ago, but I couldn't hit a target from here. How far is the front of the building?"

"About seventy-five yards—three-quarters of a football field."

"Could you hit someone from here, Tony?"

"Most likely, but if Fred does his job, I won't have to."

MaryAnd looks around. "Fred—where is he?"

"In those bushes," Tony says, nodding toward the opposite side of the street.

"I don't see him."

Tony chuckles. "That's the idea. When the van comes, stay low. These tinted windows should help keep anyone from spotting us."

MaryAna turns her gaze back to the building. "Do you think the Russians will be shootin' back at us?"

"If everything goes according to plan, the guards won't know what hit them."

For several minutes, they sit in silence, each lost in their own thoughts.

MaryAna notices Tony's left hand twitching. He grabs it with the other hand and the tremor subsides.

The same thing happened when he told me about his military missions two years ago.

I guess I'm not the only one who's nervous.

Lord, please help us save these girls. Make Fred's aim true and forgive us for anyone who gets hurt.

"Here they come," Tony says, clutching the pistol. "Get down."

The van pulls in front of the building and stops, as before. A curious MaryAna peeks just above the dashboard. When the driver glances in their direction, she ducks back down.

Half a minute later, the teenager again sneaks a peek. Both guards are now at the rear of the van. The taller man wears a shoulder holster and holds a set of keys. The other man stands behind his partner with an AK-47.

He suddenly jerks and slaps at his neck, before sinking to the pavement and drawing the attention of the taller man. He too jerks, then slumps to the ground.

Tony opens the driver's side door. "Wait here until I signal for you."

He springs from the car and moves toward the van, his head on a swivel as he goes. He is slowed by his all-too-noticeable limp.

MaryAna watches as Tony reaches the downed guards, his gun at the ready. He kicks both their weapons out of arm's reach and motions for MaryAna and Isadora to join him.

The girls scramble from the Mercedes and sprint to Tony, with Fred close behind. Tony opens the van's rear door and hands the guard's keys to MaryAna. He says something in Russian, and Sofia gets out.

"Izzy, get in the van and tell the other girls to stay put." Tony nods toward the building. "MaryAna, find the key for the front door."

MaryAna tries each key until she locates the correct one.

"Got it!" she says, pushing the door open.

"Help Fred drag these guys inside while we get Elena," Tony tells her. Once again he speaks in Russian to Sofia and they enter the building.

"Good job, Fred," MaryAna says, "but I don't see any blood. Are these guys dead?"

"The weapon you got for me is a tranquilizer rifle." He nods toward a strange-looking rifle propped against the building. "Those two will be out cold for an hour or so. As an officer of the law, I can't very well go around killing people. Not even this Euro trash."

Fred picks up the taller guard under the arms, while MaryAna takes his legs. They dump him inside, then do the same with the other guard, before tying and gagging them.

"Check these guys for phones," Fred says as he grabs the AK-47. "I don't want to take a chance on them contacting anyone when they come to."

MaryAna finds two cell phones in their pockets and hands them to Fred. He tosses both to the concrete and then crushes them with the heel of his boot.

Two minutes later, Tony and Sofia reappear through the front door, holding up Elena between them. Her face is puffy and bruised, and her eyes are mere slits. Blood has soaked through her sweatshirt, and her bare legs are covered in small cuts.

Tony gently sets Elena in the back of the van with Isadora and the other girls. "Make her as comfortable as possible, Izzy."

"Are all the girls going with us?" Isadora asks.

"Sofia assured me they all want to go." Tony closes the back door of the van and turns to MaryAna. "Keys?"

She points to the building. "Still in the door."

Tony retrieves them and tells Sofia to get into the front passenger seat of the van. Fred grabs the tranquilizer gun and the guard's assault rifle before heading off to his vehicle.

"Do you need some pain meds for Elena?" MaryAna asks, ready to offer the oxycodone. "I've got some if you need it."

Tony stops and locks eyes with MaryAna.

He probably thinks I'm hooked on drugs again.

"I already gave Elena something." He picks up the taller guard's pistol and hands it to MaryAna. "You know how to handle a Beretta?"

She nods. "I've shot one before."

"The key to my car is still in the ignition." He gets in the driver's seat of the van. "Just follow us."

MaryAna dashes over to Tony's Mercedes, pistol in hand.

At least that went smoothly. Thank you, Lord.

Chapter 66

EMERALD ACRES

At the rendezvous point near the beach, the Ukrainians are transferred from the van to the other vehicles. Wyatt's Lincoln Continental, with three of the girls, leads the small convoy to Andre's cottage. Behind them are Fred's SUV with four Ukrainians, followed by Mel's limousine carrying Izzy and six other girls. MaryAna brings up the rear in Tony's Mercedes.

Sofia sits in the front passenger seat, and Tony is in the back treating Elena. Although he has not completed med school, his experience patching up Marines in Iraq and Afghanistan is invaluable. Elena is groggy from both her injuries and the pain medication.

MaryAna glances back at her. "Will she be all right?" she asks while keeping one eye on the limousine ahead.

"I hope so," Tony answers. "Somebody did a job on her. She has multiple contusions, and there are cuts all over her body. Not deep, but they would've been extremely painful. From her bruises, I suspect internal injuries as well. She needs a hospital."

"Can we take her to one?"

"There'd be too many questions, but we may not have a choice."

"Wyatt will know where the nearest hospital is to the cottage. Do you want me to call him?"

"Let's get the girls safe first, then we'll decide how best to help Elena. So, how does Wyatt fit into all this?"

"He works for Jacqueline designs. That's where I met him and his friend Andy who owns the cottage."

"It's great that they let us use it. So, they're just your *friends*, like the CEO driving the limo?"

"Yes, all just friends."

Sofia asks Tony something in Russian, and he responds.

MaryAna glances into the rearview mirror. "What'd she say?"

"She wants to know if we've contacted the Ukrainians at the UN. I told her we hadn't yet but would soon."

"I'll make sure Izzy takes care of that," MaryAna tells him.

"Are you sure your friends can keep all this secret? We've got quite a group involved."

"I'd trust them with my life."

And I'm trusting God too.

***

When they arrive at Andre's cottage, Tony and Fred carry Elena to a downstairs bedroom. Everyone else filters in to the kitchen and living room. Wyatt lays out a spread of deli-meats, breads, and chips for the girls, who quickly dig in.

"Thanks for doin' all this, Wyatt," MaryAna tells him. "It's still hard to believe sex traffickin' goes on here in the U.S."

He shakes his head. "You said you reported it to the police, but that they wouldn't help?"

"The girl we took to the bedroom, Elena, was beaten badly. We couldn't wait for the police to get involved."

Mel, who is drinking a Coke in the kitchen, heads over to them. "Does Elena need a doctor?"

"Tony's a med student and was a medic in the military. He said she needs a hospital."

"My brother's a doctor and lives close by," Mel says. "Maybe he can help."

"Good idea, that would be wonderful. Again, I owe you big time, sir."

"I'm just glad I could lend a hand, Miss Lindley. I'll tell Tony about my brother."

Once Mel has left, MaryAna turns to Wyatt. "Thank you so much for bringin' us here and gettin' all this food."

"No problem. Why don't you eat something?"

"I'm too keyed up after the rescue—and worried sick about Elena."

Isadora comes over to them. "Those girls told me quite a harrowing story."

Fred joins the group, and MaryAna makes the introductions all around.

He shakes hands with Wyatt and nods to Isadora before saying. "I'd like to get my hands on whoever did that to the girl we carried in here."

"She was punished for just talkin' to me," MaryAna explains. "I don't think it was the guards who beat her though."

"Speaking of the guards," Fred says, "they should be coming to about now, if someone hasn't found them already."

"By the way, Wyatt," Isadora says, "what's the address here? The Ukrainians at the UN will need it. I'll request they pick up the girls as soon as possible."

He gives it to her, and she puts it into her phone.

"I'll go check on Elena," MaryAna says.

In the bedroom, Tony sits on the edge of the bed next to his patient, and Sophia is perched on the opposite side holding Elena's hand. Mel is on his cell phone in a chair near the window.

"How is she?" MaryAna whispers.

"I've done all I can do here." Tony says, standing up. "Mr. Rubenstein is talking to his brother."

A moment later Mel hangs up. "Isaac's on his way over to examine Elena. If she needs a hospital, he'll help us conceal her identity from the authorities."

"Thanks," Tony says. "You have some awesome friends, MaryAna."

She smiles. "And you're one of them."

***

Twenty minutes later, Dr. Isaac Rubenstein arrives at the cottage. While Tony takes him to examine Elena, MaryAna talks to Fred in the living room.

"Will the Russians be able to find us?" she says.

"Maybe in a few days, if they can figure out who pulled this off. By then we'll be gone, and the girls should be on their way back to Ukraine."

"Do you think they'll want revenge for what we've done?"

"I doubt it. Chances are they'll suspect the Ukrainian government ordered it, and they're already at war with them."

"If I don't show up for work Monday, the Russians might think I'm involved."

"Do they know where you live, MaryAna?"

"The only address they have for me is the Plaza. I didn't leave a forwardin' address."

"Then you should be safe." Fred smiles. "With their prostitution business in shambles, they'll be more concerned about rival gangs encroaching on their territory. I doubt they'll give you a second thought."

"What about the NSA? Will they try to hunt us down?"

"Tony doesn't think so," Fred replies. "Whatever their deal is with the Russians, I don't believe they'd come after U.S. citizens."

"I hope you're right."

If there's a problem, we'll just cross that bridge when we get to it.

***

When the doctor completes his examination of Elena, he confers with Tony, MaryAna, and Mel.

"That young lady definitely needs to go in a hospital," Isaac informs them. "She has serious internal injuries and will likely need surgery."

"Could we get her admitted to Emerald Acres?" Mel asks. "Money is no problem. I'll cover any expense."

"It isn't a matter of money," his brother explains. "That facility is particular about who they treat and more about who you are and who you know."

"What's Emerald Acres?" MaryAna asks.

"It's a hospital and rehab center not far from here," Mel notes. "The Acres caters to the super-rich and the well-connected. It assures them complete privacy. Don't you have contacts there, Isaac?"

His brother nods. "I've been asked to consult on some cases. Their medical care is cutting-edge, and they have state-of-the-art security."

"Will you contact them, Dr. Rubenstein?" Tony asks. "If you explain our situation, maybe they'll help Elena."

"I'm not sure, but I'm willing to try. It would certainly help if my last name was Kennedy."

MaryAna's ears perk up. "Why would that matter?"

"The Kennedy family owns Emerald Acres," the doctor explains. "Bobby Kennedy had it built when he was a senator from New York. It was intended to be a research hospital, but after he died, its purpose changed."

"I know one of Bobby's granddaughters," MaryAna says. "Wyatt's engaged to her."

"Could she help us get Elena into Emerald Acres?" Tony asks.

"Wyatt is outside with Fred." MaryAna heads to the front door. "I'll ask him to call her."

The nineteen-year-old joins the two men, who are discussing the New York Yankees' prospects for the remainder of the season.

"How can you guys think about sports at a time like this?"

"There's always room for baseball." Fred chuckles. "Or is that Jell-O?"

She turns to Wyatt. "I need another huge favor."

"Sure."

"Dr. Rubenstein says Emerald Acres is the perfect hospital for Elena."

"I'm familiar with it," Wyatt tells her. "You want me to ask Regina to get Elena in there, don't you?"

"Yep."

Wyatt whips out his phone and dials her number. "Regina is unpredictable about anything related to her family."

"I understand," MaryAna says. "We have that in common."

"Can I tell Regina what's going on?"

"If she's gonna help us, she needs to know. Tell her to give Emerald

Acres only the information they have to have."

Wyatt puts his phone to his ear. "Regina . . ." He listens a moment. "I know what time it is—listen, I need your help." He steps away and explains the situation to his fiancée.

MaryAna crosses her fingers.

Please, God. Help us save Elena.

Chapter 67

THE CALM

Less than an hour later, the administrator of Emerald Acres calls Wyatt to inform him Elena has been accepted as a patient. Upon hearing the news, Dr. Rubenstein and Tony load Elena into the backseat of the limousine.

Mel takes his place in the driver's seat. "What's the quickest way to get there?" he asks his brother.

"Catch the parkway," he says, getting into the back. I know a couple shortcuts from there."

Wyatt is standing nearby. "I should probably go with you since they called me."

"Hop in," Mel tells him.

Before Wyatt gets in the front passenger seat, he turns to MaryAna. "Regina is on her way here."

"Your fiancée totally came through for us."

"She's a good person. That's the main reason I love her."

"I don't know when we'll be back," Tony tells MaryAna from the backseat. "I'll keep you updated."

"I hope they can help Elena," she says. "Everything seems to be goin' so well."

"Let's not celebrate just yet . . ." Tony says as the door closes.

***

A half an hour later, Regina arrives at the cottage. MaryAna greets her with open arms, giving Wyatt's fiancée a big hug.

"You're a lifesaver. I mean for real."

"Glad I could help." Regina glances at several of the young Ukrainian women gathered in the living room. "Wyatt told me they only have the clothes on their backs, so I brought some of mine."

"I should've thought of that," MaryAna tells her. "Need some help bringing them in?"

Regina nods. "Sure, thanks."

Out front, they pass Fred who is sitting on the edge of a planter. The AK-47 he appropriated from the Russians is propped against it.

"Are you on guard duty?" MaryAna asks.

He smiles. "Just getting some air. Too many females in that house for me."

"Did you meet Regina?"

"Sure did."

"We're goin' to fetch some clothes from her car for the ladies."

"Need help fetching?"

"We've got it," MaryAna tells him. "Just make sure nobody shoots us."

"They'll have to get past me first," he says. "Everything is nice and calm—hope it stays that way."

MaryAna and Regina each gather up an armful of clothes from the car. "How did you manage to get Elena into Emerald Acres?" MaryAna asks.

Regina grins. "I told them she was a European princess on holiday who had been mugged and that it had to be kept quiet to avoid an international scandal."

"And they bought it?"

"I have the administrator's private number. I think he was half asleep when he answered. My family is always going on about doing the right thing. So, that's what I did."

They take the clothes into the house and set them onto the sofa. The Ukrainian girls just stare at them.

"Where's Izzy?" MaryAna says. "We need her to translate."

Sofia points to the back of the house. The teenager goes through the kitchen and opens the back door. Isadora is talking on her phone

354

outside near the boathouse.

MaryAna yells to her. "We need you."

"Be right there," Isadora yells back. She soon hangs up and joins MaryAna in the house. "There's better reception out there. I left a message for the Ukrainian delegation at the UN. I hope they call me back tomorrow morning, but it may not be until Monday."

"We should be fine until then," MaryAna assures her. "Regina brought some clothes for the girls. Could you explain it to them?"

They go to the front room where Isadora speaks to the women, who then begin to pick through the dresses, shorts, blouses, and skirts.

Regina and MaryAna head back to the car for more clothes. Fred is now clutching the assault rifle and watching the road.

"How long will the girls be here?" Regina asks as they gather up another load of clothes.

"Hopefully, only a couple days. The Ukrainians at the UN should provide transportation back to their country."

"If they won't help, what will you do?"

"We'll figure something out."

"I could talk to my family," Regina offers as they carry the clothes inside. "We have contacts all over the world."

"I hope it doesn't come to that, but thanks," MaryAna says with a yawn.

"Wyatt said you talked to Andy but didn't tell him what was going on. Why?"

"Tony thinks the less people who know, the safer it will be for all of us. I'm sorry we had to get you involved, Regina. I didn't want Andy flyin' back here to help."

"Where is he? Wyatt said he was on a job interview."

"Andy's in Mississippi. He wants to coach football, and I helped him get an interview at Southern Miss, and it looks like they might hire him."

Regina's eyes grow wide. "I thought he was done with football. Are you going back to Mississippi to be with him?"

"No, no. He and I are just friends, Regina. If I go back to Mississippi, it won't be because of Andy."

After they add the clothes to the batch on the sofa, MaryAna finds an armchair in the corner of the room and collapses into it and watches the Ukrainians as they try on the apparel.

Regina pulls up a straight-back chair beside her. "I just want Andy to be happy."

"I know about your history with him—your suicide attempt, the cocaine, and the get-togethers you two had in Boston."

"Wow, he told you all that, did he. Why would he do that, MaryAna, unless he has romantic feelings toward you?"

"Believe me, Regina, there'll never be a romance between Andy and me. I've got my own secrets."

"Care to share?"

"Maybe when we know each other better."

"So, are you a lesbian like Isadora?"

"No, but one time it was up for debate." MaryAna tries to smile. "It's a long story. I'd tell you, but I'm too exhausted to think at the moment."

Apparently satisfied, Regina rises from the chair. "I'm going to make a sandwich. Want anything?"

"No, thanks. I just need to rest my eyes a minute."

She tries but is unable to get comfortable.

Great, my back's acting up again.

She takes an oxy from her purse and swallows it.

Maybe it'll just knock me out.

She leans back in the chair, and—despite the chatter from the excited Ukrainians, the nineteen-year-old drifts off to sleep.

Thank you, God, for all your help.

I think we've got it from here.

Chapter 68

THE STORM

Faint rays of a pre-sunrise glow peek through the curtains of the cottage's living room as MaryAna wakes with a start.

Hmm? What was . . .

The room's plate glass window shatters as a bullet rips through the room. MaryAna lies unmoving for a second until her brain catches up to what her ears are telling her to do—hit the dirt!

She dives to the floor and scrambles to the sofa for cover.

Oh my God, they've found us!

Did Rufus sell us out?

Tony bursts through the front door, pistol in hand. Fred follows firing the AK-47 back through the doorway. They join MaryAna behind the sofa.

"You OK?" Tony asks, breathing hard.

"Yeah," she responds, as gunfire rings over their heads. "Where're the others?"

"Most of the girls are upstairs with Isadora." He slips over to the window and fires twice. "The rest are with Wyatt and Regina on the boat."

Fred moves to shut the door, but he is struck by a round. He staggers backward and slumps against the wall.

"Oh my God, Fred!" MaryAna starts to run to him, but Tony holds her back. He crawls to his fallen comrade and yanks him back to the relative safety of the sofa.

"Where you hit, man?"

"Left shoulder."

"Let me see." Tony says, starting to pull up Fred's shirt.

Fred pushes him away. "Leave it." With his right hand, he props the AK-47 on the arm of the sofa to cover the doorway. "I'll hold them off while you two get out of here."

"I'll be back," Tony tells him.

Automatic weapons fire fills the room again. The walls are pulverized before the barrage subsides.

Tony grabs MaryAna's arm. "Move, while they're reloading!"

They scoot to the kitchen, then scramble to the back door. Tony peeks out a window where early morning fog blankets the backyard. When no hail of bullets greets him, he eases the door open and signals for her to follow.

Using the fog to conceal their movement, they make their way around the boathouse and into the woods beyond. More gunfire sends them scurrying behind a fallen tree.

"I hope the neighbors called 911," she whispers.

"I'm sure someone did," he whispers back as he reloads. "Stay here while I find out what we're up against."

He heads back toward the cottage, which is still semi-shrouded in fog. The nineteen-year-old tries to follow his movements but soon loses him in the haze.

I wish I had a weapon—I'm completely exposed out here.

A single shot rings out a moment later, followed by more automatic weapons fire.

Is Tony picking the Russians off one by one?

Gunshots again disturb the murky silence, this time, from farther away. A minute later, a light goes on in an upstairs bedroom, followed by shouts and screams.

They got past Fred and found the girls!

MaryAna keeps her attention on the upstairs windows. Shadows against the curtains come and go, but nothing is clear. Then, movement on the roof catches her eye.

Is that Tony?

The teenager blinks and rubs her eyes.

No, not Tony.

Am I hallucinating, or . . .

Transfixed by what she sees, MaryAna fails to hear movement in the brush behind her. A second later, cold steel is pressed against the back of her skull.

"Hands up, or I blow head off." The accent is unmistakable.

"Helga?" MaryAna raises her hands.

"Stand up, Miss Lindley."

"How did you find us?"

"Shut up and walk to house."

Terrified, MaryAna steps over the fallen tree and starts for the cottage, her hands high. Helga now has the barrel of the AK-47 poking into the middle of the teenager's back. Then, something clicks in MaryAna's subconcious, and, with the flip of a switch, the fear disappears.

We practiced this very scenario in karate class.

"Aren't you afraid of the angel?" MaryAna says, deliberately slowing her pace.

"I tell you shut up," Helga growls. "What angel?"

"The one on the roof."

The barrel of the gun rises to between MaryAna's shoulder blades, telling her that Helga is looking up. The teenager whips around, ducking in the process. She grabs the barrel of the AK-47, directing it away from her as Helga pulls the trigger, firing wildly into the trees. She loses her grip on the weapon, and MaryAna yanks it away from her, flinging it into the brush. Before the Russian can react, a side kick to her midsection sends her to the ground.

MaryAna scrambles to recover the rifle, but by the time she retrieves it, Helga has disappeared into the heavy mist.

The teenager hears footsteps behind her and wheels around. A bullet whizzes past her head, and she hears a thud. She scans the area but sees only trees, bushes, and fog. Then, a twig snaps and she whips around with the gun ready.

"It's me."

"Tony?"

He steps into view and she lowers the weapon.

"Thank God you're safe," MaryAna says. "Helga's here somewhere."

"She was trying to sneak up on you with a knife, but she won't bother you again," he says, nodding to a spot behind MaryAna.

She turns to see Helga's body lying ten feet away, a single bullet hole in her forehead.

Tony gestures toward the assault rifle. "You know how to use that thing?"

"Point and pull the trigger?"

"Close enough. Just don't point it at me."

"Did you see the angel?"

"The what?"

"On the roof." MaryAna turns and points to the cottage, but the apparition has disappeared.

"Did you say 'angel'?"

"I prayed and it appeared. It had wings—what else could it be?"

"The fog can play tricks on you, MaryAna. Not to mention all the stress you're under."

From beyond the cottage, the sound of vehicles starting up catches their attention.

"Are they leaving, Tony?

"It sounds like it."

"What do we do?"

"First, we need to check the cottage and make sure all the Russians have left. After that, we'll play it by ear."

If that was my guardian angel, where did he go?

Chapter 69

THE FACTORIES

Tony signals for MaryAna to follow him. "I need to go inside and check things out."

They move around the boathouse to get a clearer view of the cottage. A body lies near the back door.

MaryAna freezes. "Oh my God, who's that?"

"A bad guy. Cover me from here. If you see any more of them, take them out. Don't hesitate."

Tony hurries over to the door. He steps over the body and peeks in the window before slipping inside. MaryAna keeps vigil, scanning the area for movement.

Two minutes later, he reappears and waves for her to join him. He leads her to the living room where she sees blood stains on the rug.

"Do the Russians have Fred?" the teenager asks.

"They must've taken him—and some of the girls."

"Is anyone else here?"

Tony shakes his head as he surveys the front yard through the shattered window.

"How about Izzy?"

"They must have her too." He walks out the open door.

MaryAna follows and hears sirens in the distance. "What about our friends on the sailboat?"

"They most likely heard the gunshots and are staying put. Get in my car."

"Where's Mel and his brother?"

"The doc stayed at the hospital with Elena. You were zonked out when the rest of us got back. Mel went home."

"At least some of them are safe." She sets the AK-47 in the back seat. "How is Elena?"

"She had surgery last night." Tony starts his car and pulls out of the circular drive. "She'll recover, but it'll take a while."

"Where are we goin'?"

"To find Fred and the girls."

"So, you know where they are?"

"Your guess is as good as mine." Tony speeds away in the opposite direction from the sirens.

"Shouldn't we wait for the police?"

"Do you want to explain the gunshots and the bodies?"

"No. So, how did the Russians find us?"

"No idea."

"I'm the only link to them, Tony. Could they be trackin' me?"

"You got your phone?"

She hands it to him, and he tosses it out the window. "If they're tracking you, they'll think you're still here."

"What will the Russians do to our friends?"

"Make them reveal who was involved in the rescue and the location of the other girls."

"You mean they'll torture them?"

"Probably. Don't think about it."

"How are we gonna find them?"

"If the NSA is helping them, they'll want to avoid publicity. That'll take planning and coordination."

"How does that help us find them?"

"Plans take time, MaryAna. We can check out places where they might be."

"Maybe they're at the club, waiting for instructions."

"It's as good a place to start as any." Tony turns onto a highway.

"If the Russians are there, won't they be expectin' us?"

"Yep."

It's time to pray again.

***

Tony drives to the Matryoshka Club, but it appears deserted. Next, they try the place where the girls had been kept. But the building is dark and no vehicles are parked outside.

Tony slams his hand on the steering wheel. "Dammit, we're running out of options."

"What about Rufus? He does business with them. They supply him with weapons."

"Would he help us?"

"He might. Rufus heard me mention the Matryoshka Club and made the connection to the Russian mob."

"Did you tell him where we were taking the girls?"

"He wanted to know what was goin' down. It was his price for not tellin' the Russians about us."

"You trusted him and didn't tell me? I'm betting he sold us out."

"He promised to keep our secret."

"You and him seem pretty tight. What *unfinished* business did you two need to transact?"

"I paid him to rent the gun for Fred."

"Is that all? Tell me the truth."

"I got oxy to help with my back pain."

"Are you high now?"

"No. I've only taken a couple. If I only use them for the pain, I won't get addicted again."

"Who told you that?"

"I read it on the internet."

"Maybe the oxy explains why you think you saw an angel. You're unbelievable."

"Me? You should talk. You're married, yet all you want is to get me into bed. Is that why you agreed to help rescue the girls?"

Tony glares at her and hands her his iPhone. "Call the arms dealer."

MaryAna looks up the bar's number and puts the phone on speaker. When Rufus answers, she explains the situation.

"Tony thinks you ratted us out, Rufus. But you didn't, right?"

"I keep my word, girl. I had nothing to do with what went down."

Tony mumbles something under his breath.

"Hush, Tony. I believe him. We need his help to find where the Russians took our friends."

"Thanks for the vote of confidence, Sunshine. The Russkies work out of several locations in Brooklyn. Your best bet is a couple of abandoned factories. It's where we pick up the weapons they smuggle in from overseas."

Tony takes the phone from her. "Exactly where are these factories?"

Rufus tells him the addresses. "You better have an army if you go there. They have all kinds of firepower and mercenaries trained to use it."

"Could you come with us, Rufus?" MaryAna asks. "We could use the help."

"No thanks, Sunshine. But if you need weapons, I can fix you up—at a price, of course."

"We'll pass," Tony tells him. "Your info better be legit."

"It is. Good luck—you'll need it."

***

Tony and MaryAna drive to the abandoned factories in silence. She knows he is upset with her, but that is not at the top of her concerns at the moment.

"Do you have a plan if the Russians are there?" MaryAna says.

"I could say I'm with the NSA and that I've been assigned to help them. It's risky, but it might get me in the front door."

"Then what?"

"Still working on that part."

"It sounds like a good way to get yourself killed. We could take Rufus up on his offer of weapons and storm the place."

Tony shakes his head. "That's a good way to get us *both* killed."

"I got you into this mess, Tony. I need to help get you out."

"I volunteered, remember? I'll figure out something."

MaryAna prays in silence as they head down the road.

Once they are close to the factories, Tony parks far enough away so as not to be spotted. Along with two trucks and several cars, the Russian's van sits behind a fence in front of the nearest factory. Two armed men guard the entrance.

"Looks like your arms dealer buddy was right," Tony says.

"I told you we could trust him. Do you think everyone is still alive?"

"If they wanted any of them dead, they would've killed them back at the cottage. The Ukrainian girls are valuable property, and Fred and Isadora would have information they want."

Movement on the roof of the nearest factory catches MaryAna's eye.

"Tell me you see that," she says, pointing to the roof.

Tony looks up, and his eyes grow wide. "What the hell . . ."

"That's my guardian angel. I saw him on the roof of the cottage."

As they watch, it spreads its wings and takes flight.

MaryAna smiles. "God sent him to help us."

"Whatever the heck it is, it wasn't much help back at the cottage."

The apparition lands on the roof of the adjacent factory. A few moments later, it is airborne once more, circling the factory, then disappearing behind it.

"He wants us to follow him, Tony."

"And you know that how?"

"Hurry up, or we'll lose him."

He shakes his head, then backs up and circles the block to avoid the guards. On the far side of the factories, he pulls into an alleyway.

They spot the apparition standing next to a metal door of the second factory. Tony parks the car, and MaryAna takes the AK-47 from the backseat. They watch as the being disappears through the closed door.

"He wants us to follow."

"I still don't know *what* we're following," Tony says, taking out his pistol.

MaryAna just smiles at him.

Gabriel.

That's who we're following.

Chapter 70

TEST OF FAITH

MaryAna goes to the door of the factory, but it is padlocked. "How will we get inside?"

"How did that . . . whatever it is get in?"

"I told you—"

"Stand back," Tony says, aiming his pistol at the lock.

She steps back. "Won't people hear the shots and call the police?"

"From the looks of this neighborhood, gunshots are probably a daily occurrence around here."

"Those two guards will hear it."

"But they won't know it's us, MaryAna. We'll just have to take our chances."

Tony fires and shatters the padlock. He swings the door open to reveal a dark, musty interior. He grabs two flashlights from his car and then enters the building.

MaryAna follows with the second flashlight and the AK-47 gripped tight in her hands. The cold, dank air makes her cough.

"What did they make here, Tony?"

"From the lint on everything, I suppose it was some kind of textile mill."

"There he is," MaryAna says, pointing at the whitish figure in the distance. "He's goin' toward those stairs."

Tony and MaryAna follow him down two flights of stairs to a sub-basement.

"Holy . . ."

MaryAna stops. "What?"

"That thing just walked through the door."

"You saw it do that with the outside door, Tony."

"Yeah, but—"

"But what?"

"I don't know what to believe, that's what."

MaryAna angles her flashlight toward him. "This is a test of faith."

Movement on the floor causes her to whip the light around.

"Oh my gosh, what was that?"

Tony snickers. "Probably a rat."

"Can I shoot it?"

"I wouldn't. I want to conserve our ammo. Plus, we're inside the building, so firing off a round could give us away. Don't worry about the rats—they're more scared of you than you are of them."

"Don't bet on it," MaryAna says, shuddering.

They ease through the door into another darkened room and look around.

"There he is," MaryAna says, flashing her light on the opposite wall, just as the figure disappears through it.

Tony and MaryAna approach the spot where they saw the figure. "OK, he went through the wall this time? It's all boarded up here."

"You saw it with your own eyes, Tony."

"Well, *we* can't just pass through. Help me here," he says, trying to get a handhold on the boards. They struggle with the stubborn wood, and after a moment finally loosen them enough to pry off several of them. He peers though the now-open space, shining his light on the other side.

"It's a passageway," he says, stepping through it. MaryAna follows.

She shines her light in one direction, then the other. "Where does it go?"

"I'm hoping to wherever the Russians are holding our friends."

"Did the Russians build it?"

"I doubt they even know it exists," Tony answers, moving forward. "I've heard stories about secret passageways between buildings throughout the city. They were constructed by bootleggers during Prohibition."

"So, we can sneak up on them?"

"Maybe. If we can get out the other end."

"The angel wouldn't have led us here otherwise."

"I hope that's the case," Tony says, as they start walking.

They soon reach the end of the tunnel, which is also boarded up. They switch off their flashlights and see dim light filtering through cracks between the boards. Tony peers though one of the tiny gaps to see what is on the other side.

"Looks like the sub-basement of the other factory," he says.

"Do you see the angel?"

"I don't see anyone. Just another stairwell. I'll try and kick these boards loose."

"Let me do it, Tony. You've got a bad leg."

"All right." He steps back to let MaryAna get into position.

She slips off her shoes and whacks the first board with a swift kick. The next kick loosens it enough that they are able to detach the board. She repeats the process until they can squeeze through.

They move to the bottom of the stairs. "Stay here," he whispers. "I'm going upstairs to see what we're up against. If I can find and free our friends, I'll bring them down."

"I'm going too."

"I need you here, MaryAna. I may need to send some of them down while I free the others."

"But—"

"You promised to do what I said, OK?"

She sighs. "OK."

Tony sets down his flashlight and hands her his cell. "If I'm not back in fifteen minutes, retrace our steps to get out of here and call the police."

She shakes her head. "I won't leave without you."

"Yes, you will," he says, putting his hand on her shoulder. "Now hang tight, OK?" He starts up the stairs and disappears into the gloom.

Please protect Tony and our friends.

She paces for nearly ten minutes until several shots ring out. Someone yells in Russian, and an explosion rocks the building. More yelling, then silence.

Five minutes later, but no more voices—or Tony.

Two more minutes go by. No Tony.

He said to get the police, but I can't leave him.

Footsteps from above in the stairwell get her attention. She grips the rifle tight, ready for whoever is coming. She peeks around a corner and up the stairs. Two pairs of legs appear on the floor above.

Vladimir and Izzy!

MaryAna ducks back out of sight as they stop walking.

Where is he taking her?

A metal door opens, then closes on the level above. The teenager peeks around again before easing up the stairs.

I've got to help Izzy.

Chapter 71

BLUFFING

Still barefoot and holding the assault rifle, MaryAna tiptoes to the landing, eases open the door to the basement, and peeks down a long hallway. She sees Vladimir and Isadora disappear into a room at the far end.

What is he gonna do to Izzy—torture her to get info?

MaryAna tiptoes over to the closed door. She puts one ear to the metal and hears Vladimir talking.

"Speak English, Dimitri," Isadora tells him. "You know I hate speakin' Russian."

Nathan was right—Vladimir is Dimitri.

"Just pack everything in these two boxes."

"Do we have to take all this junk with us?"

"We might not be back here any time soon," he answers. "Make sure you wrap each piece in a cloth to protect the blade."

Why is she helping him?

"Whatever." Isadora huffs. "I think you love these devices more than you love me."

"I'd love you more if you'd gotten us the address of that place sooner. By the time we got there, Elena was gone and some of the Ukrainians were on that sailboat where we couldn't get to them."

"I told you about the rescue yesterday evening," Isadora says. "Not my fault you and Uncle Ivan didn't want to stop it at the time."

So, it was Izzy who betrayed us?

"Uncle Ivan wanted to find out who all was involved. Why didn't you call us sooner with the location? We waited half the night to hear from you."

"I didn't know the address until I got there," Isadora explains. "Then, it was a while before I could get away to call."

"Ivan believes Lindley and her people are from either Russian Security Service or are Ukrainian agents."

"That's ridiculous," Isadora assures him. "Tony and Fred are ex-military, but MaryAna and the others are civilians. She still believes I work at the UN and wanted me to contact the Ukrainian government there."

What the hell? Izzy is one of them.

When we relocate," Isadora asks, "will the NSA continue protecting us?"

"As long as my father keeps passing Kremlin secrets to them."

Dimitri's daddy is some kind of spy?

"Careful with that knife," Dimitri says. "I use that when I need to extricate information from difficult subjects. It's my favorite tool. Elena certainly enjoyed it."

"You and your perverse games."

"My little con game with MaryAna Lindley proved lucrative."

"She fell for your art dealer shtick pretty quick. If she'd had access to her trust fund, we could've gotten that too."

"We came out pretty well." Dimitri chuckles. "You did a great job keeping tabs on her. She truly believed you were her friend."

They both laugh.

"When Kira and I followed her from Jacqueline Designs to Boots 'n Heels, we had no choice but to pretend we belonged there. What else could we do?"

So, Izzy and Kira were in on it the whole time.

"That night she showed up drunk at the apartment was a close call," Dimitri says.

"She thought it was my place, not Kira's. If I hadn't drugged her coffee, who knows what might have happened. She didn't remember much of anything the next morning."

What—Izzy drugged me?

"The night she seduced me was so weird," Dimitri says. "It was like an out-of-body experience. I only went along to get her to transfer the money. I certainly didn't enjoy it."

Liar! He enjoyed every second.

"You got her money. That's what counts."

I've had enough of this crap.

MaryAna bursts through the door, rifle ready. "Don't move, or I'll . . . I'll blow you away."

Isadora steps toward her. "Oh, thank heavens you're here!"

"Stow it, Izzy." MaryAna says, turning the gun toward her. "I can't believe you betrayed us. And for what? Money?"

Isadora steps back and raises her hands.

"Put your hands up too, Vladdy, or should I call you Dimitri?"

He scoffs at her but raises his hands.

MaryAna glances around the room. Shelves line the back wall. There is an old table with two cardboard boxes sitting on it next to the wall. A blood-stained straight-back chair which appears to be bolted to the floor sits in the middle of the room.

This is where Elena was when I had the vision through her eyes.

"What is this place?"

"My workshop." Dimitri answers. "Would you like to take a seat?"

"What's in those boxes?"

"The tools of my trade."

"And what exactly would that be?" she asks while deciding upon her next move. "You're certainly no art dealer."

"I extract information from people with secrets."

"You torture people."

"That's what I said."

MaryAna spots a ball of twine on a shelf. "Take that twine, Izzy, and tie his hands behind him."

"If you want to leave this building alive, Miss Lindley, I suggest you give me that *Kalashnikov*."

"You should be worried about your own life. Turn around and

put your hands behind your back. Tie them tight, Izzy, or I swear I'll shoot you both."

Dimitri smiles. "You'd better give me that rifle before you lose your head."

"And why would I do that?"

"Because a girl with purple hair has a gun pointed at you."

"Nice bluff, Dimitri."

"Not bluff. Give weapon to my cousin."

Kira!

MaryAna turns to see Kira in the open door with a handgun aimed at her. As she raises her hands, Dimitri snatches the rifle from her.

Isadora marches up to MaryAna and slaps her across the face.

"That's for seducing my husband, you slut!"

MaryAna rubs her cheek. "Your husband? So what—you're bi, is that it?"

"I'm not bi or gay. And my name is Delaura."

"Your husband's a liar," MaryAna says. "He seduced me and enjoyed every minute of it. Wanna hear the details?"

"Be quiet." Dimitri pokes the barrel of the rifle into her chest.

"Dimitri's quite the lover," MaryAna continues. "Did he mention we did it a second time after I told him I'd wire the money?"

Delaura glares at him. "Is that true?"

"She's lying," Dimitri says, his face crimson. "Now take a seat in that chair, Miss Lindley, and shut up."

MaryAna sits down, then smirks at Delaura. "If he were my husband, I'd—"

Dimitri jams the butt of the rifle into the nineteen-year-old's chest. It takes her breath away and she gasps.

"Ignore her," he tells his wife and turns to Kira. "Why are you here?"

"My father wants you to hurry up. The NSA has a plane waiting for us."

"You and Delaura each take one of those boxes upstairs. I will catch up after I deal with Miss Lindley."

"Don't let your guard down," his wife warns, taking the pistol

374

from Kira. "MaryAna knows karate."

"If she tries anything, I will put several holes in her," Dimitri says. He reaches into one of the boxes to remove a large serrated knife. "She'll soon tell me everything I need to know."

"Don't be long, my love." Delaura kisses him on the cheek and picks up a box.

She and Kira leave the room, closing the door behind them.

"It's just you and me, Dimitri," MaryAna says. "Wanna fool around some more? I'd love to see that snake tattoo one more time."

"Shut up. If we had more time, I'd make you suffer like Elena."

Dimitri sets the assault rifle on the table, then holds the knife point under MaryAna's chin, forcing her to look up at him.

"What are these bruises on your neck? I certainly wasn't that rough when we had sex."

"I got into an accident."

"How unfortunate. So, who do you work for?"

"Since Helga is dead, I assume I'm unemployed."

Dimitri slowly presses the knife upward, breaking the skin of her throat, but MaryAna does not cry out.

Dimitri withdraws the knife, and blood trickles down the nineteen-year-old's neck from the small wound.

"I said, who do you work for? Is it the Russian government or the Ukrainians? Maybe the FBI or the American police?"

"I don't work for anyone."

Dimitri makes two small cuts at the base of her throat. MaryAna grits her teeth, trying to ignore the pain.

I won't give him the satisfaction of screaming.

"I wish we had more time, Miss Lindley. I'd love to demonstrate 'death by a thousand cuts.'"

"Is that what you did to Elena?"

"I'd started to, but the bitch kept passing out—no tolerance for pain. You, on the other hand . . ." He says, making another cut, this time to her shoulder. "Where is Elena, by the way? I'd love to get together with her once more."

"She's somewhere you'll never find her."

"That's a shame. In that case, how about you and I pick up where I left off with her."

"I thought you were in a hurry to catch a plane."

Just then, MaryAna hears the metal door slam shut at the other end of the hallway.

They're gone.

Now just make one mistake, Dimitri.

That's all I need.

Chapter 72

SMITE

Dimitri steps back. "First things first. Be a good girl and give me your phone. I don't want anyone using GPS to interrupt our situation here."

"I've got a question." MaryAna says, stalling for time.

He grunts. "What?"

"Are Natasha and you even related?"

"She's Kira's sister, Uncle Ivan's other daughter. We're a family business."

"I can't believe the NSA lets girls be sex-trafficked just to learn some Russian secrets."

"So, you were listening to us. Your country is as corrupt as mine."

"It sounds like the devil is at work in both of them. Are you one of his minions?"

"Enough. Give me your phone."

MaryAna pulls out Tony's phone but holds it in her lap.

"This isn't my phone—it belongs to a friend."

Dimitri sets the knife down on the shelf and reaches for the AK-47. "Hand me the damn phone."

Seeing her chance, MaryAna delivers a swift kick to Dimitri's groin. He drops to his knees, and the rifle is flung out of arm's reach. A second kick shatters his cheekbone, sending him crashing backwards into the shelf, knocking him unconscious.

With Dimitri sprawled out on the floor, MaryAna binds his hands and feet with the twine. She retrieves the phone, rifle, and knife.

These might come in handy.

377

MaryAna wipes the blood from her neck and makes her way back down the hallway. Once through the metal door, she finds herself on the landing with a decision to make.

I doubt I can bluff my way through the rest of the Russians. I don't even know how much ammo is left in this gun.

The teenager tries to call 911 but gets no signal. She starts down the stairwell toward the tunnel, then stops.

Tony said to leave, but I can't abandon my friends.

Please, God, help me save them.

MaryAna spins around to see the stranger on the stairs above her. As in Max's painting, he is wearing a white tailored suit.

"Are you here to help me save my friends, Gabe?"

"I am. Leave the weapons and come with me," he says, climbing the stairs.

"But I need them for protection."

He stops and turns around. "You do not need them. Follow me."

She sets down the rifle and knife and hurries up behind him.

"So, you've got a plan?" she asks when they reach the landing on the ground floor.

"Our Lord has one." Her friend disappears through the metal door as before.

I'm with him now, so maybe I can do that too.

She reaches out and pushes hard on the door, but nothing happens. In a huff, she flings the door open.

"You could've opened it for me," she says to Gabriel in the distance. She hurries to catch up with him. "Be careful," she whispers. "These Russians want to kill us."

"Fear not, young lady. I am aware of the danger."

"Oh, I'm not afraid anymore, but they've got a lot of firepower. Can you stop bullets in midair? You know, like Neo in *The Matrix*?"

He smiles. "I once destroyed 185,000 Assyrians before breakfast. I believe I can handle a few of these individuals. Stay here," the angel tells her, before easing around the corner.

After he disappears into the other hallway, she hears shouts in

Russian, followed by automatic weapons fire. Then there are two bright flashes followed by an eerie silence.

"Come," the angel tells her.

Two bodies lie on the floor, one of which was the taller guard who drove the van. The other is similarly dressed.

"Did you—"

"I did what I had to."

MaryAna walks over to them. "There's no blood. Did you—what do they call it—*smite* them, like Sodom and Gomorrah?

"On rare occasions, God sends us to intervene in human affairs. The destruction of Sodom was one of those times. This is another."

"Why now?"

"I am not provided that information."

MaryAna picks up an AK-47 next to the dead men. "He won't be needing this." She notices her friend's frown and sets it back down. "Neither will I, right?"

"No." The angel points to a door further down the hallway. "Stay here."

When he steps inside the room, gunfire erupts once more. There are two more flashes and the firing ceases.

When the angel returns to the hall, MaryAna hears footsteps behind her.

"You two, raise hands."

"Close your eyes," her friend tells her.

As she squeezes them shut, her body tingles, and through her eyelids, she perceives a momentary flash.

"You may open your eyes now, MaryAna."

She turns to see the Russian sprawled on the floor, pistol still in hand.

"Thanks for savin' my life, Gabe. May I see what you did in there?" she says, nodding toward the room Gabe had entered.

"If you wish, but you should know that—"

But MaryAna has already rushed into the room. Again, two Russian guards lie dead on the floor, but there are also two naked male bodies face down in pools of blood.

"What happened to them?"

"I am sorry, MaryAna. That was the Russians' doing."

She steps over to the two men and delicately turns one and then the other's body over to confirm her worst fears.

Tony and Fred.

Her body shudders and she collapses to her knees. "Oh my God . . . why would they strip off their clothes and cut their throats?"

"Evil people do evil deeds, MaryAna."

"But can't you bring them back? They're good people who were just tryin' to save the girls. They don't deserve this."

"Only Our Lord has power over death."

Tears cascade from MaryAna's eyes. "Please, God. Don't make them pay for my mistakes."

The angel places a hand on her shoulder. "They were warriors. Soldiers know all too well the risks associated with war."

"What war?"

"The war that has raged for eons and will continue to the end of time. Come," he tells her, helping her to her feet. "There is still much to do."

"We can't just leave them there, Gabe."

"There will be time to grieve for the dead. Right now, we must save the living." The angel steps to the door, motioning for her to follow.

"I've made such a mess of things. Just go save the girls. You don't need me."

"There is much for you to do. Come."

Do I even have a choice?

Chapter 73
UNCLE IVAN

MaryAna wipes her blood-stained hands on her clothes and follows the angel to the next door.

"Enter and save whoever you wish," he tells her. "Then we will confront evil."

She wipes away her tears. "I thought that's what we were already doin'."

When the teenager enters the room, she sees ten of the Ukrainian girls huddled in the far corner. "Are you all OK?" she asks, rushing over to them.

Sofia shakes her head and points to the opposite corner of the room, behind the open door.

MaryAna whirls around to see Delaura, Kira, and Natasha together. Dimitri's wife points a pistol at MaryAna and the girls.

The nineteen-year-old takes a step toward the three women. "You need to put down that gun."

"S-stay where you are, MaryAna," Delaura says, her hand trembling. "How did you get past the guards?"

"Divine intervention. I have a friend outside who is fond of smiting bad guys, so I suggest you drop that gun before he smites you."

The three Russians look at each other, confused.

Delaura points the pistol directly at MaryAna's head. "Where is Dimitri?"

"He's tied up at the moment." MaryAna steps closer, holding out her hand. "Now, put it down."

"Stay back, or I will shoot."

"Gabe, that's my angel friend, went through your guards like a knife through butter. Do you really want to challenge him?"

Kira says something to Delaura in Russian.

"What did you tell her?" MaryAna asks.

"I say if you get this far, we no gonna stop you."

"Good advice. Delaura, put it down now."

Delaura slowly kneels down and sets the gun on the floor.

MaryAna steps closer and kicks the pistol aside. "Now, what should I do with you? Maybe tie you all up and leave you for the police."

"When Dimitri tell my father about you," Kira says, "they make us part of scam. We have no choice."

"We sorry we steal money," Natasha adds. "Dimitri hurt us if we no help."

MaryAna thinks for a few moments. "You could be just pawns, caught up in their schemes. So, where's my money?"

"Dimitri give us only little," the purple-haired Kira answers. "He keep rest. We are sorry."

"Please, let us go," Natasha pleads. "We no want to do bad things."

"I'd like to believe you. What about you, Delaura? I thought you were my friend. You lied to me about everything."

"They made us do it."

"My angel friend has lectured on forgiveness for a while now. I suppose I could let you go."

"What about Dimitri," his wife asks. "Can he go too?"

"Your no-good husband has more to answer for than just conning me out of my money. We'll leave him for the police. Now, if you don't want to share his fate, you better skedaddle."

The three Russians look at each other.

"That means *leave*."

They scramble out of the room but stop in their tracks when they encounter the angel in the hall. He motions for them to proceed to a metal door with an exit sign above it.

Once they are gone, MaryAna motions to the Ukrainian girls.

"Follow me. Don't be afraid—the man in the white suit is here to protect us."

Once everyone is in the hallway, Gabriel leads the group toward the exit. Before they reach the metal door, it swings open, and a short, unarmed man struts through. He has salt and pepper hair, a gray mustache, and a nasty scar across his forehead. The door slams shut behind him.

They all stop, except for MaryAna, who eases ahead.

"Get out of my way, young lady." The little man's voice is deep with a distinct Russian accent. "Or suffer the consequences."

MaryAna stops. "Uncle Ivan, I presume?"

"So, we meet at last, Miss Lindley. Give me those girls. They belong to me."

"Step back, MaryAna," Gabriel warns.

"I've got this, Gabe." She takes another step forward. "One well-placed kick in his pot belly, and he'll run home to Mother Russia."

Uncle Ivan puffs out his chest. "Step aside, yourself, or I'll rain hell upon you."

"We're turnin' you and Dimitri over to the cops, old man."

Ivan steps back and is swallowed by an unnatural darkness.

MaryAna turns to the angel. "Where did he go?"

The man in the white suit changes, revealing his true nature. He spreads his ivory wings and begins to glow.

A tall man with sandy-brown hair emerges from the shadows where the Russian had been. He limps forward, shading his eyes.

"MaryAna? Is that you?"

Her eyes go wide. ". . . Daddy? What are you doin' here?"

"I came to visit you, darlin'."

"But you were in jail."

"Sarah bailed me out so I could help you. Come give your old man a hug."

"Do not approach him," the angel warns. "He is not your father."

The man points to an open cooler at MaryAna's feet. "I brought you a present."

She stares down at the ice-cold cans of beer.

"How about tossing your old man a cold one."

Aghast, MaryAna turns back to the angel. "What is happening?"

"Stand beside me, MaryAna."

This time, she heeds Gabriel's advice and steps back.

What have I gotten myself into?

Chapter 74

SATAN

Gabriel's glow fades as his voice reverberates down the hallway. "Reveal your true nature, Lucifer."

The unnatural darkness returns, and MaryAna's father fades from view. In his stead appears a beast with horns like a minotaur and the scaly skin of a snake. Surrounding it are red and orange flames that swallow the darkness like a hungry monster.

"Gabriel, so nice to see you again." Something akin to a laugh emanates from the horned beast. "I see you brought a sidekick."

The angel covers MaryAna with one of his wings. "Begone from this place, Lucifer. We are on a mission for our Lord."

"Your lord, not mine." The beast scowls, showing his fangs. "God has no claim on that mortal."

"This child is under my protection. Do not attempt to harm her."

"Be gone yourself, Gabriel. Leave this plaything to me. She has served me well, and I have plans for her."

MaryAna steps from under Gabriel's wing, her anger trumping her fear. "Go back to the pit where you belong, Satan. I've never served you."

The beast snorts. "My little puppet is a feisty one."

"I'm nobody's puppet."

"Do not deceive yourself, Mary Anabella Lindley. Your desire for drink, your vanity, and your carnal desires are the strings I hold in my hands. You dance to my tune."

"Liar!"

"Remember your first beer? What were you, twelve? I knew you would succumb to temptation. You have followed me down a merry path indeed."

"I could never follow you."

"Who nudged you into the arms of all those rutting men? A dozen in the last two years? Or is it two dozen? You're adding them so quickly I lost count."

"Do not converse with him, MaryAna," Gabriel warns. "He will play with your mind and your emotions."

"But how does he know all this? Has he really been part of my life?"

"I've pulled your strings for years but wanted more," Satan says. "I possessed Dimitri's body to sample your charms. You are a lustful creature indeed and did not disappoint."

"What are you talkin' about?"

"Don't you remember our *romantic* carriage ride? Our unholy pact for youth and beauty? Our unbridled passion?"

"That was *you*?"

"Of course." Satan says, mimicking Vladimir's voice. "Miss Lindley, I want your soul!"

"It *was* you!"

"Yes. Henpecked Dimitri was more interested in your money than either your body or your soul. I, on the other hand . . ."

MaryAna shudders at the revelation.

The horned beast seems pleased with himself. "I practically told you who I was, but you were too goo-goo-eyed in lust over that would-be art dealer to put two and two together. I still can't believe you made me wear a condom."

"You got me drunk on champagne and took advantage of me."

The devil laughs. "No one forced you to drink or spread your legs. I just threw in a little romance to stoke your fire."

"You tricked me."

Satan growls. "It's what I do. Some are harder to deceive, but most never catch on. Your thirst for alcohol and desire for pleasure made you easy prey. Hardly even a challenge."

How could I be so stupid?

"I've got some revelations for you, Miss Lindley. Some nice juicy secrets. You'll be glad to know Samson got the part in *Hamilton*. Of course, he traded his soul for stardom. Carson is returning to New York next week and itching to get back with you. It's a chance for you to make some serious cash."

"I'm not a prostitute!"

"Keep telling yourself that, honey. And don't expect any more financial help from your CEO buddy Mel. He's about to make a move on the new girl in the marketing department."

"How do you know all this?"

"I'm the Devil, bitch. Oh, I almost forgot—Andy traded his soul for the coaching job, and I threw in a hot date with your girlfriend Coree. And last but not least—Tyler got Meghan pregnant."

"You're lyin'!"

"Why would I lie to you, young lady, when the truth is so sweet?"

"Is he tellin' the truth, Gabriel?"

"Lucifer sprinkles it with lies to serve his purposes."

Satan steps closer to MaryAna and lowers his voice as if sharing a secret.

"Here's another fact hot off the press. Rodney used the money he stole from you to get heroin. The icing on the cake is that he overdosed and is now a full-time resident of hell."

MaryAna recoils in horror. "Why are you tellin' me this?"

"When you join us down there, you and Rodney are gonna be roommates. You two deserve each other."

Tears fill her eyes. "I don't want to hear any more."

"Don't be down, baby girl. Just pop some oxy and chug a beer, and everything will be fine and dandy in the morning."

"I've stopped drinkin', and the oxy is for my back."

"Don't kid yourself, hon. Before long, Rufus will have you swimming in opioids and camped out in his bed to pay for it. Then when oxy isn't enough to satisfy your needs, he'll upgrade you to meth or heroin. Your family will disown you, and you'll be humping any guy who throws you a few bucks."

"Do not listen to him," Gabriel tells her. "Jesus died for your sins. His love can save you from such a fate."

The devil's flames burn scarlet red. "Gabe's been pushing that line for two millennia. Who do you think makes your fantasies come true? I'll give you a hint—it ain't the Nazarene."

MaryAna steps forward. "You're just upset because the Lord chose me to disrupt your plans. You won't destroy my life or the lives of these Ukrainians. I'll stop you."

"Do you and God have such a strong bond? You only turn to him when you're in trouble. The rest of the time, it's sex, drugs, and rock 'n roll—and the minibar, of course."

"Burn in hell, Satan, and leave us alone."

"Is that any way to talk to the guy who owns your soul?"

MaryAna turns to Gabriel. "Is that true?"

"I am afraid you gave it to him."

She turns back to the fiery beast. "I want it back."

"This ain't Georgia, girly," the Devil says in a Southern drawl, "and you ain't no fiddle player."

"I'll fight you for it."

"You think you're tough, little girl—I'll show you tough."

A ball of fire erupts from the beast and explodes in front of the Ukrainians. They scream and jump back in terror.

"Leave them alone. This is between you and me. First, some rules."

The beast laughs. "Rules?"

"You have to fight fair. No fiery bolts, no magic, none of that CGI stuff. Agreed?"

"You expect me to fight fair? I'm the devil."

"Gabriel will be the referee. If you cheat, you forfeit, and I get my soul back."

"And if you lose?"

"You keep my soul."

"I already have it. I want more."

"What more is there?"

"Your free will," he says with a laugh that curls MaryAna's toes. "When you lose, you'll surrender it and become my handmaiden."

"What does that even mean?"

"When I take human form, you'll serve me like a slave. Obedience will be your only option, no matter what I ask of you. No protests, no complaining—and no condoms."

"How long would I be your handmaiden?"

"For eternity."

"OK, Satan, but you must take human form when we fight."

"As you wish."

The flames die out, and the beast fades into the background. From the gloom steps a shirtless young man wearing loosely fitting black pants. Although not tall, he has bulging muscles. She gulps, recognizing the individual from his movies.

Bruce Lee? Satan made himself look like Bruce Lee?

MaryAna blinks and finds herself in the center of a crowded arena. She is wearing a stylish pink karate gi with a black belt around her waist. An eight-sided cage, an octagon, surrounds her and the ersatz Bruce Lee.

Thousands of onlookers cheer and chant Bruce's name. Then, above the din of the crowd, a voice echoes through the arena: "Are you ready to rumble!"

MaryAna looks around, taking in the scene, sweat pouring off her. "Someone needs to turn down the thermostat."

"Welcome to the Helldome." Bruce chuckles and bows to her. "You'll get used to the heat."

Like a warrior princess, MaryAna bows back. "I won't be here that long." She raises her fists and prepares to fight for her soul.

I've got a secret weapon.

My faith in God.

Chapter 75

AWAKENING

"Miss?" the flight attendant says. "Miss, wake up."

"Huh?" a bleary-eyed MaryAna takes out her earbuds.

"You need to bring your seat back to an upright and locked position."

"Oh, yeah." MaryAna pushes the button on the armrest to adjust the seat.

As she sits upright, pain shoots through both sides of her lower back. She winces, then glances around in disbelief.

What happened? Where's Bruce?

"So, you're finally awake," Mel says, closing his laptop.

MaryAna grabs the blanket covering her and holds it up. "Where did this come from?"

"The overhead bin. You zonked out as soon as we left Atlanta. I noticed the goosebumps on your arms and figured you were cold."

"You mean, I was asleep the entire flight?"

He nods. "We land in New York in a few minutes."

MaryAna thinks about pinching herself to see if she is dreaming, but the ache in her back is real enough to prove she is awake. Instead, the teenager closes her eyes, half-expecting to be back in the sweltering arena fighting for her soul. But when she opens them, she is still on the plane.

She turns to Mel. "What's the date today?"

"August first."

This is the day I flew from Mississippi to see Tyler.

"When was it you offered me the job?"

The CEO checks his Rolex. "About four hours ago. Why?"

"Just checkin' to make sure I didn't dream it."

"The job is very real." He chuckles. "The limousine service will pick us up at the airport and drop you at the Plaza."

"You don't own the limo?"

"No. It's a service."

"Sir, are you married?

Mel seems taken aback by the question. "I have a life partner, a wonderful man by the name of Pierre, whom you'll meet tomorrow."

"Oh, I see. So, who's the 'Jacqueline' the company is named after?"

"That would be my sister, Jackie. Since we were young, she and I have designed clothes together. Our marketing people selected the company's name to sound French." He grins. "Mel and Jackie Designs doesn't have the same *savoir faire*."

MaryAna giggles. "I guess not."

Is this all true? Everything seemed too real to be my imagination.

Maybe God took me back in time so I can make better choices. What if I'm in my own Groundhog Day?

As the plane makes its final descent, MaryAna makes a quick decision. "I'm sorry, sir, but I have to turn down your job offer—at least for now."

"I'm sorry to hear that, Miss Lindley. You sounded excited about joining our team. What changed your mind?"

"I need to talk it over with my boyfriend before makin' such a life-alterin' decision. I need to discuss it with my mama too. She deserves to have her opinion heard. When we land, I'm gonna book a flight to Scranton."

That is, if Tyler's still my boyfriend.

"Please let me know what you decide, Miss Lindley. I believe you would be an asset to our company, but I understand how important of a decision it is for you."

"I'll give it more thought, sir, and contact you in the next few days if I change my mind."

That's step one in changing my life around, or at least, not turning it upside down any more than it has to.

***

While Mel checks on her luggage, MaryAna purchases a ticket to visit Tyler. On her way to baggage claim, she sends him a text: ANOTHER CHANGE OF PLANS. ARRIVING SCRANTON TOMORROW MORNING FROM NYC. LOVE YOU SO MUCH.

"It appears your luggage didn't make it onto our flight," Mel informs her. "They're probably in Scranton."

"I'll contact Delta and have them hold them there for me. May I still catch a ride to the Plaza?"

Once in the limousine, MaryAna calls her boyfriend and brings him up to speed.

Tyler seems surprised. "That job is an awesome opportunity for you. Maybe you should go ahead and take it."

"Our relationship is far more important to me than any job," she tells him. "I won't jeopardize it. There's a lot for us to discuss."

"I wish you were here right now, MaryAna."

"Me too. The first flight to Scranton is tomorrow, or I would be. I can't wait to see you, Tyler."

He has no idea how much I've missed him.

***

The CEO accompanies MaryAna into the Plaza. He offers to pay for her one-night stay, but after verifying her money is still in her checking account, she declines his offer.

"Thanks for the ride. You've been very kind."

"I look forward to hearing from you, Miss Lindley. Have a nice trip to Scranton."

"For sure, sir. Someday I'll be back here with plenty of new ideas about fashion."

MaryAna's room is nice but not a suite overlooking Central Park. She digs through her backpack to find her bipolar medication.

No more skipping meds.

After settling in, the teenager places a call to Tony Russo. When he answers, she is relieved.

393

"I'm in New York City. I'll only be here for one night and would love to see you and Dori."

"I wish I had time to get together, MaryAna. Between med school, volunteering at the hospital, and a baby coming, I afraid I don't have a spare moment."

Tony doesn't sound like someone madly in love with me.

"I understand. How's Fred?"

"He's doing well. I talked to him yesterday. Are you on your way to visit your grandparents up in Fulton?"

"Goin' to see my boyfriend in Pennsylvania. I'll holler at you next time I'm up this way."

"Maybe after the baby is born, Dori and I could visit you and your family in Mississippi. My wife would like that."

Don't bet on it.

"Bye, Tony."

The teenager plops onto the bed and for a moment, her eyes stop on the minibar.

But only a moment.

How did I dream up an entire new life for myself?

I really liked those Ukrainian girls, especially Elena and Sofia.

MaryAna closes her eyes and pictures their faces.

It's hard to believe Leon, Max, Andy, Samson, Kristen, and the others weren't real.

She wipes away a tear.

If I made them all up, how come there's an empty spot in my heart?

The teenager sighs.

On the plus side, there is no Vladdy, Izzy, or Rodney.

MaryAna uses her phone to search for the Guardian Baptist Church. She finds their website, and a photo of Gabriel's statue is the same as the one in the magazine article. Indeed, its face resembles the mysterious stranger she has seen before.

If the church and the statue are real, what else might be?

She checks Leon's address, but there is no such street in Brooklyn. The teenager also comes up empty on the Made Fresh Bakery, T.J.

Morgan's Irish Pub, Boots 'n Heels, and the Black and Blues Jazz Bar. About to give up, she tries Matryoshka.

Bingo—it's a real club in Brooklyn.

I've got to check it out.

MaryAna changes back into her jeans and T-shirt.

If it is the same Matryoshka club, I don't want anyone to recognize me.

Chapter 76
A MEMENTO

Once in the lobby of the Plaza, MaryAna buys a Yankees baseball cap from the gift shop to cover her hair. From there, she walks to the hotel exit on Fifty-Ninth Street.

This is Leon's station. I didn't see him on the way in.

When another doorman approaches, she asks, "Is Leon workin' today."

"I don't know anyone by that name at the Plaza, Miss."

"How about a bellman named Samson or Sam?"

The doorman shakes his head. "I've only worked here a year. There could've been employees by those names before I started. I could ask around."

"Thank you, but it's not that important. Would you hail me a cab, please?"

***

On the way to the club, MaryAna considers what she might find.

Am I really expecting sex-trafficked girls?

No, but I still need to check it out.

The taxi pulls up near the front of the Matryoshka Club, where a pickup is parked. A panel on its door says JB Construction.

MaryAna asks the cabbie to wait and takes a long look at the building with its red-flashing light. She notices that the front door is propped open.

I hope my guardian angel is still with me.

Just inside the entranceway, the teenager sees a hostess station, but no one is there. She holds her breath and makes her way around the wall toward the club's interior.

It's the same club all right.

On the left wall is the bar, along with the doors to the restrooms. The red door is still the only thing on the rear wall. However, the rest of the dimly lit place is empty. No chairs, no tables.

A tall man with a three-day beard and dressed in bib overalls comes through the red door, but MaryAna does not recognize him.

"May I help you?"

"Uh, yeah . . . I kinda used to work here."

"We're doing a remodeling of the place," he says with a thick Brooklyn accent.

"Do you know the people who ran this club?"

"Nope. The new owners hired me. But if you're looking for a job, they won't open for at least another month. You can come back then."

"Do you know what kind of club it'll be?"

"Ain't gonna be no club anymore. It's a day care."

"Thanks for the info."

When MaryAna turns to leave, her mouth drops open.

Her eyes are locked onto the wall before her.

How did Max's painting of the angels get here?

She points to it. "What are you gonna do with that?"

"The owners told me to clean everything out, so we'll just trash it. You want it?"

"Please."

The man takes the painting down. "So, what—you know the artist?"

"I might. Thank you."

MaryAna leaves the club with her memento. As she rides away in the taxi, she holds up the painting in front of her. It reminds her of her friends in New York City, both real and imaginary.

If Dorothy can have her Oz, and Alice her Wonderland—why can't I have my Big Apple?

Secrets, Secrets, Secrets

Book One: *JoeE*

Book Two: *MaryAna*

Book Three: *Coree*

Book Four: *Shameful Truths*

Book Five: *Family Enigmas*

Book Six: *Drama Blitz* (Volume One)

Book Seven: *Drama Blitz* (Volume Two)

Book Eight: *Angels in the Big Apple*

For information & publication dates: www.secrets3.com

For questions, email us: books@secrets3.com

Find us on Social Media:

On Facebook: facebook.com/secrets3books
On Twitter: @secret3books

Made in the USA
Monee, IL
19 November 2023

46809611R00239